PENGUIN BOOKS

The CSIRO and Baker IDI Diabetes Diet and Lifestyle Plan

Baker IDI Heart and Diabetes Institute is an independent, internationally renowned research facility working on diagnosis, prevention and treatment of diabetes and c: cular disease. The main laboratory facilities in Melbourne are complemented by a national network that includes a research facility in Alice Springs dedicated to Indigenous health and a research node in South Australia focused on community interventions and nutrition. The five main research areas are: population studies and profiling, metabolism and obesity, diabetic complications, vascular and hypertension, and cardiology and therapeutics. The Institute also runs a multidisciplinary, evidence-based diabetes clinic, diabetes education services, and a world-class Healthy Hearts Clinic that provides cardiovascular disease risk assessments. Baker IDI also trains health professionals and collaborates on international research projects into heart disease and diabetes. In 2010 the Institute launched the Healthy Lifestyle Research Centre, where researchers will examine the role of nutrition, physical exercise, genetic and environmental factors in disease. For more, visit bakeridi.edu.au.

The CSIRO Preventative Health National Research Flagship aims to improve the health and wellbeing of Australians through the prevention and early detection of chronic disease. As populations age, preventing or delaying chronic disease is the key to improving health and wellbeing. The Flagship's research focuses on: colorectal cancer and diseases of the gut; neurodegenerative diseases such as Alzheimer's disease; and excess weight and obesity. The main thrust of the research is to develop: better screening for and early detection of disease; better understanding of how diet and environment contribute to disease; new protective foods and personalised nutritional and lifestyle approaches to disease prevention; and better ways to monitor and measure health, incorporating improved use of health data. CSIRO is working in partnership with a range of prominent clinical, research, government and industry organisations to ensure these research findings have a positive impact on the health of all Australians. For more, visit csiro.au/org/PreventativeHealthFlagship.html.

Windsor and Maidenhead

3806710056 9401

the CSIRO and BAKER IDI

Diabetes
Diet and Lifestyle Plan

CSIRO

Baker IDI
HEART & DIABETES INSTITUTE

PENGUIN BOOKS

Published by the Penguin Group
Penguin Group (Australia)
250 Camberwell Road, Camberwell, Victoria 3124, Australia
(a division of Pearson Australia Group Pty Ltd)
Penguin Group (USA) Inc.
375 Hudson Street, New York, New York 10014, USA
Penguin Group (Canada)
90 Eglinton Avenue East, Suite 700, Toronto, Canada ON M4P 2Y3
(a division of Pearson Penguin Canada Inc.)
Penguin Books Ltd
80 Strand, London WC2R 0RL England
Penguin Ireland
25 St Stephen's Green, Dublin 2, Ireland
(a division of Penguin Books Ltd)
Penguin Books India Pvt Ltd
11 Community Centre, Panchsheel Park, New Delhi – 110 017, India
Penguin Group (NZ)
67 Apollo Drive, Rosedale, North Shore 0632, New Zealand
(a division of Pearson New Zealand Ltd)
Penguin Books (South Africa) (Pty) Ltd
24 Sturdee Avenue, Rosebank, Johannesburg 2196, South Africa

Penguin Books Ltd, Registered Offices: 80 Strand, London, WC2R 0RL, England

First published by Penguin Group (Australia), 2011

10 9 8 7 6 5 4 3 2

Design by Elissa Webb © Penguin Group (Australia)
Food photography by Alan Benson
Food styling by Sarah O'Brien
Recipes and food preparation by Grace Campbell
All other images by Getty Images
Typeset in Sabon and Avenir by Post Pre-press Group, Brisbane, Queensland
Colour reproduction by Splitting Image Colour Studio Pty Ltd, Clayton, Victoria
Printed and bound South China Printing Co Ltd, China

National Library of Australia
Cataloguing-in-Publication data:

The CSIRO and Baker IDI diabetes diet and lifestyle plan / CSIRO;
Baker IDI Heart and Diabetes Institute.
978 0 14 320226 4 (pbk)
Includes index.
Diabetes – Diet therapy. Diabetes – Nutritional aspects.
Diabetes – Social aspects. Lifestyles.
CSIRO.
Baker IDI Heart & Diabetes Institute.

616.4620654

penguin.com.au

The CSIRO and Baker IDI Diabetes Diet and Lifestyle Plan is the result of collaboration between the Commonwealth Scientific and Industrial Research Organisation (CSIRO) and Baker IDI Heart and Diabetes Institute. The following researchers have contributed to its writing.

CSIRO Preventative Health National Research Flagship
Dr Grant Brinkworth, Research Scientist, Exercise Physiologist
Jing Hui (Jillian) Chin, Research Dietitian
Dr Lance Macaulay, Theme Leader Obesity and Health
Dr Phil Mohr, Psychologist, Research Team Leader
Associate Professor Manny Noakes, Research Program Leader for Diet
    and Lifestyle Programs
Pennie Taylor, Senior Research Dietitian

Baker IDI Heart and Diabetes Institute
Professor Peter Clifton, Head, Nutritional Research and Co-Director
    Healthy Lifestyle Research Centre
Associate Professor David Dunstan, Head, Physical Activity and Physical
    Activity Project Leader – Healthy Lifestyle Research Centre
Associate Professor Jennifer Keogh, Honorary Research Fellow
Sonia Middleton, Senior Dietitian
Professor Merlin Thomas, Head, Diabetic Complications
Professor Paul Zimmet AO, Director Emeritus, Director International Research

Acknowledgements
The Editorial Committee is grateful to the many people in both organisations who assisted in the production of this book. The people who independently reviewed this book were: Professor Lesley Campbell, Garvan Institute; Professor Bob Atkins, Monash University; Professor Stephen Twigg, University of Sydney; Professor Martin Silink AM, International Diabetes Federation.

The CSIRO and Baker IDI Diabetes Diet and Lifestyle Plan makes reference to a number of products and trademarks throughout. Neither CSIRO nor Baker IDI has received financial contributions or other benefits in return for these references from the companies that own these products or trademarks, or from any other entities associated with their promotion. The information contained in this book is of a general nature. It is not intended to constitute professional medical advice and is not a substitute for consulting with your doctor or other health care provider. The publisher, CSIRO, Baker IDI and their employees are not responsible for any adverse effects or consequences arising from the use of any suggestions, preparations or procedures contained in this book. All matters relating to your health including diet, medication and appropriate physical activity should be discussed with your doctor.

Contents

Congratulations

You have taken an important step in regaining control of your health. This book is a great initiative from two very fine Australian research institutions – Baker IDI Heart and Diabetes Institute and CSIRO – that are committed to preventing chronic disease and assisting you to improve your health.

The good news is that type 2 diabetes can be prevented. In fact, you can take steps to actively prevent it and to help others in your family from developing the disease.

And if you have already been diagnosed with diabetes, there are many ways to control and manage it in order to avoid complications, including a combination of diet, physical activity and excellent medical care that may or may not involve medication. Evidence-based research has also demonstrated that it's possible to reverse the effects of diabetes and lessen your reliance on medication by following the various programs Baker IDI and CSIRO have developed.

It is always heartening to see scientific organisations translate their research into practical advice for ordinary people. I recommend this book to you. Read it carefully and keep coming back to it over the years. It contains wise advice and clear information that will help you take care of yourself and those around you.

Professor Martin Silink AM MB BS MD FRACP
IMMEDIATE PAST PRESIDENT, INTERNATIONAL DIABETES FEDERATION

Foreword

If you have diabetes, you are not alone. More than 1.5 million Australians have diabetes. And more than twice this number are at significant risk of developing diabetes in the next five to ten years. But a diagnosis of diabetes need not seriously affect your health and wellbeing. With good medical care, healthy nutrition and regular physical activity, most people with diabetes lead full and healthy lives. It requires effort, willpower and persistence, but the rewards are considerable.

This book is your guide to diabetes, and the many opportunities you have to maintain and improve your quality of life. In these pages, experts from our respective organisations examine what diabetes is, how it comes about and what you can do to reduce its severity. We look at optimal diets for people with diabetes, and some of the different ways they can be achieved. Our researchers provide ideas for increasing physical activity and how exercise can maintain and improve health. We also shed light on the medical aspects of diabetes care, including the best ways to achieve control of blood glucose, blood pressure and cholesterol levels, and how to reduce the risk of developing major complications.

The CSIRO and Baker IDI Diabetes Diet and Lifestyle Plan provides options for living well with diabetes, but there are no generic solutions. The advice here is based on current Australian science and clinical practice. However, this book is not a substitute for medical advice. The book aims to help Australians make the best diabetes management choices for themselves in order to live full and satisfying lives. We hope you and your family will benefit from our collaboration on this lifestyle resource.

Dr Megan Clark
CHIEF EXECUTIVE, CSIRO

Professor Garry Jennings
DIRECTOR, BAKER IDI HEART
AND DIABETES INSTITUTE

PART 1
Living with diabetes

1 All about diabetes

Type 2 diabetes usually starts out as a silent disease.
Most people with diabetes are unaware they have it.

What is diabetes?

Our brain runs on glucose as its preferred fuel. Without glucose, other parts of our body could keep going, but our brain would slow down and eventually stop. So in a healthy body, day and night, feeding or fasting, blood glucose levels are kept almost constant.

When we eat, our body releases insulin from the pancreas, which signals cells to take up glucose as fast as they can. These hormones also tell the liver to stop releasing glucose into the bloodstream. The net result is that blood glucose levels rise only very slightly after a meal. When all the food is used up and we stop absorbing glucose, our body stops releasing these hormones. This halts the uptake of glucose and tells the liver to release its glucose stores slowly back into the bloodstream, like a kind of drip-feed. The release of glucose into the blood occurs at roughly the same rate at which the body (particularly the brain) uses it up, so the glucose concentration in the blood stays roughly the same.

Diabetes occurs when there is not enough insulin to keep glucose under control and glucose levels start to rise. There are several forms of diabetes. This book is largely for people with type 2 diabetes but is also useful for those with a family history of diabetes, who are overweight, or have type 1 diabetes.

TYPE 1 DIABETES

In children and adolescents, the immune system can inadvertently destroy the insulin-producing cells of the pancreas. This is called type 1 diabetes or insulin-dependent diabetes mellitus (IDDM) because insulin injections are needed to survive.

TYPE 2 DIABETES

In type 2 diabetes the insulin-producing cells of the pancreas have burnt out and can't produce enough insulin. This is the most common form of diabetes, and most cases of type 2 diabetes occur in adults, particularly those over the age of 65. It is also called non-insulin-dependent diabetes mellitus (NIDDM), because the body still produces some insulin, at least initially. This amount may be enough to cope with small meals, but not with additional demands.

The first sign of type 2 diabetes may be when glucose levels remain elevated for too long after a meal that is high in carbohydrate. This is called impaired glucose tolerance or prediabetes, and is detected very simply – you drink sugar and we measure your blood glucose levels two hours later. If your glucose levels are elevated, the insulin you produce is insufficient for the demands of a carbohydrate-rich meal. If they are elevated by a large margin, the insulin you produce is almost always insufficient to deal with the sugary demands of meals and you have type 2 diabetes. The passage from prediabetes to diabetes usually takes years, but some people can go from having a normal glucose level to type 2 diabetes in less than five years.

GESTATIONAL DIABETES

Some women become diabetic during pregnancy. This is known as gestational diabetes and is thought to be caused by the hormones and other factors released during normal pregnancy causing resistance to the actions of insulin. This means that insulin production needs to be almost doubled to keep glucose levels under control. Some women, however, do not have the capacity for this increase, especially older women and overweight women, and their glucose levels rise. Although levels usually return to normal after delivery, women with gestational diabetes have a substantially increased risk of developing type 2 diabetes as they get older.

Why is diabetes so important?

When glucose levels rise, the effects on health and wellbeing are numerous. The most obvious is that it means making more urine, as the body tries to get rid of the excess glucose. Urinating more frequently also dries you out, so you become thirsty and drink more. In fact, the word diabetes means 'a siphon'.

Continued high blood glucose can also damage susceptible parts of the body, such as the kidneys, eyes and blood vessels. Preventing these complications is the main reason diabetes is medically monitored and treated and why the measures described in this book are so important. With good diabetes care, lifestyle and dietary modifications, most people with diabetes are able to stay healthy and free of any complications.

How to tell if you are at risk of health complications

	FEMALE WAIST CIRCUMFERENCE		MALE WAIST CIRCUMFERENCE	
	Non-Asian	Asian*	Non-Asian	Asian*
Increased risk	88–100 cm	80–90 cm	102–110 cm	90–100 cm
Substantially increased risk	More than 100 cm	More than 90 cm	More than 110 cm	More than 100 cm

*The term 'Asian' here covers Indian subcontinent, Middle East, North Africa, Southern Europe.

Who gets diabetes?

In Australia, one in every twelve adults has diabetes and it is becoming increasingly common. The number of Australians with diabetes has increased threefold over the last 20 years and it is expected that there will be more than 2 million Australians with diabetes by 2020.

The people most likely to develop diabetes are those with impaired glucose tolerance or prediabetes. They are more than 15 times more likely to develop diabetes in the next five years than people with normal blood glucose levels.

The most powerful contributor to developing diabetes is becoming overweight or obese. Diabetes is not caused by eating too much sugar or other carbohydrates. Excess energy from too much fat, sugar, and protein alone or in combination will all work the insulin-producing cells in the pancreas much harder. Anytime the intake of your kilojoules is greater than your body's energy needs, the excess is stored as fat, initially under the skin, and in the buttocks and breasts. If the excess of kilojoules continues, the body creates additional storage, particularly around the internal organs, called visceral fat. This kind of fat is far more dangerous. All fat, but especially visceral fat, leaks chemical factors that hold back or *resist* the glucose-lowering effects of insulin. This 'insulin resistance' makes the pancreas work even harder, even when it should be resting between meals. Eventually something has to give.

Unless they are very old, few people whose waist circumference is within the healthy reference range will become diabetic. If you are obese, however, you are four times more likely to develop type 2 diabetes than people whose waist circumference is within the healthy reference range (see the table above). Sixty per cent of Australians are now overweight or obese, and this is the main reason why rates of diabetes are rising. Diabetes is also influenced by genetic, hormonal, gender and environmental factors.

Being inactive significantly increases your risk of diabetes, partly because regular exercise is an important means of weight control, and can burn off dangerous visceral fat. Regular physical activity also improves the body's sensitivity to insulin, meaning the pancreas needs to work less to do the same job.

Getting older increases your risk of diabetes, in some measure because people tend to get fatter and less active as they get older. One in four people over the age of 75 has diabetes. The regenerative capacity of the pancreas is not limitless. A lifetime of maintaining blood glucose levels ultimately reduces the body's capacity to make insulin. The greater the demands on the pancreas over time, the more likely it is that age will eventually catch up with it. Whether this results in diabetes depends on how much insulin production is reduced and how much insulin is required to keep glucose levels under control. Weight control, a healthy diet and regular physical activity still play an important role, even in advanced age.

Diabetes tends to run in families, partly due to genes and partly due to similar diet and lifestyle habits and exposure to similar environmental factors. If either of your parents or your siblings has diabetes, you are five to six times more likely to develop diabetes yourself. If three family members are affected, you're more than 15 times more likely to develop diabetes yourself than someone without a family history. A third of people with type 2 diabetes also has a close family member with diabetes.

Diabetes is more common in certain ethnic groups, such as Aboriginal and Torres Strait Islanders, Polynesians, Canadian and American Indians, Asians, Hispanics, Afro-Americans and people from the Middle East. One in six Indigenous Australian adults has diabetes. This is partly due to increased susceptibility to factors that cause diabetes more generally, such as obesity. For example, a weight gain of 5 kilograms almost doubles the risk of diabetes in Asian people, compared with non-Asians.

Other factors associated with an increased risk for type 2 diabetes include the following.

- Gestational diabetes (see page 4).
- Polycystic ovary syndrome (PCOS).
- Heart disease and high blood pressure.
- Chronic depression.
- Heavy smoking (more than 20 cigarettes a day).
- High (more than 5 kilograms) or low (less than 2.5 kilograms) birth weight.
- Some medications, including steroids, beta-blockers, diuretics and some antipsychotics.

The Australian Diabetes Risk Assessment Tool

You can estimate your own risk of developing type 2 diabetes in the next five years using this risk calculator (AusDRISK) developed by Baker IDI Heart and Diabetes Institute. It is used by the Australian Government Department of Health and Ageing, general practitioners and health workers.

1	What is your age group?	
a	Under 35	0 points
b	35–44	2 points
c	45–54	4 points
d	55–64	6 points
e	65 or over	8 points

2	What is your gender?	
a	Female	0 points
b	Male	3 points

3 What are your ethnicity and country of birth?

   i Are you of Aboriginal, Torres Strait Islander, Pacific Islander or Maori descent?

      a No   0 points
      b Yes   2 points

   ii Where were you born?

      a Australia   0 points
      b Asia (including the Indian sub-continent), Middle East, North Africa, Southern Europe   2 points
      c Other   0 points

4 Has either of your parents, or any of your brothers or sisters, been diagnosed with diabetes (type 1 or type 2)?

      a No   0 points
      b Yes   3 points

5 Have you ever been found to have high blood glucose (sugar) (for example, in a health examination, during an illness, during pregnancy)?

      a No   0 points
      b Yes   6 points

6 Are you currently taking medication for high blood pressure?

      a No   0 points
      b Yes   2 points

7 Do you currently smoke cigarettes or any other tobacco products on a daily basis?

      a No   0 points
      b Yes   2 points

8 How often do you eat vegetables or fruit?

      a Every day   0 points
      b Not every day   1 point

9 On average, would you say you do at least 2½ hours of physical activity per week (for example, 30 minutes a day on five or more days a week)?

      a Yes   0 points
      b No   2 points

10 What is your waist measurement taken below the ribs?

(The correct place to measure your waist is halfway between your lowest rib and the top of your hipbone, roughly in line with your navel. Stand up, measure directly against your skin, breathe out normally, make sure the tape is snug, without compressing the skin.)

   i For those of Asian, Aboriginal or Torres Strait Islander descent

     Men

      a Less than 90 cm   0 points
      b 90–100 cm   4 points
      c More than 100 cm   7 points

     Women

      a Less than 80 cm   0 points
      b 80–90 cm   4 points
      c More than 90 cm   7 points

   ii For all others

     Men

      a Less than 102 cm   0 points
      b 102–110 cm   4 points
      c More than 110 cm   7 points

     Women

      a Less than 88 cm   0 points
      b 88–100 cm   4 points
      c More than 100 cm   7 points

YOUR RISK OF DEVELOPING TYPE 2 DIABETES IN THE NEXT FIVE YEARS

Check your total score against the three possible point ranges below.

5 or less: Low risk

If you scored 5 or less you are at low risk of developing type 2 diabetes within five years – approximately one person in every 100 will develop type 2 diabetes.

6–11: Intermediate risk

If you scored 6–11 you are at intermediate risk of developing type 2 diabetes within five years – for scores of 6–8, approximately one person in every 50 will develop diabetes. For scores of 9–11, approximately one person in every 30 will develop diabetes. Make a copy of pages 6–8 and take it to your doctor. Discuss with your doctor your score and your individual risk. Improving your lifestyle may help reduce your risk of developing type 2 diabetes.

12 or more: High risk

If you scored 12 or more you are at high risk of developing type 2 diabetes within five years or you may have undiagnosed type 2 diabetes. For scores of 12–15, approximately one person in every 14 will develop diabetes. For scores of 16–19, one person in every seven will develop diabetes. For scores of 20 and above, approximately one person in every three will develop diabetes. Make a copy of pages 6 and 7 and take it to your doctor. Ask your doctor about having a fasting blood glucose test.

* The overall score may overestimate the risk of diabetes in those aged less than 25 years.

Do you have diabetes?

Type 2 diabetes usually starts out as a silent disease. Most people with diabetes are unaware they have it. They may dismiss their symptoms – fatigue, lethargy, poor vision, irritability, reduced libido, passing urine more frequently or having to get out of bed at night to go the toilet – as part of getting older or other problems. Most people who are diagnosed with diabetes have probably already had it for five to ten years. In the recent AusDiab survey of the general Australian population, for every one person who knew they had diabetes, there was another who had diabetes but had never been diagnosed. The sooner you know about diabetes the more you can do about halting its progress and avoiding complications. If the questionnaire on pages 6–7 shows you're at risk, you should see your doctor for a test.

The most common way to test for diabetes is an oral glucose tolerance test (OGTT), which involves an initial blood test, then drinking a large amount of glucose, then another blood test two hours later, to determine how quickly the glucose is cleared from your blood and balance restored. The OGTT is usually performed in the morning after fasting overnight. You are allowed to drink water beforehand, but no coffee, tea or juice.

In healthy people the blood glucose level from the second test should be below 7.8 mM. Modestly elevated glucose levels (between 7.8 and 11.1 mM) indicates impaired glucose tolerance (prediabetes). Glucose levels above 11.1 mM confirms diabetes. Two random blood glucose level results above 11.1 mM, or a fasting glucose result greater than

7.8 mM on separate occasions, confirms a diagnosis of diabetes mellitus. An OGTT is not required to confirm diagnosis.

Reducing your diabetes risk

Each day in Australia, 275 people develop type 2 diabetes. Although this book focuses on the management of diabetes and its complications, an equally important strategy is preventing diabetes in the first place. Everyone can reduce their chance of developing diabetes. The most important way to do this is to control your weight by eating less (if overweight) and being more active. Contrary to popular belief, cutting out sugar alone is not enough without also reducing your overall kilojoule intake.

Most Australians consume more kilojoules from food than they need. A healthy diet, lower in kilojoules but with all the nutrients we need, will reduce our waistlines and our risk of diabetes. The most practical way to achieve this is to follow an eating plan. All of the dietary advice in this book is just as effective for people who wish to reduce their risk of diabetes as for those who already have established diabetes.

Regular physical activity is an important means of achieving and maintaining weight control and of improving the body's composition. Even without any weight loss, regular exercise can substantially reduce your risk of diabetes. But you will achieve best results if you manage both. You don't need to become a fitness fanatic. Even a modest change in activity, such as more walking or riding a bike, combined with a weight loss of only 2 kilograms, can significantly reduce your chance of developing diabetes.

2 The diabetes healthy eating plan

Eating well is about establishing a workable routine
so that it becomes a part of your everyday life.

WHAT YOU CHOOSE TO eat can be powerfully important for your health and wellbeing. Your diet can make a tremendous difference to your blood glucose levels, your blood pressure and your cholesterol levels.

It used to be thought that a diet for controlling diabetes was all about cutting out sugar. These days the nutritional recommendations focus more on weight control and a healthy eating pattern low in saturated fat and high in fibre, with a moderate intake of less refined wholegrain carbohydrate foods, and of healthy fats such as those in oils and nuts. A small amount of added sugar is not a problem, since we now know that starchy carbohydrate foods cause a greater increase in blood glucose levels than does sugar. The quality of the carbohydrate foods you choose and the type of fats you eat are important.

After we eat carbohydrate-rich foods such as sugar, bread, pasta, rice, fruits and cereal-based foods, the carbohydrate they contain is converted into glucose and absorbed into the bloodstream, causing blood glucose levels to rise, reaching a peak 30–60 minutes later. Eating fewer carbohydrate foods can help prevent the rise in blood glucose levels after meals without affecting your insulin resistance – so cutting out carbohydrate foods altogether is not the solution.

Different types of carbohydrate cause different responses in our blood glucose levels. The glycaemic index (GI) is a measure of that response and we recommend eating moderate amounts of lower-GI carbohydrate foods (for more on the glycaemic index, see page 26).

The eating plans in this book (coming up on pages 14–23) are aimed at anyone who wants to improve their lifestyle but particularly people with a family history of diabetes, high cholesterol or high blood pressure. The eating plans are adaptable for weight loss or long-term weight maintenance, and allow you to enjoy good food while keeping your diabetes under control.

Determining your daily energy needs

You may or may not need to lose weight, but there are versions of the eating plan to suit everyone. To work out which level of the eating plan you should follow, first calculate the kilojoules you need to maintain your current weight. You will need to know your height in centimetres and your weight in kilograms. You will also need to select an appropriate activity factor from the table below.

Women should use this equation:

[655.1 + (9.56 × weight in kg) + (1.85 × height in cm) – (4.68 × age in years)] × 4.2 × activity factor

Men should use this equation:

[66.47 + (13.75 × weight in kg) + (5 × height in cm) – (6.76 × age in years)] × 4.2 × activity factor

Example

Donna is 50 years old, 170 cm tall and weighs 78 kg. She walks her dog 2–3 times a week, giving her an activity factor of 1.375. Donna's daily energy requirements to maintain her current weight will be:

[655.1 + (9.56 × 78) + (1.85 × 170) – (4.68 × 50)] × 4.2 × 1.375)

= [655.1 + 745.68 + 314.5 – 234] × 5.775

= 1481.28 × 5.775

= 8554 kJ (rounded down)

Many people will find it hard to calculate their daily energy requirements (BMR) and their BMI, so there are websites with calculators to do it for you. The Baker IDI website (bakeridi.edu.au) has calculators, or type 'BMR' and 'BMI' into your search engine.

Activity factors

ACTIVITY LEVEL	DESCRIPTION	ACTIVITY FACTOR
sedentary	little or no exercise each day, probably have a desk job	1.2
lightly active	light exercise or sport on 1–3 days a week	1.375
moderately active	moderate exercise or sport on 3–5 days a week	1.55
very active	hard exercise or sport on 6–7 days a week	1.725
extremely active	hard daily exercise or sport or a physical job or hard training (marathon, triathlon, etc.)	1.9

Body Mass Index (BMI)

BMI is used to measure whether you are under- or overweight or fall within the healthy range. You can calculate yours by dividing your weight in kilograms by the square of your height in metres. It is easy to calculate, but it can be misleading (see note below), so if you are worried you can always discuss your BMI with your diabetes care team.

$$BMI = \frac{\text{weight in kilograms}}{(\text{height in metres})^2}$$

What your BMI tells you

BODY CONDITION	NON-ASIAN BMI	ASIAN* BMI
Underweight	18.5 or less	18.5 or less
Healthy	18.6–24.9	18.6–22.9
Overweight	25–29.9	23–27.4
Obese	30 or more	27.5 or more

* The term 'Asian' here covers Indian subcontinent, Middle East, North Africa, Southern Europe.

EXAMPLE

Donna's height in metres is 1.7 and she weighs 78 kg. Her BMI is therefore:

78 divided by 1.7 squared

$= 78/(1.7)^2 = 27$ (rounding up)

Note that BMI measures can be misleading for children and elite athletes.

YOUR DAILY KILOJOULE REQUIREMENTS FOR WEIGHT LOSS

If your body mass index (BMI) indicates that you need to lose weight, subtract 2000–4000 kJ from the current daily kilojoule intake you calculated above. To reduce your weight by 0.5 kilogram (500 grams) each week, subtract 2000 kJ; to reduce your weight by 1 kilogram each week, subtract 4000 kJ. To calculate your BMI, see the box above.

Example

Donna now knows that her energy requirement (basal metabolic rate, or BMR) is 8554 kJ/day and that her BMI is 27, which places her in the over-weight category. Donna is aiming for a small weight loss so she reduces her kilojoule intake by 2000 kJ per day. Her daily kilojoule intake for weight loss is:

8554 – 2000

= 6554 kJ

HOW MUCH WEIGHT SHOULD YOU LOSE?

Aiming to reach a target weight that brings you into the normal BMI category is a guide but in reality this may not be easily achievable. Even a 5 per cent weight loss can improve diabetes control and may even prevent diabetes in some people.

The eating plans

SOMETHING FOR EVERYONE

One of the key features of the eating plans is that there are two options you can follow. Option 1 is a higher-protein plan with moderate amounts of carbohydrate foods. Level 2 of this eating plan provides you with 2 units of carbohydrate foods at breakfast and lunch and limits carbohydrate foods to 1 unit at dinner with a higher protein-food allowance (50–100 grams for lunch and 150–200 grams for dinner). This is very similar to the eating plan in the *CSIRO Total Wellbeing Diet*. The advantages of it are that the higher protein levels can help reduce hunger while lower carbohydrate levels can help keep blood glucose levels down.

Option 2 Level 2 offers smaller serves of protein-rich foods (50–100 grams for lunch and 50–100 grams for dinner) but includes 2–3 units of low-GI carbohydrate foods at breakfast, lunch and dinner.

Which option you choose is up you. If you prefer more meat, then Option 1 would suit you, but you don't need to follow the same option each day. Mixing and matching allows plenty of variety and flexibility while you stay healthy. In Part 2 you will find six weeks of menu plans for each option.

WEIGHT LOSS OR MAINTENANCE?

We have developed four different levels of the eating plan for you to choose from, depending on your sex and whether you wish to lose weight or maintain your current weight. To select the correct level of the eating plan that suits you, follow these three basic steps:

1 Determine your energy needs for either weight loss or weight maintenance using the information on pages 12–13.
2 Select the eating plan level that suits your energy needs from the table opposite.
3 Select your preferred eating plan – Option 1 or 2 or a combination of both.

In general, levels 1 and 2 are suitable for many women, and levels 3 and 4 for most men. But which is best for you will depend on your size and activity level.

EXAMPLE

Donna decides to try Level 2 (6500 kJ) to start with but to move up to Level 3 (7500 kJ) if she feels hungry or down to Level 1 (5500 kJ) if she is not losing weight (see table opposite). To assist with her weight loss and blood glucose control Donna should also consider increasing her physical activity level to moderate.

If this is all too complicated, the menu plans (see Part 2) and recipes (see Part 3) are a pretty good guide to the general eating style we recommend. Once you understand the basic principles, you can be more flexible in your food choices. Your dietitian can certainly help you with this.

The diabetes healthy eating plan, levels 1–4

EATING PLAN LEVEL	1	2	3	4
total daily energy intake (kilojoules)	5500	6500	7500	8500
OPTION 1 – HIGHER PROTEIN				
protein foods (units*/day)	2	2½	3	3½
low-GI wholegrain bread and cereals (units/day)	4	5	5	6
OPTION 2 – HIGHER CARBOHYDRATE				
protein foods (units/day)	1	1½	2½	2½
low-GI wholegrain bread and cereals (units/day)	5	7	7	8
BOTH OPTIONS				
reduced-fat dairy (units/day)	3	3	4	4
fruit (units/day)	2	2	2	3
Free List vegetables and salad (minimum units/day)	5	5	5	5
nuts, seeds and oils (units/day)	4	6	6	7
indulgence foods (units/week)	2	4	4	4

* What constitutes a unit for each food type is explained on pages 18–19.

Some people may wish to develop a personalised eating plan and others may need to have their medications adjusted either before or after they start to make lifestyle changes. If your diabetes is very well controlled, before making radical changes to what you eat we recommend talking to your diabetes care team. A diabetes care team generally consists of your doctors and various allied health professionals such as dietitians and podiatrists. See the Total care checklist (page 260) and Glossary (page 268) for further details about diabetes care teams.

ONE DAY ON THE EATING PLAN

Following is a sample day for both Option 1 and Option 2. As you adjust to the eating plan you will learn how to alter your daily intake to suit your medication regime and even your personal preferences, including swapping lunch and dinners if that suits you. To help guide your intake, you will need to monitor your blood glucose regularly and identify any hyperglycaemic or hypoglycaemic events (see Chapter 6). If you feel you need help at any time, talk to your diabetes care team.

The recipes referred to below are all from this book (see Part 3) and all suit the diabetes eating plan. Refer to individual recipes to see how many units each provides.

A sample day on Option 1 or 2

OPTION 1 – HIGHER PROTEIN

Breakfast
40 g low-GI high-soluble-fibre cereal (e.g. Guardian, Healthwise) with 250 ml skim milk; 1 small serve fruit *or* 10 g dry-roasted almonds
2 units bread, 1 unit dairy, 1 unit fruit *or* 1 unit fats (NSO)

Lunch
turkey, avocado & salad sandwich (2 slices low-GI wholegrain bread with 30 g avocado, 50 g shaved turkey, 1 cup mixed salad leaves & 20 g reduced-fat cheese)
2 units bread, ½ unit protein, 1 unit dairy, 1 unit vegetables, 1 unit fats (NSO)

Dinner
Thai Beef Salad (p 148) with an additional 1 cup Free List vegetables (p 20); 1 slice low-GI multigrain bread topped with 1 tsp light margarine
1 unit bread, 2 units protein, 4 units vegetables, 2 units fats (NSO)

Core food snack options
tea or coffee with skim milk – **Free List**
200 g low-fat yoghurt – **1 unit dairy**
1 piece fresh fruit – **1 unit fruit**
20 g raw, unsalted nuts – **2 units fats (NSO)**

Note: NSO refers to nuts, seeds and oils.

OPTION 2 – HIGHER CARBOHYDRATE

Breakfast
2 slices low-GI wholegrain toast with 2 tsp light margarine, 50 g low-fat reduced-salt cottage cheese; 125 ml unsweetened juice
2 units bread, 1 unit dairy, 1 unit fruit *or* 1 unit fats (NSO)

Lunch
4 wholegrain crispbread (e.g. Vita-Weat) with 30 g avocado & 50 g grilled chicken tenders; 1 cup mixed salad with low-joule balsamic dressing
2 units bread, ½ unit protein, 1 unit dairy, 1 unit vegetables, 1 unit fats (NSO)

Dinner
Penne with Tuna and Tomato Sauce (p 155) with ½ cup cooked spinach mixed in and 1 cup side salad
2 units bread, 1 unit protein, 4 units vegetables, 2 units fats (NSO)

Core food snack options
tea or coffee skim milk – **Free List**
200 g low-fat yoghurt (e.g. Nestlé diet or Yoplait formé) – **1 unit dairy**
1 piece fresh fruit – **1 unit fruit**
20 g raw, unsalted nuts – **2 units fats (NSO)**

YOUR DAILY FOOD GUIDE

For the first few weeks we suggest you try to stick as closely as possible to the menu plans in Part 2. This will give you a good chance to familiarise yourself with the key features of the eating plan and establish a good routine. Once you feel confident with the mix of foods, you can start to be creative. It is important to include each of the required units each day – each food group provides key nutrients and benefits.

Your daily core food allowance
(Level 2 – 6500 kilojoules)

1 LOW-GI, HIGH-FIBRE BREAD OR CEREAL FOODS

Either Option 1 = 5 units a day
or Option 2 = 7 units a day

**1 unit bread provides 300–400 kilojoules
and is equal to:**

- 20 grams low-GI, high-fibre breakfast cereal,
  e.g. Kellogg's Guardian, Komplete or Sustain;
  Uncle Toby's Oatbrits; untoasted natural muesli
  (including gluten-free); rolled oats,
  Freedom Quick Oats Porridge
- 1 × 35 grams slice low-GI wholegrain bread
- 1 large slice fruit loaf
- 1 × 40 grams slice wholewheat Mountain Bread
- ¼ cup cooked basmati rice
- ½ cup wholemeal pasta, noodles
  or couscous
- 100 grams cooked legumes*,
  e.g. lentils, baked beans,
  any cooked bean mix
- 100 grams sweet potato
- 200 grams pumpkin
- 70 grams sweet corn
- crispbread – 3 × Ryvita or
  4 × Vita-Weat

* We recommend cooked legumes for lunch or dinner at least
twice a week (counted either as a protein or carbohydrate unit).

2 LEAN PROTEIN FOODS

Either Option 1 = 2½ units a day
or Option 2 = 1½ units a day

**1 unit protein provides 500–600 kilojoules
and is equal to:**

- 100 grams any raw lean meat,
  including fish* and chicken
- 100 grams tofu
- 100 grams TVP (textured vegetable protein)
- 150 grams cooked legumes, e.g. lentils,
  baked beans, any cooked bean mix
- 2 eggs (up to 6 eggs a week)

* We recommend fish for lunch or dinner at least twice a week.

3 LOW-FAT DAIRY

3 units a day

**1 unit dairy provides 350–450 kilojoules
and is equal to:**

- 250 millilitres skim, low-fat or soy milk
- 200 grams low-fat, diet or soy yoghurt,
  e.g. Nestlé diet or Yoplait formé
- 200 grams low-fat custard or dairy dessert
- 20 grams reduced-fat (less than
  10 per cent) cheese
- 10 grams full-fat cheese

4 FRUIT

2 units a day

1 unit fruit provides 250–350 kilojoules and is equal to:

- 150 grams fresh or tinned, unsweetened fruit
- 150 millilitres unsweetened fruit juice
- 30 grams dried fruit

5 VEGETABLES

At least 5 units a day
from the Free List (see page 20)

1 unit vegetables provides 80–100 kilojoules and is equal to 1 cup salad vegetables or ½ cup cooked vegetables
We recommend 1 cup salad and 2 cups cooked vegetables each day. Aim to include orange and green vegetables, such as carrots, spinach and broccoli, to boost your intake of a range of nutrients.

6 FATS (NUTS, SEEDS AND OILS)

Up to 6 units a day

1 unit fats provides 200–250 kilojoules and is equal to:

- 1 teaspoon any liquid oil, such as canola, olive, grapeseed or sunflower oil
- 1 teaspoon polyunsaturated or monounsaturated margarine
- 2 teaspoons fat-reduced polyunsaturated or monounsaturated (light) margarine
- 10 grams nuts or seeds
- 20 grams avocado

7 INDULGENCE FOODS

4 units a *week**

1 unit indulgence is equal to any food or drink providing approximately 450 kilojoules,
such as 150 millilitres wine or 20 grams chocolate. (See page 36 for snack options and pages 138–144 for recipes.)

* If you are aiming to lose weight, you may wish to make this 2 units a week.

If you don't need to lose weight, you can be more liberal with your core foods, including nuts, seeds, fruit, cereals and low-fat dairy foods.

THE FREE LIST

Free List foods contain minimal carbohydrates and kilojoules, so eat them freely to spice up your meals and help control hunger. Recipes made completely with Free List foods are highlighted with a 'Free' tag in Part 3 of this book.

Vegetables – all vegetables *except* potato, pumpkin, sweet potato and sweet corn.

Drinks – water, cocoa (*not* drinking chocolate), coffee, diet cordial, diet soft drinks, herbal tea, unflavoured mineral water, tea.

Condiments – barbecue sauce, chilli sauce, clear soup, curry powder or paste, diet jelly, diet topping, garlic, ginger, herbs, hoisin sauce, horseradish, lemon, low-kilojoule sweeteners, mint sauce, mustard, oil-free dressings, parsley, pickles, salt-reduced soy sauce, spices, salt-reduced stock, tomato paste, tomato salsa, tomato sauce, Vegemite, verjuice, vinegar, wasabi.

Note – Many condiments and sauces are high in salt, so avoid these. A small amount of cornflour, custard powder or sugar is fine to thicken or sweeten dishes: 1 level teaspoon of cornflour, custard powder or sugar contains 40–60 kilojoules. This is low enough not to worry about if you use them only occasionally.

If nuts are used in a recipe in small amounts it is okay to consider their kilojoule contribution as negligible. Alternatively, you could treat them as part of your fat allowance.

The weight maintenance plan

Weight maintenance after weight loss can be challenging, mainly because in the relief of reaching our target weight we forget the healthy habits that helped us get there. Make your new eating and exercise habits a way of life from the beginning, to ensure you can maintain your healthy weight in the long term.

The people who are most successful at maintaining their weight loss are more likely to:

1 monitor their weight and food intake with a food diary

2 maintain or seek additional supports, including fitness or weight-loss groups

3 exercise regularly, at least 30 minutes four days a week

4 accept that they are responsible for their own health

5 monitor their hunger and be aware of appropriate portion serves

6 have three meals a day and snack on healthy foods between meals if needed

7 set small and realistic goals and review these at suitable times

8 maintain a positive attitude and get back on track after dietary lapses

9 develop interests and hobbies to help them focus on things other than food

10 develop creative ways to manage stress effectively, including seeking help.

Sample 500-kJ blocks*

CORE FOOD GROUP	FOOD	500-KILOJOULE BLOCK	UNITS
bread	pasta	⅓ cup cooked	1 unit bread
	sweet potato	150 grams	1 unit bread
	bread – wholegrain, wholemeal, fruit	1 × 35 gram slice	1 unit bread
protein	tofu or TVP (textured vegetable protein)	100 grams	1 unit protein
	canned beans	150 grams cooked	1 unit bread *or* 1 unit protein
	dried chickpeas or legumes	40 grams	1 unit bread *or* 1 unit protein
	cooked fish, chicken, beef, lamb or turkey	100 grams	1 unit protein
	boiled egg	1	½ unit protein
dairy	low-fat milk or flavoured milk	250 millilitres	1 unit dairy
	low-fat ice-cream	70 grams	1 unit dairy
	low-fat yoghurt or custard	200 grams	1 unit dairy
	Frûche, fromage frais	150 grams	1 unit dairy
	full-fat cheese	10 grams	1 unit dairy
	reduced-fat cheese	20 grams	1 unit dairy
fruit	fresh fruit salad	300 grams	2 units fruit
	unsweetened fruit juice	250 millilitres	2 units fruit
	dried fruit – apricot, mango	60 grams	2 units fruit
fats	sunflower, pumpkin or sesame seeds	20 grams	2 units fat
	tahini paste	3½ tsp (20 grams)	1 unit fat
	light peanut butter	3½ tsp (20 grams)	1 unit fat
	unsaturated oil	3 teaspoons	3 units fat
	dry-roasted, unsalted nuts	20 grams	1 unit fat
	avocado	¼ (40 grams)	2 units fat
indulgence	wine	150 millilitres	1 unit indulgence
	beer	375 millilitres	1 unit indulgence
	spirits	60 millilitres	2 units indulgence
	chocolate	20 grams	1 unit indulgence
	crisps – potato, chickpea, pita, soya, Peaz – cooked in canola or sunola oil with no added salt	1 × 21 gram packet	1 unit indulgence
	air-popped popcorn, no added salt	4 cups	1 unit indulgence
	honey	30 ml	1 unit indulgence
	sugar	30 g (6 tsp)	1 unit indulgence

* Choose low- or reduced-salt options whenever possible.

We all have different energy needs, so there will be a period of trial and error as you work out how much you should eat to maintain your new weight. We suggest keeping to the basic structure of the eating plan and slowly adding new foods to your daily allowance in 500-kilojoule 'blocks', relying more frequently on the core foods – see the table below for suggestions and check food labels for kilojoule information if you want to try a food that is not listed in the table.

It's best to weigh your portions – it is easy to become complacent and underestimate the amounts we are eating.

ADDING 500 KJ BLOCKS ON THE MAINTENANCE PLAN

The idea is to add one 500-kilojoule block to your daily allowance each week until you are maintaining your weight. You can vary the 500-kilojoule blocks within the week or, if you are planning to eat out, you can save them up. Here's how to add the blocks to your daily allowance over a three-week period and beyond.

week 1	Add 1 × 500-kilojoule block to your basic eating plan each day
week 2	If you're still losing weight, add another 500-kilojoule block to basic eating plan each day
week 3	If you're still losing weight, add another 500-kilojoule food block to your basic eating plan each day and continue doing this each week until you maintain your weight.

If you start to gain weight again, do not add any foods the following week. If your weight gain is more than 1 kilogram, drop back to the previous week's plan. Once you reach a stage where your weight becomes stable, that should remain your eating plan for long-term weight maintenance. You will need to weigh yourself weekly during this transition phase to judge the effect of adding extra foods to your diet. Once you have achieved a stable weight, however, weighing yourself once a fortnight at the same time and in the same state of dress or undress is more than enough.

Five weeks on the maintenance plan

week 1 maintenance	choose any 1 block, e.g. 1 × 35 gram slice toast at breakfast
week 2 maintenance	choose any 2 blocks, e.g. 1 × 35 g slice toast + 20 grams nuts as a snack
week 3 maintenance	choose any 3 blocks, e.g. 1 × 35 g slice of toast + 20 grams nuts + 20 grams dark chocolate
week 4 maintenance	choose any 4 blocks, e.g. 1 × 35 grams slice toast + 20 grams nuts + 20 grams dark chocolate + 150 millilitres wine
week 5 maintenance	choose any 5 blocks, e.g. 1 × 35 g slice toast + 20 grams nuts + 20 grams dark chocolate + 150 millilitres wine + 1 piece fruit

Don't forget to stay active. If you change how much you exercise, you may also need to alter your food intake. This will be the key to maintaining your healthy weight and staying in control of your diabetes forever.

Note: Only continue to add blocks if you are still losing weight. As soon as your weight stabilises, stop adding blocks.

KEEPING A FOOD DIARY

One of the most important tools for losing weight successfully *and* maintaining weight loss in the longer term is a food diary. Recording your daily food intake not only makes you more accountable and aware of what you're eating, it also helps you monitor your eating patterns and identify any problem areas that may lead to weight regain or that cause problems with your blood sugar levels.

Once you have achieved your target weight and feel in control of your eating, you will find that you don't have to monitor your intake as much. A weekly or even monthly food diary may then be enough to help you maintain your weight. If you find you are slowly regaining weight or feeling out of control with your eating, you may need to go back to recording your intake on a daily basis to get yourself back on track.

3 Low-GI foods and diabetes

Timing, amount and type of carbohydrates are what matters.

Carbohydrates and diabetes

Carbohydrate foods are broken down to release glucose. Glucose then enters the bloodstream to be distributed throughout the body as fuel. Some carbohydrate foods, such as high-GI white bread, are digested quickly and cause a rapid increase in blood glucose levels. Others, such as porridge, are digested more slowly and cause a slow and gentle increase in blood glucose levels.

Breads, cereals, fruit and dairy (except cheese) all contain carbohydrates, so it is important to spread these foods out over your day.

TIMING, SPREAD AND AMOUNT OF CARBOHYDRATE

To help achieve good blood glucose control, it is important to have regular meals, to maintain an even spread of carbohydrate intake throughout the day and to balance the carbohydrates with protein foods. Skipping meals then over-loading on carbohydrate foods may cause large increases in your blood glucose levels, which increases your risk of complications in the long run. Controlling your weight and exercising can make a big difference to how well your body can use carbohydrate foods.

The Glycaemic Index (GI)

Different types of carbohydrate foods are digested at different rates, causing different responses in your blood glucose level. The glycaemic index (GI) is a measure of that response, with the reaction to glucose as a point of reference. It indicates how your blood glucose level will react if you eat a particular carbohydrate food. In general, it is best to choose low-GI carbohydrate foods, which will increase your blood glucose levels slowly, and to avoid high-GI carbohydrate foods, which cause a rapid increase in blood glucose levels.

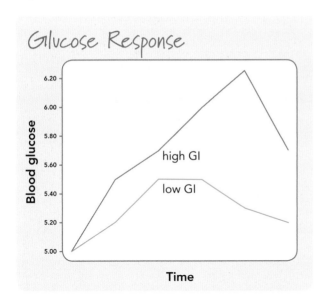

Glucose Response

The Glycaemic Index

GI	EFFECT
Low – 55 or less	slow rise in blood glucose levels
intermediate – 56–69	moderate rise in blood glucose levels
high – 70 or more	fast rise in blood glucose levels

Note that the glycaemic index is only a guide and that different people can respond differently to different foods. This means you still need to monitor your blood glucose levels to ensure optimal diabetes management.

It is important to bear in mind that you cannot always be sure of a food's GI. Many factors can change the GI – although pasta falls into the low-GI category, the more it is cooked, the higher its GI becomes. For this reason it is best to eat pasta and potatoes al dente.

GLYCAEMIC LOAD (GL)

Although the GI of a carbohydrate food can provide information about how quickly that carbohydrate increases blood glucose levels, the *amount* of carbohydrate in the food will affect how long this increase lasts. The glycaemic load (GL) attempts to quantify the amount of glucose 'loaded' into the bloodstream by a carbohydrate food. It takes into account *both* the type of carbohydrate (GI) and the amount of the carbohydrate in the food eaten.

GL = (GI × amount of carbohydrate in grams)/100

Having lots of a low-GI food can cause a long rise in blood glucose levels similar to that caused by a small serve of high-GI food. This makes GL a more useful indicator of how a food will affect your blood glucose levels. Even though the GI of watermelon is in the high range, the total amount of carbohydrate in watermelon is very low, so eating it will not affect your blood glucose levels very much. When selecting starchy foods such as bread, however, it's always best to go for low-GI options.

Eating moderate amounts of low-GI carbohydrate foods can help control blood glucose levels, but it is even more important to restrict your kilojoule intake and keep your weight in check.

FOOD COMBINATIONS AND GI

GI and GL values apply only to carbohydrate foods, but their values change when the carbohydrate food is consumed with other carbohydrate foods, or with protein foods or fats. Protein foods and fats can lower the GI of a carbohydrate food by slowing its digestion, so mixing food groups at each meal is an important way of ensuring your blood glucose levels don't fluctuate too widely. Always choose lean protein foods and healthy fats.

The GI symbol

To help you to identify healthy low-GI foods at a glance while shopping, the Glycemic Index Foundation has created a GI symbol. Food products carrying the symbol must not only have a low GI, but also meet other criteria concerning their energy, fat, saturated fat, sodium, calcium and fibre content.

Common foods carrying the GI symbol include breads, breakfast cereals, fruit, frozen desserts, sweeteners and products containing sweeteners, dairy foods, pasta, rice and snack foods.

For more information, visit glycemicindex.com or gisymbol.com

4 Shopping, food labels and eating out

Healthy eating starts with what you
put in your shopping trolley.

Shopping

You don't need to buy special foods for diabetes, you just need to make healthy choices. Before you go out looking for new foods, though, conduct a pantry audit, to see which foods you already use and if you can make healthier choices.

Use the table below as a guide to foods you might want to include on your shopping list. Some are staples, but others are low-kilojoule foods that might help provide a little more variety in your eating plan. Beware of 'diabetic' foods in the confectionery aisle – these are rarely necessary.

SEVEN TIPS FOR SMART SHOPPING

1 Be prepared – A shopping list will save you time and money, and can help prevent impulse buying. Keep a notepad in the kitchen and write down the items you need as you run out of them.

2 Don't shop on an empty stomach or if you're hungry – People who shop on an empty stomach tend to buy more – particularly things they really don't need. Try to go shopping just after a meal.

3 Get to know your supermarket – Once you know the layout, write your shopping list in categories that resemble the aisles. This keeps you out of aisles you don't need to visit and can eliminate unnecessary shopping time.

4 Buy fruit and vegetables in season – This is the smartest and cheapest way to reach your goal of eating two serves of fruit and five serves of vegetables a day.

5 Occasionally take your time – Every so often, take time to compare brands and investigate new products. The quietest times to shop are early in the week and late at night.

6 Skip that aisle – If you don't need food from a particular aisle, don't visit it. This applies especially to the confectionery, biscuits, pastry and soft-drink aisles.

7 If you're in a hurry, shop on the edges – Foods kept on the perimeter of the supermarket tend to be *core foods* – meats, vegetables, salads, breads and chilled items such as dairy foods and spreads.

Food labels

NUTRITION INFORMATION PANELS

Nutrition information panels allow us to compare products of the same nature. *Always* check the 'per 100 g' column. The serving size given on the label is determined by the manufacturer and is not necessarily the right one for you.

For dairy products, check the fat and saturated-fat content and choose lower-fat varieties. If you do choose full-fat versions, simply eat smaller portions. As a general rule, choose foods with less than 10 grams *total fat* per 100 grams, but with dairy products choose foods with less than 2 grams total fat per 100 grams. Aim for as low a *saturated-fat* content as possible.

For breads, you need to check whether it is a wholegrain, and is high in fibre (more than 5 grams fibre per 100 grams) or has a low GI. For breakfast cereals, check the fibre content and choose higher-fibre cereals (3 grams fibre per serve). Some cereals are higher in fat, but this comes from nuts, which contain healthy fats. Don't let the fat content of these foods put you off – as they can be healthy choices in controlled amounts. Do look out for the sugar content – some breakfast cereals are very high in sugar.

Sample breakfast cereal nutrition information panel

NUTRITIONAL INFORMATION (AVERAGE) SERVING SIZE: 30G (2 BISCUITS)		
	Quantity per serving	Quantity per 100 g
Energy (kJ)	447kJ	1490kJ
Protein	3.7g	12.4g
Fats – Total Fat – Saturated Fat	 0.4g 0.1g	 1.4g 0.3g
Carbohydrates – Total – Sugars	 20.1g 1.0g	 67g 3.3g
Fibre	3.3g	11.0g
Sodium	87.0mg	290mg
Potassium	102mg	340mg

Ingredients:
Wholegrain wheat (97%), Raw sugar, Salt, Barley malt extract, Minerals [Zinc gluconate, Iron], Vitamins [Niacin, Thiamine, Riboflavin, Folate], no artificial flavours.

Food type	Healthy examples*
vegetables	• fresh and plain frozen vegetables – all varieties are suitable • canned vegetables – choose reduced-salt varieties • buy sweet potato instead of potato
fruit	• fresh fruit – all varieties are suitable • tinned fruit – choose varieties in natural juice or water rather than sugar syrup
breakfast cereals	• choose high-fibre varieties, such as rolled oats, Mini-Wheats, All-Bran, Sultana Bran, Weet-Bix, Vita Brits, Shredded Wheat, Weeties, Goodness BARLEYmax cereals
bread	• choose low-GI varieties, such as Bürgen, and wholegrain or white high-fibre varieties over white bread • choose low-salt varieties – Bürgen Wholegrain & Oats is lower in salt (280 milligrams per 100 grams) than other breads • choose brands with small to moderate slices rather than very large ones
biscuits	• crispbread – Ryvita, Rice Thins, Corn Thins, Kavli rye crispbread • sweet biscuits – Arnott's Snack Right
cheese	• cottage cheese, quark or quarg, ricotta • Devondale Seven, Coon Light & Tasty, Bega So-Light, Bega Super Slim, Bonlac fat-reduced, Perfect Italiano light grated mozzarella cheese (all have less than 15 per cent fat)
milk	• choose fat-reduced varieties, such as Skinny, REV, PhysiCal, So Good Lite, Pura Light Start, Feel Good flavoured milks
yoghurt	• choose fat-reduced varieties, such as Ski D'lite, Dairy Farmers Thick & Creamy, Yoplait formé, Weight Watchers, Jalna Low Fat or Fat Free, Nestlé Diet
jam	• St Dalfour, Monbulk 100% fruit, Weight Watchers • you may use regular jam in small amounts as part of a mixed meal
salad dressings	• Kraft 100% Fat Free salad dressings, Kraft 99% Fat Free Coleslaw Dressing, Kraft 97% Fat Free Mayonnaise, Salad Magic No Oil salad dressings, Salad Magic Low Oil Mayonnaise, Weight Watchers Mayonnaise and dressings
rice	• basmati, doongara
canned beans	• all varieties – baked beans, butter beans, red kidney beans, three-bean mix, haricot beans, chickpeas
soft drinks	• all diet and low-joule soft drinks and cordials, plain mineral water or soda water
confectionery	• Wrigley's Extra Sugarfree Chewing Gum
desserts	• low-fat dairy desserts, such as Peters Light & Creamy dairy desserts; low-joule jellies, such as Aeroplane Jelly Lite

* Choose low- or reduced-salt varieties whenever possible, or buy foods with the Heart Foundation Tick.

The Heart Foundation Tick

The Heart Foundation's Tick symbol tells shoppers that a particular product is a healthier choice than similar products without a Tick. Foods that carry the Tick have been independently tested to ensure they meet the Heart Foundation's strict standards for saturated fat, trans fat, kilojoules, salt and fibre content.

Once a food has earned the Tick, it will be subject to random testing. This means that at any time, without the manufacturer being warned, the food will be purchased from a supermarket or food outlet by Tick and sent to an independent lab for testing, to ensure that it still meets Tick's standards.

The Tick appears on over 1100 supermarket foods as well as on restaurant and takeaway meals. For more information about the Tick Program, visit heartfoundation.org.au/tick.

CERT TM

Sweeteners

A moderate intake of sugar (10 per cent of total daily energy needs) is acceptable in a healthy diet, but diabetic diets often include sweeteners to replace sugar in foods and beverages. There are two types of sweetener: non-nutritive (also known as 'artificial' or 'intense') and nutritive. Non-nutritive sweeteners, such as saccharin, have a minimal or no effect on blood glucose levels, making them popular among people trying to lose weight and control their blood glucose levels. They are generally much sweeter than sugar, so you need to use much less of them. Nutritive sweeteners, however, still contain kilojoules and can affect blood glucose levels. Some, such as honey and fructose, should be considered as providing plentiful energy without much nutritional value.

NON-NUTRITIVE SWEETENERS

Here are the most common non-nutritive sweeteners. Their properties are summarised in the table opposite.

- Saccharin was one of the first non-nutritive sweeteners, created in 1879. Because of its bitter aftertaste, it is often used in combination with other non-nutritive sweeteners.
- Aspartame is made up of two amino acids – aspartic acid and phenylalanine – found in natural proteins. People with the rare genetic condition phenylketonuria have to avoid foods containing phenylalanine, including aspartame. It does not have a bitter

aftertaste, but can interact with other foods and may not always taste like sugar.

- Acesulfame potassium is also known as Acesulfame K and is similar in structure to saccharin. It is not metabolised in the body, so it passes out unchanged in the urine. It is also heat stable and so can be used in cooking and baking. It is often used in combination with other non-nutritive sweeteners.

- Sucralose is created by modifying the structure of ordinary sugar (sucrose). Only negligible amounts are absorbed by the body. It is heat stable, which makes it suitable for use in cooking and baking.
- Steviol glycosides are most commonly known as stevia and are extracted from the leaves of the South American herb *Stevia rebaudiana*. They were approved for use in Australia and New Zealand in 2008.

Common tabletop non-nutritive sweeteners

NAME (code number)	BRAND NAMES	AVAILABLE IN	SUITABLE FOR COOKING?	ENERGY CONTENT*	APPROXIMATE SWEETNESS**
saccharin (954)	Sugarine Sugarella Sweetex Hermesetas Mini Sweeteners	• table-top powder, tablet or liquid	no – usually leaves a bitter or metallic aftertaste	nil	300
cyclamate (952)	Sucaryl	• tablet, usually	no	nil	30
aspartame (951)	Nutrasweet Equal Hermesetas Gold Equal Spoonful	• diet products, including sugar-free gum, and diet soft drinks, cordial, yoghurts • table-top powder	no – breaks down at high temperatures	17 kJ/g	180
Acesulfame K (950)	Hermesetas Gold	• diet products, including sugar-free gum, and diet soft drinks, cordial, yoghurts • table-top tablets	yes – stable at high temperatures	nil	200
Sucralose (955)	Splenda	• diet products, including sugar-free gum, and diet soft drinks, confectionery • table-top tablets or powder	yes – very heat stable and no aftertaste	nil	600
Steviol glycosides (960)	Hermesetas Stevia Sweet	• table-top powder or liquid	Yes – heat stable; does have an aniseed aftertaste	negligible	30

* Sucrose (table sugar) contains 16 kilojoules/gram and has a GI of 65.

** Sweetness is calculated relative to sucrose, where sucrose has a sweetness of 1.

NUTRITIVE SWEETENERS

Common nutritive sweeteners include fructose, sugar alcohols (such as sorbitol), polydextrose and maltodextrin. Some may have a laxative effect, especially if consumed in large amounts. All contribute kilojoules to your diet and can cause rises in blood sugar levels.

ARE NON-NUTRITIVE SWEETENERS SAFE?

The non-nutritive sweeteners available in Australia have been tested and approved by Food Standards Australia and New Zealand (FSANZ) and are safe for consumption. You should never use more of them than indicated by the acceptable daily intakes (ADI). Bear in mind that the ADI is not an absolute indicator of where safety ends and possible health concerns begin – we each react differently to sweeteners.

Common nutritive sweeteners

NAME (code number)	BRAND NAMES	AVAILABLE IN	SUITABLE FOR COOKING?	ENERGY CONTENT*	COMMENTS
Fructose – fruit sugar (nil)	Sweetaddin	• fruit, fruit juices, honey, maple syrup • soft drinks, yoghurt • table-top tablets	yes	16 kJ/g	large amounts may cause diarrhoea in children and some adults with fructose intolerance
Sugar alcohols – sorbitol (420), xylitol (967), mannitol (421), maltitol (965), isomalt (953)	nil	• chewing gums, confectionery (with other sweeteners)	no – will commonly leave a bitter/ metallic aftertaste	16 kJ/g	can cause wind and bloating; large amounts can have a laxative effect
polydextrose (1200)	Litesse	• baked goods, dairy products, confectionery, salad dressings, cereals, jams	yes	16 kJ/g	large amounts may have a laxative effect
maltodextrin (nil)	nil – also called hydrolysed corn syrup or glucose syrup	• soft drinks, canned fruits, chewing gum, cereals	yes	16 kJ/g	maltodextrin has a very high GI
thaumatin (957)	Talin	• dairy products, jams, coffee and tea drinks, chewing gum • toothpaste	yes	17 kJ/g	—

Women who are pregnant or breastfeeding can safely consume foods containing non-nutritive sweeteners in small amounts. There is no clinical evidence that artificial sweeteners cause cancer.

'LOW-GI' SUGAR

Recently CSR released a 'low-GI' sugar called LoGIcane. It has a GI of 50 compared with sucrose, which has a medium GI of 65. This difference between LoGIcane and regular sugar is not significant, since they have the same number of kilojoules. If you are watching your weight, the best strategy is to use sugars in moderation. If you want to reduce the overall GI of your diet and *not* lose weight, then LoGIcane will help you do that.

Snacks

It is a common belief that people with diabetes must snack regularly, but most people with type 2 diabetes don't need snacks between meals. A snack often just means unnecessary kilojoules and weight gain.

If you like to have snacks, it's best to choose a piece of fruit, a tub of yoghurt or another healthy snack from your daily core foods (for more see below). Healthy snacks can help you stay focused throughout the day and prevent uncontrollable hunger in the evening.

Be aware that many 'snacks' provide as many kilojoules as a normal meal – look at the example over the page of coffee and a muffin versus a ham and salad sandwich.

SNACKS AND INSULIN

If you need insulin injections to manage your blood glucose levels, you may need to have a snack between meals or at supper to help keep your blood glucose levels under control and avoid the risk of hypoglycaemia (see page 64). If your blood glucose levels are frequently low, your doctor may review your drug dose. In many cases it may be best to reduce your medication rather than snack all the time.

HEALTHY SNACKS

Unless you are taking insulin, it is generally not essential to have snacks. If you prefer to do so, the healthiest snacks come from your core daily food allowance (see pages 18–19). Examples include fruit, reduced-fat yoghurt, nuts, fruit toast or even a slice of wholegrain bread. If you decide to snack on one of your indulgence foods, keep it to a very small amount.

Snack versus lunch

regular-milk mugaccino with 1 × 80 g sultana & bran muffin (7 cm in diameter by 4–7 cm high)	ham & salad sandwich (2 × 35 g slices wholegrain bread, 50 g lean sliced shoulder ham, 20 g reduced-fat cheese, ½ cup mixed salad vegetables, 1 tsp oil-free dressing) with 150 ml unsweetened fruit juice
total energy – 1450 kJ **total carbohydrate – 45 g** **GI – 53 (low)**	**total energy – 1440 kJ** **total carbohydrate – 39 g** **GI – 50 (low)**

TIPS FOR SNACKING SENSIBLY

1 Identify if you *need* a snack or just want one.

2 Keep your snacks to 500 kilojoules or less and monitor your weight.

3 Beware of overindulging in low-fat or low-sugar foods – check the label for energy content.

4 Make a list of your daily snacks and place it on the fridge to remind you of your plan.

5 Place your planned snacks in reusable single-serving containers or resealable bags so that you only have in front of you what you want to eat.

6 Small quantities of nuts are a healthy and quick option – they contain monounsaturated fats, which help lower cholesterol and reduce the risk of heart disease, and are a good protein source.

7 Snack on Free List foods, such as raw vegetables, or see the Free List recipes marked with the 'Free' tag in Part 3.

8 Blend a fruit smoothie using foods from your daily core allowance – blend half a chopped banana, 75 grams mango, 100 grams of low-fat plain or vanilla yoghurt and a non-nutritive sweetener (optional) with ice until smooth, then sip it slowly.

Cravings and hunger

There are many physiological reasons why we experience cravings and hunger, and some relate to our hormone levels. The hormone ghrelin, which is produced in the stomach, generally increases before a meal and drops again after meals. It is known as the hunger stimulator. Other hormones work in an opposite fashion, making us feel full when we've eaten a meal. The best way to ensure you eat only when you are hungry is to establish a dietary regime and take your time to sit and enjoy your meals. Slowing down your food intake allows your body to produce and respond to fullness cues.

There can also be psychological reasons for cravings and hunger. Food commercials, cooking programs or even cooking smells can trigger cravings, as can stress, boredom and a low mood. To change your habits you need to understand the triggers for your cravings.

TIPS FOR BEATING HUNGER AND CRAVINGS

1 Keeping a food diary – Writing it down can help you become aware of what situations are risky for you so that you can avoid them.

2 Don't be afraid of change – Alter your routine and seek support from those around you.

3 Deal with stress and strong emotions – A short burst of exercise when you are under stress can improve your mood and help control your cravings. Seek help if your stress or emotions are overwhelming.

4 Use Free List foods and core foods – This will help make you feel fuller without the danger of excessive kilojoule intake.

THE HUNGER SCALE

Many people have forgotten what physical hunger feels like, just as they have forgotten what comfortably full and overfull feel like. One of the best ways to control your cravings is to ask yourself what is triggering them and to rate your hunger and fullness on a scale of one to ten.

If you think you're hungry, check with your body before you eat. Aim to eat whenever your hunger is between 1 and 3 and to stop when you are at 5.

0	1	2	3	4	5	6	7	8	9	10
0 = starving			3 = peckish		5 = COMFORTABLE			8 = overfull		10 = uncomfortable

Eating out

Just because you have diabetes doesn't mean you can't enjoy eating out. You just need to make healthy food choices. Many restaurants and take-aways offer a wider range of healthy meals. Some even have symbols or nutritional information on their menus to assist you.

If you eat out very frequently, you will have to be more careful with your food choices. If you dine out only occasionally, you can be less strict and allow yourself a moderate treat now and then.

Use the following tips to avoid overeating when eating out.

Healthier restaurant meals

CUISINE	HEALTHIER OPTIONS
Western	• hamburger – order a standard hamburger rather than one with the lot • fish and chips – order grilled or baked fish fillets and a small serve of chips • chicken – remove the skin and fat, especially if the chicken is deep-fried • salad – order a salad with every meal and ask for oil-free dressing or the dressing on the side • sandwiches – choose wholegrain or wholemeal bread and lean protein, ask for lots of salad and take care with portion sizes
Italian	• avoid cream-based soups or creamy pasta sauces • pasta – order an entrée-sized serve • pizza – choose a thin crust and lots of vegetables as toppings and avoid adding extra cheese
Greek	• dips – choose hummus or yoghurt-based dips • meats – choose grilled red meat, fish or chicken and order vegetables or salad and beans on the side • desserts – give them a miss or stick to small serves
Mexican	• tortillas – choose soft rather than hard • avoid refried beans • limit your intake of cheese, sour cream and guacamole
Indian	• order from steamed rice, saffron rice or naan for your carbohydrate serves • limit dishes based on coconut cream or coconut milk • avoid or limit anything deep-fried – pappadams, poori, samosas, bhaji
South-East Asian	• order steamed rice or noodles rather than fried rice or crispy noodles • order dishes that are not fried, especially for entrées • order at least one vegetable-based dish • limit dishes based on coconut cream or coconut milk

TEN TIPS FOR EATING OUT

1 Plan ahead – Find out before you go what food will be on offer. Know your portion sizes and stick to them.

2 Watch your portion – Order an entree for your main meal or ask for an entree-size main course.

3 Include some carbohydrate in your meal – and keep it within your eating plan. If you have some bread, you don't really need the butter or margarine too.

4 Practise visualising bread, protein and fat units – Weigh your foods at home and get used to estimating a unit. If you are served too much, just leave it on your plate.

5 Order salads or vegetables as the bulk of your meal – Request oil-free salad dressings such as balsamic vinegar or for the dressing to be served separately.

6 Limit your alcohol intake to 2 standard drinks or less – If you're not sure how many standard drinks are in your glass, stick to just one glass (most places serve 1½–2 standard drinks). Order water and drink it between sips of wine.

7 Stop and ask yourself if you need dessert – If you do order one, think about sharing it or opt for a skim-milk coffee instead.

8 Choose the nibbles – If a friend invites you for dinner, suggest that you bring nibbles to ensure they are low energy.

9 Don't let yourself get over-hungry before you go – When you arrive at a restaurant or dinner party, ask for a glass of water and sip it slowly while looking over the nibbles or the menu and considering your options. When your food comes, eat it slowly and focus on the conversation.

10 Switch lunch and dinner – If you eat out regularly for work during the day, you can enjoy the midday meal but maintain your new eating plan by having a simple sandwich or salad for dinner. If the rest of the family is eating dinner, have some too, but make yours a smaller portion and serve it on a side plate.

Alcohol

You need not avoid alcohol altogether – you just need to drink sensibly. Alcohol provides kilojoules, just as fats, carbohydrates and protein do. In fact, alcohol provides almost as much energy (29 kilojoules/gram) as fat (37 kilojoules/gram). Alcohol can also stimulate the appetite and remove inhibitions, which can make it easier to overeat. It can also cause weight gain, make it difficult to manage diabetes, trigger hypoglycaemia with certain medications, increase blood triglycerides, increase blood pressure, damage major organs and systems over time, and increase cancer risk.

RECOMMENDED ALCOHOL INTAKE

The current daily recommendations for people with diabetes are:

- 1 standard drink or less for women
- 2 standard drinks or less for men
- at least 2 alcohol-free days per week for everyone

TIPS FOR DRINKING ALCOHOL

1. Do not drink on an empty stomach.
2. Set yourself a limit before you start drinking.
3. Sip your drink slowly.
4. Alternate sips with water or a diet soft drink.
5. Treat alcohol as indulgence units and stick to your eating plan.

For more information on the alcohol guidelines visit nhmrc.gov.au/your_health/healthy/alcohol/index.htm

What is a standard drink?

1 standard drink contains 10 grams of alcohol. Serving sizes in restaurants, pubs and bars are usually *not* equivalent to 1 standard drink, but usually 1½–2 standard drinks.

1 standard drink is equal to:

- 285 millilitres regular beer (4.9 per cent alcohol)
- 375 millilitres mid-strength beer (3.5 per cent alcohol)
- 80 millilitres table wine (12–14.5 per cent alcohol)
- 30 millilitres spirits (40 per cent alcohol)
- 60 millilitres fortified wine, such as port

5 Active living

Sit less, move more, move more often.

REGULAR PHYSICAL EXERCISE is one of the most effective ways of improving your health and managing your diabetes. It is particularly effective in controlling blood glucose levels and reducing the risk of heart disease, stroke and diabetes complications. In this chapter we look at the benefits of exercise and suggest a simple exercise program to get you started. This program, which encompasses light- to moderate-intensity activities, would generally be considered safe for most people. If you have concerns, however, you should speak with your diabetes care team before commencing any exercise plan.

Living an active life

There are two sorts of physical activity: purposeful exercise and incidental movement. We tend to think of physical activity as planned exercise, but it is also important to keep active and moving during our day-to-day lives. The less we sit, the healthier we'll be.

Incidental movement includes walking to the bus stop, moving around the office, vacuuming the lounge room or walking up stairs. As a general rule, incidental movement is a non-sweaty form of physical activity. In fact, any type of movement that requires us to use our muscles, even standing up, uses energy and contributes to our overall health and wellbeing.

Try to maximise opportunities for both purposeful exercise and incidental movement in your daily routine so that it becomes a lifelong healthy habit.

Exercise and hypoglycaemia

Exercise often decreases blood glucose levels towards normal levels, so it helps you avoid hyperglycaemia throughout the day and reduces your blood glucose levels to normal in the long term. Contrary to popular belief, people with type 2 diabetes who are not taking antidiabetic medications very rarely suffer hypoglycaemia during exercise, and don't usually need snacks before, during or after exercise. For more on hypoglycaemia and medications, see Chapter 6.

If you *are* using insulin, exercise is still one of the best ways to improve your health, but it is important to monitor blood glucose levels in response to exercise, to understand how the timing of your insulin dose affects your blood glucose response, and to carry a carbohydrate snack with you in case your blood glucose gets too low during or after exercise. In general, you should have your insulin injection at least 1 hour before exercise. Once the exercise starts to improve and lower your blood glucose levels, ask your doctor about reducing your dose.

THE BENEFITS OF ACTIVE LIVING

We all know that regular exercise is good for us, but its benefits are greater than you might think. It can help:

- control your body weight and reduce abdominal fat
- reduce the need for blood glucose and blood pressure medications
- reduce the risk of premature death
- reduce the risk factors for diabetes complications, such as high blood pressure and high blood cholesterol levels
- improve your fitness and your capacity for enjoying daily life
- improve the health and function of your blood vessels
- improve your mental health, including your mood, self-esteem, cognitive function and quality of life
- reduce the risk of some cancers, osteoporosis and depression
- maintain your ability to look after yourself.

People who maintain an active lifestyle live longer and healthier lives than those who do not, regardless of age, sex, race or environment. Exercise provides all of these benefits no matter what your weight and regardless of whether you lose weight or not. In fact, physical activity is one of the best 'medicines' there is. It also helps improve our personal appearance, is fun, and allows us to enjoy the great outdoors and spend time with family and friends. Best of all, physical activity can cost you nothing except time. By being creative and making some slight modifications to your daily routine, you can achieve great benefits from physical activity without much effort at all.

Exercise and glucose control

Exercise is very effective in lowering glucose levels. If you are particularly well controlled and using insulin or sulphonylureas (see pages 61–62), then exercise can act as a double dose of medication, leading to hypoglycaemia. This shouldn't stop you exercising, but you may need to work with your doctor or someone from your diabetes care team on the best insulin dose and food regime for your exercise program.

Exercise can reduce blood glucose by 3–4 mmol/litre per hour by increasing muscle metabolism and blood flow to muscles, but intense exercise can *elevate* blood glucose by activating the sympathetic nervous system and increasing adrenalin and noradrenalin. The net result is not predictable without some trial and error. You will need to test your blood glucose levels more often and it's always a good idea to have a healthy snack on hand if your blood glucose tends to drop during and after exercise.

OUR SEDENTARY LIFESTYLE

In just three generations, sweeping technology, social and lifestyle changes have ushered in a highly sedentary lifestyle for more and more Australians. Widespread car ownership, energy-saving devices, prolonged periods of television viewing and the modern office environment have all contributed to a culture in which many of us sit for long periods during the day. Increasingly, our leisure and recreation also involve physically inactive pastimes such as watching sporting matches, watching movies, playing video games and surfing the internet rather than surfing waves, playing golf, gardening or walking the dog. This relatively new phenomenon in human evolution has coincided with a sharp increase in obesity and related health complications such as type 2 diabetes.

Think about what you did yesterday: there's a good chance you spent eight to ten hours of your waking day just sitting.

WHAT'S WRONG WITH SITTING?

Sitting might feel comfortable, but people who sit for long periods are at greater risk of weight gain and have poorer blood glucose control, no matter how much physical exercise they do. Sitting, also known as sedentary time, reduces muscle movement and therefore the amount of energy we burn. When we sit for long periods, not only do we expend hardly any energy, which can contribute to weight gain, but the body's ability to metabolise carbohydrates is likely to be greatly diminished. This is of particular concern for people who have type 2 diabetes.

How sedentary is your lifestyle?

Kathy has a desk job. She sleeps for eight hours on most days, so she has 16 waking hours. This is how she spends them.

TIME SPENT ...	KATHY	YOU
sitting in car or public transport	1 hour	
sitting watching TV	3 hours	
sitting at a desk at work	8 hours	
sitting using the computer at home	1 hour	
sitting reading a book or newspaper	30 minutes	
sitting at a table for meals	1 hour	
sitting talking with friends	30 minutes	
sitting talking on the phone	15 minutes	
other sedentary activities	—	
total time spent sitting	15¼ hours	

Now, take a moment to calculate how much time *you* spend sitting every day.

Incidental movement

The great thing about incidental movement is that it requires little or no planning. You don't have to think about the weather, what route you'll take or wearing special clothing, and it can be incorporated into your existing schedule. It may require some creativity at first to come up with ideas for increasing your movement throughout the day, but over time it will become second nature.

BREAK UP YOUR SITTING TIME

It helps to break up your prolonged sitting time with even short periods of movement. At the office, get up as often as you can and walk around. Get up and speak to your colleagues rather than sending an email, get up and collect your printing rather than waiting for someone to bring it to you, and use the stairs instead of the lift. Even standing up while you're on the phone is an effective way to move your body and reduce your sitting time.

Try moving from your sitting position at least once every half-hour. Even if you just stand up for a short while, this will help reduce the detrimental effects of sitting for extended periods without movement.

SET YOURSELF CHALLENGES

Whenever you can, try to maximise your day-to-day movements by setting yourself mini-challenges. Try parking further away from the entrance to the shopping centre so that you have a slightly longer walk. Consider walking home from the station one, two or even five nights a week rather than being picked up. Avoid sitting at your desk during lunch breaks. Instead, go out for a short, brisk walk – it will not only help regulate your blood glucose levels but will increase your metabolism and have a positive effect on blood flow to the brain, thus helping with concentration and focus when you return to your desk.

Use television commercial breaks as an opportunity for movement – get up and do household chores, or get your things together for the next day or simply walk to the other end of the house and back.

Start small. Try to reduce your total daily sitting time by 10 per cent. If you spend 15 waking hours doing sedentary activities, aim to reduce this to 13.5 hours. What Kathy did is in the table below.

Although incidental movement is an important component of a healthy, active lifestyle, it does not replace purposeful exercise. To enjoy real and lasting benefits, you need to combine incidental movement with purposeful exercise on a daily basis.

Purposeful exercise

Purposeful exercise is more structured, requiring a higher level of physical intensity over a more sustained period. It is the cornerstone of a healthy lifestyle and essential for physical health and wellbeing. There are two main types of purposeful exercise: aerobic exercise and strength training. You should aim to incorporate both types into your exercise regime.

ACTIVITY	TIME SPENT	NEW ACTIVITY PLAN	REVISED SITTING TIME
sitting in car or public transport	1 hour	park further away or get on and off public transport a stop early	50 minutes
sitting watching TV	3 hours	get up during each commercial break and walk around the house	2¼ hours
sitting at a desk at work	8 hours	get up every 30 minutes and walk to the other side of the building and back	7 hours and 45 minutes
sitting using the computer at home	1 hour	—	1 hour
sitting reading a book or newspaper	30 minutes	—	30 minutes
sitting at a table for meals	1 hour	—	1 hour
sitting talking with friends	30 minutes	walk and talk with friends	0 minutes
sitting talking on the phone	15 minutes	stand up while talking on the phone	0 minutes
total time spent sitting	**15¼ hours**		**13⅓ hours**

Footwear for activity and exercise

It is always important to have well-fitting exercise footwear, but this is doubly important if you have diabetes. Ill-fitting or inappropriate footwear can produce abnormal pressures, inadequate blood flow or supply to the feet and inflammation from repetitive stress that can progress to wounds and become infected. Appropriate footwear protects the skin and can reduce the occurrence of ulcers. Avoid restrictive or tight footwear, and socks or stockings that can cause inadequate blood flow to the foot. Your shoes should have plenty of room around the forefoot and toes, but be snug enough around the heel to prevent rubbing and blisters. If you have an active foot ulcer, you should avoid weight-bearing activities such as prolonged walking, jogging and step exercises. We recommend doing non-weight-bearing exercise such as cycling, rowing, strength training or arm exercises during the healing process.

See pages 80–81 for more on looking after your feet.

AEROBIC EXERCISE

Aerobic exercise, such as brisk walking, swimming or cycling, is not only highly effective in regulating blood glucose levels, but it also reduces the risk of early death and reduces risk factors for cardiovascular disease and type 2 diabetes.

To ensure good health you should do at least 30 minutes of aerobic exercise on five days a week. Although the more exercise you do, the greater are the health benefits. Sometimes it won't be practical to do 30 minutes of continuous exercise. Luckily, it can be just as beneficial to do three 10-minute blocks of exercise during the day. This means that there's always time to fit your exercise into your daily routine.

The most common form of aerobic exercise and perhaps the easiest to plan is brisk walking. This might include walking the dog, walking for pleasure, walking to work or the shops or walking as a break from work. Other forms of aerobic exercise include cycling, swimming, jogging, dancing, aerobics and team sports such as basketball, football, soccer and netball.

When starting a new exercise plan:

- speak to your doctor first for medical clearance for vigorous exercise
- keep it moderate – regular, sustained, moderate-intensity exercise is fine
- make it practical, realistic and achievable so that it complements your existing lifestyle without requiring too many changes
- begin at a comfortable level of intensity and challenge yourself to work up to a more moderate intensity over time
- go no more than two consecutive days without exercise.

How hard, how long, how often?

Intensity – think of intensity on a scale of 0 to 10 where 0 is the equivalent of sitting down while 10 is the highest level of effort possible. Moderate-intensity activity is a 5 or 6 while vigorous intensity is a 7 or 8.

Frequency – exercise at least three times a week, and five times a week for optimal benefit.

Duration – exercise for 30 minutes a day, either all at once or in three 10-minute blocks.

STRENGTH TRAINING

Strength training uses weight to create resistance and build muscle tissue. Muscle is where most of our energy is burned and is the main site for glucose clearance. Building, or at the very least, maintaining muscle mass is an important part of managing diabetes. The more muscle you have, the greater your metabolic rate and the more energy you expend while resting. This also helps maintain your weight and prevent weight gain in the long term.

Muscle mass varies significantly from person to person and shrinks through lack of movement as well as age. Without maintenance, we start to lose muscle mass when we are about 45 and this decline or shrinkage speeds up past the age of 65. This also explains why there is a sharp rise in people diagnosed with type 2 diabetes from 45 onwards.

The most common and effective form of strength training is lifting weights. You can also use your own body weight or use stretch bands to create the resistance required to train your muscles.

How heavy, how often?

Although it might feel comfortable, lifting a 1 kilogram weight may not be sufficient to build muscle mass. Research shows that for best results a combination of repetition and resistance is required. Start by selecting a weight that feels heavy, and aim to complete a set of 8–12 repetitions. The final 2–3 repetitions should feel challenging. If you can lift a weight or perform the exercise 12 times easily, you probably need to consider increasing the weight in order to achieve optimum benefit. Aim to repeat 2–3 sets of each movement twice a week and to perform 8–10 different exercises that work all the major muscle groups.

As your muscle mass increases and your strength improves, it will become easier to lift the weight, so it's important to increase the weight or resistance level over time to ensure you are continually strengthening your muscle tissue and maximising the benefits of exercise.

I can't afford gym membership

You don't have to go to a gym to do strength training, nor do you need expensive equipment. You can complete a whole-body strength-training workout using your body weight as resistance or some inexpensive rubber tubing or a pair of dumbbells with adjustable weight loads.

EXERCISE TIPS

1 Physical activity is safe for most people with type 2 diabetes, but check with your doctor before you start a new intensive exercise program.

2 When doing any sort of exercise program, warm up and cool down with a light jog and some stretches.

3 Start small and build up slowly – if you haven't been active for a while, start with small amounts of physical activity and increase slowly over time as you become fitter and feel more confident.

4 Keep a journal to keep track of your progress. Record your exercise and your blood glucose levels. This will help you set physical activity goals and stay on track.

5 Mix it up to make it fun and enjoyable. If you're sick of doing the same walk every day, try a different route or go swimming instead.

FINDING HELP

People generally have greater success with exercise when they have supervision and encouragement from a third party such as an exercise specialist or personal trainer. There are lots of great programs and resources out there to support you and help you reach your goals.

Try these ideas to get you motivated and keep you enthused.

- Start or join a walking club in your local area or at work.
- Check out your local government website – most have excellent information on local walking paths, bicycle tracks, local fitness groups and community sports facilities such as pools and parks.
- Visit local gyms and ask to speak to one of their qualified fitness professionals about the services they offer and how they can support you with a tailored exercise program.
- Enlist the support of an accredited exercise physiologist. Ask for a referral from your doctor and you may be eligible for a Medicare rebate. For more see the Resources section on page 263.
- Work with a professional personal trainer on a personalised plan.
- Enrol in your local Lift for Life program. Lift for Life is a structured strength-training program developed by Baker IDI for older people with diabetes. For more see page 265.

Your easy exercise plan

This low-cost, easy-to-follow six-week exercise plan will help get you started and build up your fitness and strength. It incorporates brisk walking as your aerobic exercise and simple resistance exercises for strength training. Follow the timetable below and enjoy your growing strength, fitness and vitality.

RESISTANCE EXERCISES

Perform 8–10 of the following exercises. They target all the major muscle groups and can be done at home without any expensive equipment. Do each exercise in sets of 8–12 repetitions. Start with one set per session then move up to two sets in the third week.

To increase the difficulty of these exercises, do them with a resistance tube (a long rubber tube with handles at each end) or a pair of dumbbells with adjustable weights. These simple pieces of equipment will increase the range of exercises you can do and help maintain your interest and enjoyment.

Stay positive

Don't let a lack of confidence or fears of feeling inadequate stop you from exercising. Set yourself modest but realistic goals and maintain a positive attitude. Don't compare yourself to other people. Just think about improving your own health gradually. If you feel better, more energetic or have an improved mood, that's all that matters.

Have your blood glucose, cholesterol and blood pressure checked before you start, so that you can see how much they improve with exercise. An exercise physiologist or health care professional with exercise expertise can help tailor your exercise regimen to your individual needs and provide any guidance you may require. Ask your GP to refer you – if you have diabetes, part of the costs may be covered by Medicare.

WEEK	AEROBIC EXERCISE		RESISTANCE EXERCISE	
	DURATION (MINUTES)	FREQUENCY (DAYS/WK)	SETS (8–12 REPETITIONS/ EXERCISE)	FREQUENCY (DAYS/WEEK)
1	10	3	1	1
2	20	3	1	1
3	20	3	2	1
4	30	3	2	1
5	30	4	2	2
6	30	5	2	2

Chest press

BEGINNER

1 Stand facing a wall with your feet hip-width apart, then place your palms on the wall at shoulder height and slightly more than shoulder-width apart. Your arms should be almost straight but still slightly bent.

2 Keeping your back straight and using your arms to take your weight, slowly lean towards the wall until your nose almost touches it. Pause, then slowly push with your arms back to your starting position. Don't lock your elbows at the end of the movement; keep them slightly bent.

INTERMEDIATE/ADVANCED

1 Kneel on all fours with your back parallel with the floor. Your hands should be slightly more than shoulder-width apart and your elbows slightly bent.

2 Back straight, bend your elbows and slowly lower your body to the floor until you touch it with your nose or chest. Pause, then slowly push with your arms back to your starting position. Don't lock your elbows at the end of the movement; keep them slightly bent. For Advanced, start with your legs stretched out behind you and your weight resting on your toes.

Calf raises

BEGINNER

INTERMEDIATE/ADVANCED

1 Stand up straight with your feet hip-width apart.

2 Keeping your back straight, lift your heels as high as you can so that you are on tiptoe. Pause, then slowly return to your starting position.

1 Stand up straight with your feet hip-width apart.

2 Keeping your back straight, lift your right foot off the floor (let it hang, or rest it behind your left calf) then lift your left heel as high as you can so that you are on tiptoe. Pause, then slowly return to your starting position.

3 Repeat, lifting your left foot. For Advanced, start with your toes on a phone book and your heels hanging off the back.

Lunges

Squats

1 Stand up straight with your hands on your hips and your feet hip-width apart.

2 Keeping your abdominal muscles tight and your back straight, take a good step back with your right leg and land on the ball of your right foot.

3 Still keeping your back straight, slowly bend your knees until your right knee is almost touching the floor and your left thigh is parallel with the ground. Don't allow your left knee to go further forward than your left toes.

4 Pause, then return to your starting position.

5 Repeat with your left leg behind you. For Advanced, start with a dumbbell in each hand and your arms by your sides.

1 Stand up straight with your feet hip-width apart and your hands on your hips.

2 Keeping your back straight (focus on a spot high on the wall directly in front of you), slowly bend your knees and lower your body, until your thighs are almost parallel with the floor. Try not to allow your knees to go further forward than your toes; if this happens, push your buttocks further back. Pause, then slowly return to your starting position. For Advanced, start with a dumbbell in each hand and your arms by your sides.

Triceps dips

BEGINNER

1 Sit on the floor with your knees bent and your feet flat on the floor, hip-width apart. Put your hands just behind you, with your fingers pointing towards your body.

2 Keeping your back straight and your abdominal muscles tight, slowly and gently bend your elbows to about 90 degrees (no further) and lower your body towards the floor. Pause, then slowly return to your starting position.

INTERMEDIATE/ADVANCED

1 Stand in front of a secure chair or stable surface of a similar height. Put your hands behind your back and on the chair, slightly more than shoulder-width apart. Walk your feet out until your knees are bent at 90 degrees and your upper legs are parallel with the floor, then lift your toes off the floor. Your arms should be almost straight but still slightly bent.

2 Keeping your back straight, your elbows in line with your hands and your legs relaxed, slowly lower your buttocks towards the floor until your upper arms are parallel with the ground. Pause, then use your hands (not your legs) to slowly push yourself back up to your starting position. For Advanced, walk your feet out until your legs are straight.

Abdominal crunches

1 Lie on your back with your knees bent and your feet flat on the floor. Ensure that your lower back is pushed into the floor. Place your hands behind your head with your elbows out.

2 Leading with your chest, keeping your head and neck straight and ensuring that your motion comes from your abdominal muscles and is smooth throughout, lift your upper body off the floor, to an angle of no more than 30 degrees. Pause, then slowly uncurl to your starting position. To increase the intensity, hold your arms straight above your head or hold a weight across your chest.

Glute kickback

1 Kneel on all fours with your back parallel with the floor.

2 Keeping your right knee at 90 degrees, slowly move your right foot up until your right thigh is parallel with the floor. Squeeze your buttocks then return to your starting position. Repeat with your left leg.

The plank

1 Lie on your tummy with your hands beside your shoulders and your feet together. To get into your starting position, keep your forearms and hands on the floor then bend your elbows to 90 degrees.

2 Relaxing your shoulders and bracing your abdominals, push up on your toes so that your legs are slightly off the floor and your body is parallel with the floor. Hold this position for 30 seconds, then return to your starting position.

The swim

1 Lie on your tummy with your arms stretched over your head, parallel with the floor, and your legs straight.

2 Slowly lift your right arm and your left leg towards the ceiling, as high as you can. Pause, then slowly lower your right arm and left leg back to their starting positions. Repeat, lifting your left arm and right leg.

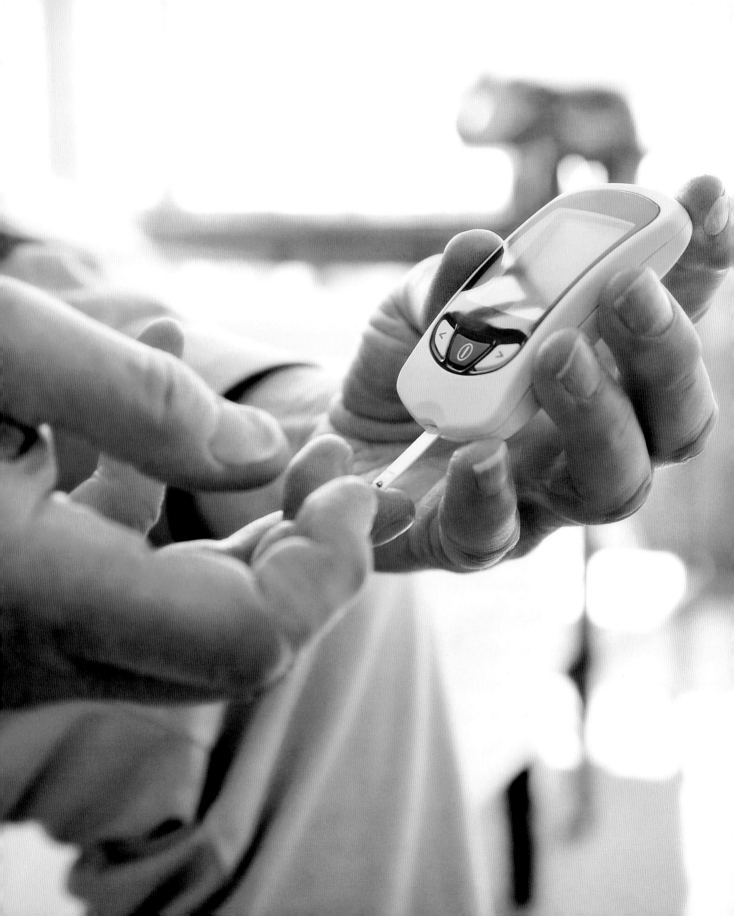

6 Diabetes medications and glucose control

Diabetes develops when the body loses its ability to maintain healthy glucose levels. A number of different medications are able to help you regain control, but you'll need to be on the watch for low blood glucose levels. Note that information about medications in this book is of a general nature and correct at the time of printing. Always check with your doctor.

PEOPLE WITHOUT DIABETES naturally keep their blood glucose levels within a very narrow range, but in diabetes this balance is disrupted. Even if you feel fine, chronically high glucose levels are potentially toxic to many parts of your body, especially your blood vessels, nerves and kidneys. Keeping your blood glucose levels within a healthy range is one important part of preventing the complications of diabetes. Good control will not only benefit you today, but will also determine your risk of serious complications in the future. For more on complications, see Chapter 7.

Staying in control

Although it may seem difficult at first, most people with type 2 diabetes can achieve a healthy level of glucose control. Many effective interventions are available, but the most important component is you. For good control you need to be engaged in managing your diabetes, be motivated and have a long-term commitment to getting the job done. Everyone with diabetes must find what works best for them.

Here are five simple steps to better glucose control.

1 Monitor your glucose control – Test your blood glucose levels regularly to keep them as close to healthy levels as possible and minimise your risk of hypoglycaemia (see page 64). This means, when possible, keeping your glucose levels within 4–8 mM when fasting and 4–10 mM one to two hours after a meal. Monitoring usually involves pricking your finger to release a drop of blood, placing the blood on a plastic strip and putting it in a small machine that gives a read-out of your blood glucose level. This process is not very complicated or painful. Newer devices that measure glucose levels through the skin are also becoming available.

Testing allows you to become aware of which foods or activities affect your glucose levels, and to look for patterns you can use to improve your control. Despite this, your blood glucose levels can sometimes change for no obvious reason.

Your doctor will also measure your haemoglobin A1C (often just called HbA1C or A1C) by doing a blood test. The A1C shows how much glucose is stuck to the haemoglobin in your red blood cells. The higher your glucose levels have been during the previous 3–4 months, the higher will be your A1C. People without diabetes have an A1C of less than 6 per cent. An A1C of more than 8 per cent suggests persistently elevated glucose levels.

2 Set appropriate short-term goals – You should aim to keep your A1C as low as possible, especially if you are young, but also to minimise your risk of hypoglycaemia. Your own targets should take into account your age, lifestyle, work practices, life expectancy, risk of complications and side effects, and a host of other factors. Most Australians with type 2 diabetes are able to safely achieve an A1C of less than 7 per cent.

3 Team up lifestyle and medications – Many people with type 2 diabetes control their blood glucose levels with increased physical activity, weight loss and coordinating their carbohydrate intake. You can also improve your glucose metabolism by managing stress, improving sleep and making other lifestyle changes. Medication should never be considered an alternative to healthy nutrition and physical activity. Even if you need tablets or injections, it is still important to eat the right foods and undertake regular exercise.

4 Develop a pattern and follow the plan – Know exactly how many tablets to take and when to take them. Medications are

most effective when they are taken as prescribed by your doctor. Most problems occur when people take their pills intermittently, especially if their meals and activity are equally haphazard. If you sometimes forget to take your tablets, ask your pharmacist about prepackaged pills. The best control comes when you can coordinate your medications with your meals and exercise.

5 Use your support team – Managing your glucose levels requires teamwork in which you are the central player. The best way to stay in control is to harness the support of your diabetes care team. Involve your whole family and work colleagues as a team to optimise your diet, organise activities and improve everyone's health.

Medications for lowering blood glucose levels

A number of medications for type 2 diabetes can help the body regulate its blood glucose levels. If your doctor prescribes any of these for you, it doesn't mean you're doing something wrong. Most people with diabetes eventually reach a point where they need some medication to prevent their glucose levels from rising dangerously. Different treatments will suit different people and different circumstances. Your doctor will advise which medications may be right for your particular needs. Keep an up-to-date list of all your medications with you.

METFORMIN

What it is – The most commonly used diabetes medication in Australia, taken by more than two-thirds of Australians with type 2 diabetes. Originally developed from an antidiabetic compound found in French lilac plants, it is distributed under several brand names (see the table on page 66).

How it works – Reduces the production of glucose by the liver and slows the absorption of glucose from a meal. It also helps your own insulin work better by increasing the body's sensitivity to insulin. Taken as directed, it can reduce the A1C by 1–1.5 per cent.

How you take it – Usually 2–3 times a day, with or after meals.

Its advantages – Can reduce the risk of heart disease, stroke and some cancers. Does not cause weight gain, and may reduce weight slightly in some people. When used on its own, hypoglycaemia does not occur.

Its disadvantages – Common side effects include nausea, diarrhoea, cramping and flatulence. Beginning at a low dose, reducing the dose, or taking slow-release preparations can help with this. Long-term use can reduce vitamin B12 levels, so vitamin supplements are recommended. People with heart conditions or impaired kidney or liver function should use it only under the close supervision of their doctor.

SULPHONYLUREAS

What they are – Used by half of all Australians with type 2 diabetes, mostly in combination with metformin. The four sulphonylureas available in Australia – glimepiride, glibenclamide, gliclazide and glipizide – are sold under a number of different brand names. Their effect on glucose levels is about the same, but some work for longer or are more quickly cleared from the body. For brand names see the table on page 66.

How they work – Increase the amount of insulin released from the pancreas. Taken as directed, they can reduce the A1C by 1–1.5 per cent. In a small number of cases, they do not control glucose levels when used on their own.

How you take them – Usually once or twice a day, with or before meals.

Their advantages – Very effective in lowering blood glucose levels, with few side effects.

Their disadvantages – Can cause hypoglycaemia by stimulating excess insulin production and release. This is more common in people who have impaired liver or kidney function or irregular eating habits or don't take their medication as directed. They can cause modest weight gain. Some doctors think they can accelerate loss of pancreas function.

GLITAZONES

What they are – Also known as thiazolidinediones and used by one in ten Australians with type 2 diabetes, mostly in combination with other medications or insulin. Two glitazones are available in Australia: rosiglitazone and pioglitazone. For brand names see the table on page 66.

How they work – Help insulin work better by increasing the body's sensitivity. Taken as directed, they can reduce the A1C by 1 per cent.

How you take them – Usually once a day.

Their advantages – Effective in lowering blood glucose levels and rarely cause hypoglycaemia when used on their own.

Their disadvantages – Can cause fluid retention and thus weight gain, ankle-swelling and sometimes even heart failure. They may also increase fat mass. They may increase the risk of heart attack and vision-threatening disease (macular oedema) compared with other medications. They can cause bone-thinning, which may increase the risk of fractures, particularly for post-menopausal women.

ACARBOSE

What it is – A natural product derived from cultured bacteria and sold as Glucobay.

How it works – Lowers blood glucose levels after a meal by inhibiting the enzymes that break down carbohydrates, slowing down their digestion as they pass through the gut. Taken as directed, it can reduce the A1C by 0.5–1 per cent.

How you take it – Up to three times a day, with the first bite of every meal.

Its advantages – Has only modest effects on average glucose levels, but is especially good at preventing a rise in blood glucose after a meal. Reduces the risk of heart attacks and strokes, over and above its effect on lowering A1C. May also reduce the risk of clots, lower blood pressure and lower lipid levels. May reduce the risk of colon cancer by feeding good bacteria in the colon.

Its disadvantages – Allows more starch to reach the colon, where it is happily digested by bacteria, and so will cause flatulence in most people, and bloating, discomfort or diarrhoea in some. This can be helped by starting at a lower dose, but generally settles down after a month or two. It does not cause hypoglycaemia when taken on its own, but can

Trade names of antidiabetic medications

MEDICATION	TYPES	SOLD AS
metformin	—	Diabex, Formet, Glucomet, Diaformin, Glucohexal, Glucophage, Metex XR, Metforbell, Metformin
sulphonylureas	glimepiride	Aylide, Amaryl, Diapride, Dimirel, Glimepiride
	glibenclamide	Daonil, Glimel, Glucovance (with metformin)
	gliclazide	Diamicron, Gliclazide, Glyade, Mellihexal, Nidem, Oziclide
	glipizide	Melizide, Minidiab, Nidem
glitazones	rosiglitazone	Avandia, Avandamet (with metformin)
(thiazolidinediones)	pioglitazone	Actos
acarbose	—	Glucobay
incretin analogues	exenatide	Byetta
DPP-4 inhibitors (gliptins)	sitagliptin	Januvia, Janumet (with metformin)
	vildagliptin	Galvus
metaglinides	repaglinide	Novonorm, Prandin
insulin	very short-acting	Humalog, NovoRapid
	short-acting	Actrapid, Apidra, Humulin R, Hypurin Neutral
	intermediate	Humulin NPH, Hypurin Isophane, Protophane
	long-acting	Lantus, Levemir
	short- and long-acting mixtures	Humulin Mix, Humalog Mix, Mixtard, NovoMix

make the effects of other antidiabetic drugs more powerful. Alcohol can cause a decrease in blood glucose levels if you are taking acarbose.

INCRETIN ANALOGUES

What they are – Natural hormones or synthetic copies of them that increase the amount of insulin released by the pancreas after eating. The only incretin available in Australia is exenatide, which is sold as Byetta.

How they work – Increase the amount of insulin released from the pancreas and slow the absorption of glucose after a meal by reducing the rate at which the stomach empties. Taken as directed, they can reduce the A1C by 1 per cent.

How you take them – Injected twice a day.

Their advantages – Weight loss as a result of loss of appetite.

Their disadvantages – Must be injected and can cause temporary dose-related gastrointestinal disturbance, such as nausea, vomiting, indigestion and flatulence. They rarely cause hypoglycaemia when used on their own, but may increase the risk of hypoglycaemia in people who are also taking sulphonylureas.

DPP-4 INHIBITORS

What they are – DPP-4 is the enzyme that breaks down our natural incretin hormones. DPP-4 inhibitors (also known as gliptins) elevate the levels of incretin hormones and thus how much insulin is released from the pancreas after eating. The only subsidised ones currently available in Australia are sitagliptin, which is sold as Januvia, and vildagliptin, sold as Galvus.

How they work – Raise levels of natural incretins, and thus how much insulin is released from the pancreas after meals. Also they slow absorption of glucose by slowing the rate at which the stomach empties. Taken as directed, they can reduce the A1C by 0.5–1 per cent.

How you take them – As tablets, usually once a day.

Their advantages – Increase natural levels of incretins rather than trying to mimic their effects. They appear to have few side effects.

Their disadvantages – Do not cause weight loss but do not usually cause weight gain either. They rarely cause hypoglycaemia when used on their own, but may increase the risk of hypoglycaemia in people who are also taking sulphonylureas.

METAGLINIDES

What they are – Also known as glinides, quick-acting synthetic compounds that trigger the release of insulin. Only repaglinide is available in Australia, sold as Novonorm or Prandin.

How they work – Stimulate the release of insulin from the pancreas, producing a healthy rise in insulin levels after meals. Taken as directed, they can reduce the A1C by 0.5–1 per cent.

How you take them – Usually taken three times a day, with the first bite of each meal.

Their advantages – Fast-working and short-acting, so effective in preventing a rise in blood glucose levels after meals. They can reduce the risk of hypoglycaemia for people with irregular meal patterns: one meal, one dose; no meal, no dose.

Their disadvantages – Can cause hypoglycaemia if not taken with a meal and can cause gastrointestinal disturbances such as nausea, abdominal pain and indigestion.

INSULIN

What it is – The most important natural regulator of blood glucose levels. If other medications are not enough to maintain glucose control, your doctor may prescribe insulin. The longer you have diabetes, the more likely you will need insulin. Different forms of insulin with different rates of action are available for different situations. Some preparations are a mixture of short- and long-acting insulin, to reduce the number of injections. For more, see the table on page 63.

How it works – Injected insulin works the same way as the natural insulin from the pancreas, stimulating removal of glucose from the blood and stopping the liver from making more glucose. Taken as directed, it can reduce the A1C by 1–5 per cent.

How you take it – Injected into the fat under the skin, usually in the abdomen or thighs. The injection site should be changed regularly within the same general area to ensure identical results. Short-acting insulin is injected immediately before meals, 1–3 times a day; intermediate and long-acting usually once a

Complementary therapies for lowering blood glucose levels

Many products are marketed for people with diabetes, but these should not be considered alternatives to managing diabetes. In fact, there are significant health risks when such 'remedies' replace standard-of-care treatment.

Some supplements may, however, have a modest impact on blood glucose control when used in addition to exercise, diet and regular medications. These include:

* chromium – which may improve the sensitivity of the body to insulin, resulting in a modest reduction of the A1C. Chromium is available in many mineral supplements as well as in brewer's yeast.

* vanadium – which may modestly improve glucose control. Vanadium commonly causes gastrointestinal irritation, but a vanadium chelate may be less troublesome.

* coenzyme Q10 – also known as CoQ or ubiquinone, this vitamin-like chemical is reduced in people with diabetes, especially in those with poor glucose control and those on statins. CoQ supplements have been shown to modestly improve glucose levels in some but not all studies.

* soluble fibre – which slows the absorption of sugar from the diet. It can improve glucose control when included in meals. A regular intake of fibre is also important for bowel health, which can be very important for people with diabetes. The most commonly used supplement is psyllium, which is made from ispaghula husks. Fibre supplements containing inulin or fructans can also be used as a sugar substitute.

* herbal supplements – including cinnamon, garlic, fenugreek and bitter melon, which may lower glucose levels in some people with diabetes. While generally safe in the short term, their long-term effectiveness and potential for side effects are unclear. Some products may provide the wrong dose or be contaminated with toxic ingredients.

* mind–body techniques – since a healthy mind may improve physical health. There is evidence, for example, that repeated and sustained yoga may reduce glucose levels, blood pressure and cholesterol levels. Secular meditation may also have beneficial effects on glucose metabolism, weight control, blood pressure levels and chronic pain in some people. These techniques take a lot of application and will not work for everyone.

day, at bedtime or breakfast. Your diabetes care team will identify the insulin that works best for you if you need it. Most people with type 2 diabetes who require insulin inject it twice a day but will often start with a single daily dose of intermediate or long-acting insulin. Most people must also keep taking some or all of their other antidiabetic medications.

Its advantages – The most effective way to lower blood glucose levels, and the dose can be adjusted to fit each person's glucose levels, physical activity and meal size.

Its disadvantages – Must be injected, although it is quite easy to become proficient at this. People taking insulin commonly experience hypoglycaemia, especially if their injections and dose are not coordinated with their meals or physical activity. Often causes weight gain initially.

Hypoglycaemia

Your brain needs a constant supply of glucose to function normally and cannot go more than a few minutes without it. Blood glucose levels lowered with medications sometimes drop too low for the brain to function normally. This is known as hypoglycaemia ('a hypo'). While controlling your glucose levels is necessary for the management of your diabetes, preventing hypoglycaemia is also very important, as low levels are potentially dangerous.

THE SYMPTOMS OF HYPOGLYCAEMIA

If your brain is starved of glucose, all of its functions slow down. This can lead to faintness, drowsiness, loss of attention or concentration, confusion or impaired judgement, anxiety or moodiness, blurred vision, disturbed sleep or nightmares, slurred speech, delayed reflexes, seizures and eventually loss of consciousness.

Low glucose levels also trigger a range of responses in the body, including sweatiness, palpitations, shaking, headache, nausea and hunger. The severity of these symptoms depends on how low the glucose levels go and how rapidly they fall. Initially the symptoms may be mild and easy to ignore, especially if your mind is focused on other matters. Not all people experience the same warning signs so it is important to discover what the early signals are for you and to do something about them.

THE CAUSES OF HYPOGLYCAEMIA

Hypoglycaemia can occur when using insulin or a treatment that lowers glucose by releasing insulin. It is most common in people who require insulin, but because it is easy to adjust and coordinate insulin doses with glucose levels, meals and physical activity, serious hypoglycaemic incidents (or 'hypos') are rare. Accidentally injecting insulin into muscle (instead of fat) or exercising after injecting into your thigh can sometimes lead to faster absorption of insulin and thus to hypoglycaemia. Sulphonylureas and metaglinides are often associated with hypos, especially in people who have impaired kidney function, are advanced in age or have an irregular lifestyle.

PREVENTING HYPOGLYCAEMIA

Most hypos are predictable and can be avoided with foresight and planning. The most common precipitants of hypoglycaemia are: skipping or delaying a meal, unplanned physical activity, eating too little carbohydrate, taking too much medication, taking medication at the wrong time and drinking alcohol. Hypos can usually be prevented by adjusting habits and changing the dose or timing of medications.

A good diet that meets your individual glucose requirements is also useful. Low-GI foods can help prevent lows during the night or after meals. Sometimes it will be important to eat meals that provide more glucose upfront, particularly before exercise and with fast-acting medications or insulin. Talk to your diabetes care team about when your blood glucose gets low and what you can do to stop this. Overeating to prevent hypoglycaemia is never a solution.

Physical activity uses up more blood glucose and at a faster rate if it is vigorous. This is why it is so effective in controlling glucose levels in diabetes, but also why it can lead to hypos, not just during exercise but also for several hours afterwards. The solution is not to avoid exercise. Most people with type 2 diabetes have glucose levels high enough to buffer the effects of exercise and never experience hypos. The minority who do can usually avoid them by better coordinating their physical activity with their diet and/or reducing their medication doses.

Preventive management is very important if you plan to drive a car. You should:

- have a supply of snacks
- eat meals and snacks before and during long journeys
- not wait until you feel symptoms of a hypo – check your blood glucose levels before you leave and every two hours during the drive, and treat falling levels straightaway (see below)
- not drive if you have low blood glucose levels, even if you are not far from home
- never drink and drive, even if you're under the legal limit.

TREATING HYPOGLYCAEMIA

Always intervene if you experience the symptoms of low glucose. It might be informative to measure your blood glucose level first, but if you suspect a hypo it is best to treat it immediately – failing to treat an episode is riskier than unnecessary treatment.

If you are having a hypo, immediately do one of the following:

- take 10–15 grams of glucose (in tablets, powder or sweets), or
- eat 1 tablespoon of jam, honey or sugar, or
- drink half a glass of lemonade or similar sugary drink.

If your symptoms persist, repeat the dose in 5–10 minutes.

When your symptoms have resolved, wait another 5–10 minutes for the glucose to be fully absorbed, then eat a carbohydrate-rich snack, such as a piece of fruit, a sandwich or your usual meal if you're due for one.

If you have had a severe hypoglycaemic incident requiring hospitalisation or other medical attention, you must have a medical review and not drive or operate machinery until after you are cleared.

7 Diabetes complications

The best way to avoid diabetes complications
is to work hard to prevent or manage diabetes.

IF BLOOD GLUCOSE LEVELS become elevated and stay high for a long time, some parts of the body may become progressively damaged. This damage is not inevitable: most people with diabetes stay healthy and free of complications. This chapter will show you why diabetic complications are worth preventing, and what you can do about them if they do occur.

Your heart

The body depends on the flow of blood for its survival. If blood flow is stopped, even for a brief period, cells and tissues downstream from the blockage will suffer and may even die. When this occurs in the heart, it is called a heart attack or myocardial infarction. When it occurs in the brain, it is called a stroke or cerebrovascular accident. Together, heart disease and strokes are the most important complications of type 2 diabetes. They are also among the most preventable. There are several ways you can prevent them happening to you.

BLOOD PRESSURE

Blood pressure is the force generated by the heart as it pumps blood through your body. The systolic blood pressure is your beating heart's maximum pressure, which you feel as your pulse. It is also the major stress on the surface of your blood vessels. Diabetes makes the blood vessels stiffer and less able to relax, increasing the pressure inside them. This condition is called hypertension. If you have diabetes, you should have your blood pressure checked every time you see your doctor. Reducing your systolic blood pressure will in turn reduce your long-term risk of heart attack or stroke. Most people can achieve this through a combination of diet, regular exercise and appropriate medication. Relaxation therapy, yoga and meditation can also lower blood pressure.

There are several ways to reduce your blood pressure:

- **Lose weight** – For every kilogram of weight you lose, your systolic blood pressure goes down on average by about 1 mmHg.
- **Exercise regularly** – This can lower your blood pressure by as much as 10 mmHg. If your blood pressure is normal, exercise can also prevent it rising as you age. For your exercise program to reduce your blood pressure, it must include aerobic activity such as brisk walking, climbing stairs, jogging, bicycling or swimming (for more see Chapter 5). Try to do at least 30 minutes of aerobic exercise on all or most days of the week.
- **Reduce your salt intake** – This will not only lower your blood pressure but also make your blood-pressure medications more effective. If you have diabetes, you should try to reduce your salt intake to less than 4 grams a day. More than 75 per cent of the salt in the average Australian diet is hidden in processed foods, such as bread, cereals, cheese, soups, sauces, stock powder and condiments. Look for fresh alternatives and products labelled as reduced-salt, no added salt or low-salt. Use herbs and spices instead of salt to add flavour to your food. Foods with the Heart Foundation Tick have less salt than similar foods without the Tick (see page 32).
- **Eat more fruit and vegetables** – Diets high in fruit and vegetables can also help reduce blood pressure. Try to include two serves of fruit and five serves of vegetables in your diet every day. One way to do this is to follow our diabetes eating plan (see Chapter 2).
- **Eat more fish and omega-3 oils** – Including oily fish in your weight-loss diet can help reduce blood pressure more effectively than weight loss alone. Fish oil supplements can also reduce blood pressure, but you need to take them regularly and in large amounts (e.g. 4 grams a day).
- **Limit your alcohol intake** – There is an established link between excessive alcohol intake and hypertension. Limit your alcohol intake to no more than 2 standard drinks each day for men or 1 standard drink each day for women (see page 41).

BLOOD PRESSURE MEDICATION

More than two-thirds of people with type 2 diabetes require medications to lower their blood pressure. To effectively reduce the risk of a heart attack or stroke, several different blood-pressure-lowering drugs are usually required, in combination with lifestyle changes.

ACE inhibitors

ACE inhibitors are the most commonly used drugs for blood-pressure control for people with diabetes. They have few side effects but can sometimes cause a troublesome cough. A number of different formulations are now available.

Diabetes and omega-3

Some fats are essential for good health. The most well known of these are the omega-3 fatty acids, which regulate inflammation, clotting and immune function. Diets naturally high in omega-3 are associated with a lower risk of heart disease and stroke. If you have diabetes, you should aim to consume a meal of oily fish (such as salmon, herring, mackerel, anchovies, sardines or tuna) 2–3 times a week. If you find this difficult, you can try supplements such as fish oils and flaxseed (linseed) oil. These are safe for some people and do not alter glucose levels. It is a matter of debate whether supplements are as effective as omega-3s in food.

Products containing ACE inhibitors

DRUG NAME	SOLD AS
captopril	Acenorm, Capoten, Captohexal, Captopril
enalapril	Alphapril, Auspril, Enahexal, Enalabell, Enalapril
fosinopril	Fosipril, Fosinopril, Monace, Monopril
lisinopril	Fibsol, Liprace, Lisinobell, Lisinopril, Zestril
perindopril	Coversyl, Indopril, Ozapace, Perindo, Perindopril
quinapril	Accupril, Acquin, Filpril, Quinapril
ramipril	Prilace, Ramace, Ramipril, Tritace, Tryzan
trandolapril	Dolapril, Gopten, Tranalpha, Trandolapril

Angiotensin-receptor blockers (ARBs)

Angiotensin-receptor blockers (ARBs) also reduce blood pressure by blocking the chemicals that cause hypertension. Although ACE inhibitors and ARBs have different mechanisms of action, recent studies suggest that they are interchangeable in blood pressure control and protecting the heart and other organs in diabetes. ARBs usually cause few side effects. A number of different formulations are available, as indicated in the table below.

Products containing angiotensin-receptor blockers (ARBs)

DRUG NAME	SOLD AS
candesartan	Atacand
eprosartan	Teveten
irbesartan	Avapro, Karvea
olmesartan	Olmetec
telmisartan	Micardis
valsartan	Diovan

Beta-blockers

These drugs reduce blood pressure by relaxing the blood vessels, slowing the pulse and making the heart beat less forcefully. This reduces stress on the heart, so beta-blockers are also used to treat angina, heart failure and some disturbances in the heart's rhythm. They can sometimes cause tiredness, depression and impotence, and precipitate asthma. They can also interfere with glucose control and the body's response to hypoglycaemia (see Chapter 6).

Products containing beta-blockers

DRUG NAME	SOLD AS
atenolol	Atenolol, Noten, Tensig, Tenormin
bisoprolol	Bicor, Bispro, Bisoprolol
carvedilol	Carvedilol, Dilasig, Dilatrend, Kredex, Vedilol
labetalol	Presolol, Trandate
metoprolol	Betaloc, Lopresor, Metohexal, Metolol, Metoprolo, Minax, Toprol
oxprenolol	Corbeton
pindolol	Barbloc, Visken
propranolol	Deralin, Inderal
sotalol	Cardol, Solavert, Sotab, Sotacor, Sotalol

Calcium-channel blockers

These effective drugs reduce blood pressure by dilating blood vessels. Some people may suffer troublesome swelling of the ankles and constipation, especially at higher doses.

Products containing calcium-channel blockers

DRUG NAME	SOLD AS
amlodipine	Amlo, Amlodipine, Norvasc, Ozlodip, Norvapine, Perivasc
diltiazem	Cardizem, Coras, Diltahexal, Diltiazem, Dilzem, Vasocardol
felodipine	Felodil, Felodur, Plendil
lercanidipine	Zanidip
nifedipine	Adalat, Adalat Oros, Addos, Adefin, Nifedipine, Nifehexal
verapamil	Anpec, Cordilox, Isoptin, Veracaps

Diuretics or water tablets

These drugs lower your blood pressure by making you lose more salt (and water) in your urine. Diuretics are safe, effective and inexpensive. They are most effective in combination with other antihypertensive drugs. In some people, diuretics can interfere with glucose control or cause gout.

Products containing diuretics

DRUG NAME	SOLD AS
chlorthalidone	Hygroton
ethacrynic acid	Edecrin
eplerenone	Inspra
frusemide	Frusehexal, Frusemide, Frusid, Lasix, Uremide, Urex
hydrochlorothiazide	Dithiazide
hydrochlorothiazide with amiloride hydrochloride	Moduretic
hydrochlorothiazide with triamterene	Hydrene
indapamide	Dapa-Tabs, Indapamide, Indahexal, Insig, Napamide, Natrilix
spironolactone	Aldactone, Spiractin
amiloride	Kaluril

Complementary therapies for diabetes complications

There is insufficient scientific evidence to prove that any supplements have a substantial effect on diabetes complications. Nonetheless, some people experience improvements in health and wellbeing from complementary therapies. Some of the best known and most studied include:

* alpha-lipoic acid – which is also known as ALA, lipoic acid or thioctic acid, and is taken for nerve pain, paresthesias and numbness
* vitamin B1 (thiamine) – which is taken for nerve pain
* Pycnogenol – an antioxidant extracted from the bark of French maritime pine, which is taken for healing of leg ulcers
* Medihoney – which is used for wound healing and prevention of infection
* zinc – which is used to reduce susceptibility to infection and improve wound healing.

If you are considering complementary therapies, it is important to be open with your doctor and other health care providers. Most practitioners are very accepting of their patients doing whatever it takes to manage their diabetes, providing the complementary therapy does no harm.

REDUCING YOUR
LDL CHOLESTEROL LEVELS

There are several kinds of cholesterol. Cholesterol contained in low-density lipoprotein particles, called LDL cholesterol, is on its way to be deposited somewhere, such as in the walls of your arteries. It is often called bad cholesterol.

The higher your LDL cholesterol levels, the greater your risk of heart attack or stroke. Reducing your LDL cholesterol to as low as possible will reduce your risk of complications. You can usually achieve this through a combination of:

1 A healthy diet – Choose low-fat foods, eggs, lean red and white meat, and fresh fruit and vegetables. You can eat up to six eggs a week as part of a healthy diet. Eat shellfish (e.g. prawns) and organ meats (e.g. liver) in moderation. Choose polyunsaturated fats over saturated-fat products. See Chapter 2 for details.

2 Plant-sterol-enriched foods – Look for margarines and dairy products marked as containing plant sterols. These products can reduce cholesterol absorption if used in conjunction with a balanced diet.

3 Regular exercise – See Chapter 5 for more.

4 Cholesterol-lowering medication – LDL cholesterol levels can be effectively lowered by drugs that prevent the body from making cholesterol. These medications, known as statins, are now used by more than two-thirds of

Australians with type 2 diabetes. Some people cannot take statins because of troublesome side effects, including muscle aches and pains. Fibrates and cholesterol absorption inhibitors can also lower LDL levels, although their effects are more modest than those of statins.

RAISING YOUR
HDL CHOLESTEROL LEVELS

Cholesterol found in high-density lipoprotein particles, HDL cholesterol, takes cholesterol from the walls of blood vessels and moves it to safer storage sites. The higher your HDL cholesterol levels, the lower your risk of heart disease and stroke. This is why HDL cholesterol is also called good cholesterol. HDL cholesterol can be increased by losing excess weight, increasing physical activity and eating more healthy fats (see Chapter 2). Lipid-lowering medications known as fibrates can also raise HDL cholesterol levels. High doses (1–6 grams a day) of vitamin B3 (niacin) may also help, but are poorly tolerated at this dose (which is much higher than that in multivitamin tablets – generally less than 100 milligrams).

LOWERING YOUR TRIGLYCERIDE LEVELS

Most of the fat stored by the body is made up of triglycerides, which is then slowly broken down between meals to ensure a constant supply of energy. Triglyceride levels are elevated in people with diabetes because they have a reduced ability to suppress the release of fats into the bloodstream. High triglyceride levels are associated with an

Lipid-lowering medications

DRUG TYPE	DRUG NAME	SOLD AS
statins	atorvastatin	Lipitor
	fluvastatin	Lescol, Vastin
	pravastatin	Cholstat, Lipostat, Liprachol, Pravachol, Pravastatin, Vastoran
	rosuvastatin	Crestor
	simvastatin	Lipex, Ransim, Simvabell, Simvahexal, Simvar, Simvasyn, Zimstat, Zocor
fibrates	fenofibrate	Lipidil
	gemfibrozil	Ausgem, Gemfibrozil, Gemhexal, Jezil, Lipazil, Lopid
nicotinic acid	nicotinic acid	nicotinic acid
cholesterol or bile acid absorption inhibitors	cholestyramine	Questran Lite
	colestipol	Colestid
	ezetimibe	Ezetrol
	ezetimibe with simvastatin	Vytorin

increased risk of heart disease and other diabetes complications.

Maintaining good glucose control (see Chapter 6) will also significantly improve triglyceride levels. Weight loss, regular exercise, limiting alcohol intake and eating a healthy diet lower in refined carbohydrates will also help lower triglycerides. Omega-3 fatty acids (see page 71) and medications called fibrates (see the table above) can also effectively reduce triglyceride levels.

GIVING UP SMOKING

Smoking significantly increases your risk of heart attack or stroke. Toxins in cigarette smoke damage the surface of blood vessels, and even passive smoking puts your heart at risk, so encourage others to stop too. Talk to your doctor or call the Quit line (see page 267) to find out the best options for you. If you quit for good, you can reverse some of the damage caused by smoking. If you can keep off the cigarettes for more than a decade, your risk of heart attack and stroke will be almost as low as that of a non-smoker.

CONTROLLING YOUR BLOOD GLUCOSE LEVELS

A high blood glucose level means you are at the highest risk of heart attack or stroke. Any effort to better control your glucose levels (see Chapter 6) will significantly reduce your heart attack risk.

BLOOD-THINNERS

If you have already had a heart attack or stroke, regularly taking blood-thinning agents such as aspirin and clopidogrel can reduce your risk of heart attack by 20–30 per cent. Some doctors also prescribe blood thinners for people who have a very high risk of heart disease, such as those with kidney damage. People with diabetes can also suffer atrial fibrillation, a condition in which the heart rhythm is erratic. This increases the risk of a stroke, and is usually treated with the blood thinner warfarin together with a combination of drugs or a pacemaker to prevent the heart from beating too fast.

Heart attack and stroke preventative medications containing a blood thinner

DRUG NAME	SOLD AS
aspirin	Aspirin, Astrix, Cardiprin, Cartia, Solprin
clopidogrel	Isocover, Plavix
dipyridamole	Persantin
dipyridamole with aspirin	Asasantin
prasugrel	Effient
warfarin	Coumadin, Marevan

DON'T IGNORE HEART ATTACK OR STROKE SYMPTOMS

There are many effective ways to treat a heart attack or stroke, all of which help to rapidly restore blood flow along blocked arteries. These are most effective when delivered as soon as possible. The longer the blockage is left, the greater the damage to the heart or mind, and the more limited any recovery. All people who have type 2 diabetes should be familiar with the warning signs of a heart attack, and call for an ambulance immediately if they experience sudden tightness, pressure or crushing pain in the chest that spreads to the shoulder, arm or jaw and doesn't go away. Some people with diabetes will not experience any pain with a heart attack, but instead suddenly feel short of breath, nauseous, sweaty or faint for no reason.

The warning signs of a stroke are more predictable and include:

- sudden weakness or numbness of the face, arm or leg on one side of the body
- sudden change in vision
- sudden change or loss of speech, and trouble talking or understanding
- sudden onset of dizziness, unsteadiness or loss of balance.

Your kidneys

Every five minutes, healthy kidneys filter all the blood in your body. They filter out everything we don't need in the blood, and get rid of the water (and any dissolved toxins) as urine. This system is so efficient that for every litre of blood filtered less than a teaspoon of urine is made. Good kidney function allows your heart, brain, bones and many other parts of your body to do the job they are supposed to do.

SYMPTOMS OF KIDNEY DAMAGE

Poor diabetes control can result in damage to many parts of the kidney. This damage is usually painless, and can be quite advanced before any symptoms are noticed. Most often kidney disease is detected incidentally when a urine test discovers elevated amounts of albumin leaking into the urine, or a blood test shows a reduced glomerular filtration rate (GFR).

Other symptoms that can be due to kidney disease are often attributed to other causes, including:

- elevated blood pressure
- swelling of your legs or around your eyes (known as oedema)
- an increase in side effects from diabetes medication – including hypoglycaemia and acidosis
- anaemia – since your kidneys regulate how many red blood cells are in your blood, damage to your kidneys can cause anaemia
- bone thinning – since your kidneys regulate the levels of calcium in your bones, damage to your kidneys can result in bone-thinning and increase the risk of fracture
- passing more urine – an early sign of kidney disease may be passing urine more frequently, and having to get out of bed at night to go the toilet

- feeling generally tired, nauseous, cold and itchy – these are all late signs of kidney disease, caused by the accumulation of toxins as kidney function fails.

REDUCING YOUR RISK OF KIDNEY DAMAGE

Although kidney damage is very common in people with diabetes, these steps usually make it possible to prevent serious decline in kidney function or complete kidney failure.

1 Regular examination of kidney function – If you have type 2 diabetes, this should be done annually, or more often if you already have early signs of damage, high blood pressure, heart problems or eye disease. The most practical tests measure both the GFR in a blood sample and the albumin level in a urine sample from your first wee of the morning. Some doctors prefer to measure protein in urine collected over 24 hours to document the protein lost over the course of a day (proteinuria). Random (spot) urine tests are more variable and may be less accurate in determining your risks.

2 Good glucose, cholesterol, triglyceride and blood pressure levels – These will all reduce your risk of kidney damage and its effects on your body. Some blood-pressure-lowering drugs, such as ACE

inhibitors and ARBs (see pages 71–72), are better than others in helping prevent kidney damage.

3 Regular fluid intake – People with healthy kidneys should aim to drink at least 2–3 litres of fluid (8–10 glasses) every day. On hot days or if you have exercised you will need to drink more to make up for fluid lost through sweat. You'll know when you've achieved it if you go to the toilet three to four times a day, making a good amount of clear to light-yellow urine with little or no odour.

REPLACING KIDNEY FUNCTION

If your kidney function declines to a point at which the accumulation of fluid and toxins threatens your life (known as end-stage kidney disease, or ESKD), you will need dialysis or a kidney transplant in order to survive. A number of different dialysis options are now available. Haemodialysis is where a machine filters your blood via a direct connection to your bloodstream. Peritoneal dialysis is where the abdomen is filled with fluid via a soft tube. Waste products then pass from your body into this fluid, allowing any toxins to be removed when the fluid is subsequently drained.

While renal replacement is effective in removing waste products and toxins from your body, even the best outcomes are far worse than those with healthy kidneys. Prevention is a much better option.

Your eyes

Diabetes is the leading cause of preventable blindness, but eye damage is not inevitable. With hard work and commitment, most people with diabetes can retain excellent vision.

DIABETES AND THE EYES

To form an image in your brain, light must pass through the iris, be focused by the lens, reach your retina and pass as an electrical signal down the optic nerve. Diabetes can disrupt any or all parts of this pathway, reducing the quality of the picture or blocking part of the image. Diabetes is especially damaging to the small blood vessels at the back of the eye, which can result in a number of complications, including the following.

• Macular oedema – The macula sits at the centre of the retina and is responsible for seeing fine details. If diabetes damages the blood vessels near the macula, they can leak fluid, causing the retina to swell (known as oedema) and your vision to be reduced.

- Retinal ischaemia – Damaged blood vessels can sometimes become blocked, reducing the supply of oxygen and nutrients to parts of the retina and reducing vision.
- Proliferative retinopathy – Diabetes sometimes triggers a proliferation of new blood vessels in the eye to take the place of the damaged ones. But far from being helpful, these new vessels can promote scarring and more damage. They are very fragile and prone to spontaneous bleeding. As scar tissue associated with the new vessels shrinks, it can also sometimes pull the retina right off, leading to permanent loss of vision in the detached area.
- Cataracts – Diabetes can cause the lens of your eye to become clouded. Nearsightedness is an early sign of cataracts. Cataracts also scatter the light entering the eye, making things appear less vivid with less contrast, especially in low light. People with cataracts may also experience glare with bright lights, such as car lights. Eventually, cataracts can obstruct the passage of light into the eye and reduce vision. Many of us will experience a degree of vision loss due to cataracts as we age, but diabetes makes it more likely and may cause it to occur at a younger age.

PREVENTING EYE DAMAGE

Although eye damage is very common in people with diabetes, it is often possible to prevent significant vision loss or blindness through the following.

1   Regular eye tests – Get your eyes examined regularly (at least yearly) by an optometrist or ophthalmologist, even if your vision is normal. In diabetes, the damage to the eyes is insidious, with no pain and few symptoms. If you notice problems with your vision, it may be too late. If you already have early signs of eye damage, high blood pressure or kidney disease, you will need to have your eyes examined more frequently.

2   Don't ignore symptoms – Rapidly report any sudden changes in your vision to your doctor or eye specialist. Treatments are most effective when damage is caught in its early stages.

3   Control your diabetes – Maintain good control of your glucose, lipid and blood-pressure levels.

4   Protect your eyes – Avoid exposure to the ultraviolet and infrared rays in sunlight, which can contribute to cataract development. Wear UVB-protecting sunglasses and a broad-brimmed hat, and avoid direct sunlight in the middle of the day.

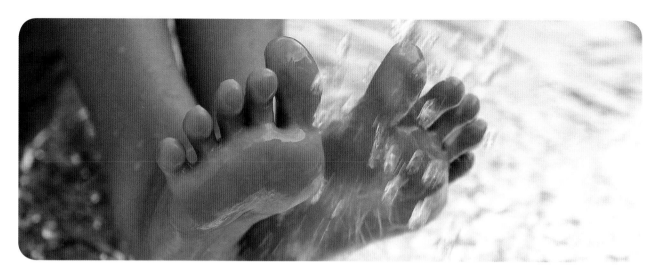

Your feet

Diabetes is the leading cause of leg and foot amputation in adults, but most foot problems are preventable.

DIABETES AND FEET

Your feet are especially vulnerable to diabetes. It can damage the nerves in your feet (known as neuropathy), which can make them numb to injuries or damaging pressure. Nerve damage can also sometimes be painful, producing pins and needles or a burning sensation, which is often worse at night. Damage to the nerves also makes the muscles in the foot weak or uncoordinated, which can cause foot deformities, such as bunions or hammertoe. These increase the stresses on your feet and can lead to corns, calluses, blisters and ulcers.

Diabetes can also damage the blood vessels that supply the feet, reducing the flow of blood, oxygen and sustaining nutrients to the furthest reaches of your body. High glucose levels also impair your ability to fight off infections that get under your skin through cracks or ulcers in your feet or into your toenails. If left untreated, these infections can spread and kill off tissues in your feet (known as gangrene). Diabetes can also alter the skin on your feet, making it thicker, drier, less resilient and more prone to blisters or cracks (especially at the heel).

PREVENTING FOOT DAMAGE

There are many simple steps you can take to avoid damage to your feet.

1 Pay attention to your feet – Inspect your feet every day for early signs of trouble or potential problem areas. Use a hand mirror to see the entire bottom of your feet and check between your toes. Before you put your shoes on, check them for stones, sticks and other foreign objects that might hurt your feet. Take off your shoes and socks every time you see your doctor. Your feet should be examined by a doctor or podiatrist every three or four months. If you already have signs of foot problems you must have regular podiatry care.

2   Look after your toenails – Many foot problems begin in an around the toenails. Thickened nails or sharp edges that dig in (without you feeling them) are often the opportunity an infection needs to get started. Keep your toenails trimmed straight across following the curve of your toes and file the edges with an emery board or nail file. Have a podiatrist do this if you need help or are unsure, or can't see or reach your toes well.

3   Keep the skin on your feet healthy – Wash and dry your feet well every day, but don't soak your feet or put them in very hot water. Moisturise dry areas, such as the heel, every day with lotions that don't contain alcohol. Keep moist areas, such as between the toes, dry.

4   Buy good shoes and socks – Many ulcers come from poorly fitting shoes or going barefoot unnecessarily. Always wear shoes properly fitted to the shape of your feet. Speciality shoe shops are usually better equipped than discount or department stores. If they don't know about diabetes, go somewhere else where they do. Choose shoes that give more room to your toes, with thick cushioning rubber soles but never high heels. Special shoes with extra cushioning or orthotics can be useful if you are at increased risk of foot problems. The right socks are also important in keeping your skin dry and cool. These are usually acrylic, not tight and don't have seams. Some also have special cushioning. Always wear clean socks and throw out damaged, tight or old ones.

5   Don't add to your risk – Maintaining good control of your glucose, cholesterol, lipids and blood-pressure levels is an important way to prevent foot damage. Smoking – even passive smoking – increases the risk of needing an amputation.

6   Don't ignore foot problems – Immediately report any changes in your feet to your doctor or foot specialist. Don't ignore them and hope they go away. The earlier you detect an infection, the better the chance of doing something about it. Important warning signs include: redness or skin discolouration, especially around corns or calluses; swelling or changes in the size or shape of your feet or ankles; pain in the feet or legs at rest or while walking (but even if you feel no pain there could still be cause for concern); blisters; bleeding; open sores (ulcers), no matter how small; and hot or cold spots. There are a number of effective treatments that can help your feet to heal. These can include: cleaning and dressing the wound; staying off damaged feet; antibiotics to help the infection heal and prevent it from spreading; and surgery, which is sometimes necessary to help ulcers heal.

Your mood

Staying healthy is about more than just keeping your glucose levels down. You also need to maintain and optimise your mental wellbeing.

DIABETES AND DEPRESSION

Depression is not just a brief period of feeling low, but a disproportionate and pervasive mood that interferes with your ability to function. It can affect your relationships, work, sleep and many other aspects of health and wellbeing. Depression can also affect your diabetes control, the likelihood of complications and their impact.

Adults with diabetes are more likely to develop depression or other forms of mental illness than people without diabetes. Various factors can contribute to the development of depression, including the following.

- The guilt and perceived stigma associated with having diabetes.
- The stress of living with diabetes and the demands of managing it successfully.
- Chronic pain or disability associated with diabetic complications.
- Low physical activity.
- A strong family history of diabetes and exposure to its consequences.
- Changes in the balance of chemicals in the brain caused by diabetes.
- Damage to the small blood vessels in the brain that regulate brain function.
- Increased levels of inflammation associated with diabetes, triggering the release of cytokines, signalling molecules that modify brain function.
- Insomnia, especially for sufferers of obstructive sleep apnoea (see pages 84–85).
- Certain medications, such as beta blockers.

PREVENTING DEPRESSION

Not everyone who has diabetes will become depressed. Simply looking after your diabetes will help reduce your risk of depression. The more competent you become at looking after yourself, the lower will be your stress and risk of depression.

Are you depressed?

Recognising and treating depression is an important and under-recognised part of diabetes care. One simple screening test is the Patient Health Questionnaire-2 (PHQ-2) that asks two simple questions:

1. Have you often had little interest or pleasure in doing things over the past month?
2. Have you often been bothered by feeling depressed or hopeless over the past month?

Most people with depression will answer yes to one or both of these questions. About half of all people who answer yes turn out not to be depressed, but it is still important to ask your doctor if you are worried.

Where possible, enlist the support of your diabetes care team, family and friends. Support groups can also help reduce the risk of depression. Find out about local diabetes meetings or consider joining one of the many diabetes organisations (see the Resources section beginning on page 263).

TREATING DEPRESSION

Depression is not something you have to put up with – it can be treated. The effective treatment of depression will also mean better diabetes control and reduced risk of complications. A number of different treatment options are available, including the following. Your doctor will decide which, alone or in combination, will work best for you.

- Antidepressant medications – These medications aim to balance disturbed chemistry in the depressed brain. Antidepressants do not blunt normal emotional reactions or turn you into a zombie, nor do they lead to dependence or addiction. About half of all people treated with a given antidepressant respond positively, mostly after a month of treatment, although it may take a few more months for a full response. Therapy is usually continued for a further 6–12 months, as stopping too soon increases the risk of recurrence. People who do not respond initially will be tried on alternative antidepressants or combinations, with or without psychotherapy.

- Psychotherapy – This treatment is effective for many people with depression, especially in combination with antidepressant medications. There are many different forms of psychotherapy, but most involve weekly structured sessions with a trained therapist that aim to retrain thinking and behaviour or develop coping skills.

- Exercise programs – Participation in exercise programs or increasing your physical activity in a social setting can also significantly improve the symptoms of depression, and has a range of other benefits if you have diabetes.

Your sleep

Without sleep we not only feel tired, but our bodies don't work as well. Inadequate sleep can lead to weight gain, and makes it harder to control blood pressure, cholesterol and glucose levels. Poor sleep is actually associated with an increased risk of developing diabetes. Sleep also affects your mood, sensitivity to pain and resistance to infection.

DIABETES AND SLEEP

Diabetes can have an impact on your nights as much as your days. Diabetes can stop you getting the sleep you need by causing:

- a need to get up at night to pee
- shortness of breath when lying down
- restless legs and cramping
- painful feet (due to ulcers, infection, nerve damage or vascular disease)

- stress or depression
- obstructive sleep apnoea.

Some diabetes medications (such as beta-blockers and antidepressants) can also disrupt sleep patterns.

PREVENTING SLEEP PROBLEMS

Some very simple things will help make it easier to get the sleep you need. First, eliminate any negative influences on your sleep, such as noise light, and too much stimulation. For example:

- block out street noise and light with the right choice of window curtain, garden planting or other simple tricks
- keep the TV and computer out of the bedroom
- replace your worn-out or uncomfortable mattress with a comfortable one that is good for your posture
- change your sheets regularly
- keep the pressure off your feet using a cradle or a short quilt
- put work away at least a couple of hours before going to bed
- avoid drinks containing caffeine after 2 p.m., and do not eat just before going to bed.

Secondly, make the most of positive sleep triggers, such as darkness, falling body temperature, quiet and routine. Finally, establish a regular pattern of going to bed and waking at the same time every day, even on weekends. Go to bed when your body tells you to and get up when you wake up.

Do you have a sleep problem?

Insomnia means different things to different people, including:

- difficulty falling asleep
- interrupted sleep with frequent or extended waking
- early-morning waking then being unable to get back to sleep
- non-restorative sleep resulting in impaired functioning during the day.

None of these things is a normal part of ageing or diabetes. If you are sleeping poorly, ask your doctor or sleep specialist for their advice and assistance.

TREATING SLEEP PROBLEMS

Insomnia typically does not go away by itself. Treating the underlying condition may resolve some symptoms but does not necessarily improve the insomnia. Sleeping pills can help re-establish a pattern and restore confidence that a good night's sleep is achievable, but they often have side effects, such as daytime sleepiness and dependence. Some effective long-term solutions include cognitive behavioural therapy and relaxation training.

OBSTRUCTIVE SLEEP APNOEA (OSA)

During every breath, we suck air into our lungs. If the airway is narrowed, extra sucking power is required. When you are asleep and your body is relaxed, this

extra power can cause the airway to cave in and obstruct the flow of air, which is heard by others as snoring. Sometimes the airway collapses completely and breathing stops. This is known as apnoea and eventually wakes you up with a start, allowing you to open your airway and breathe freely again.

Obstructive sleep apnoea (OSA) occurs when this cycle of apnoea followed by sudden waking happens repeatedly during every sleep (more than five times an hour). The resulting stress and fragmented sleep increases blood-pressure levels and the risk of heart attack and stroke. People with type 2 diabetes, especially men, are more likely to suffer from OSA. The risk of OSA also increases with age and increasing body weight, probably through fat accumulation in the neck surrounding the airway. Weight control (especially losing more than 10 kilograms) is the most effective way to prevent OSA and reduce its impact.

There is no effective drug therapy for OSA. The best treatment method is nasal continuous positive airway pressure (CPAP). This means sleeping with a device over your nose that holds your airway open

Do you have OSA?

It is hard to know what is happening when you are asleep, and feeling tired or inattentive during the day may have many causes. Sometimes you may remember choking or gasping sensations or recurrent awakenings or find yourself waking unrefreshed. More commonly, partners or family members complain about habitual loud snoring or witness your choking episodes. Talk to your doctor if you are concerned, especially if you have excessive daytime sleepiness.

through the pressurised flow of air. Not everyone can cope with CPAP because of discomfort, noise, congestion or claustrophobia, but if you can, it can lead to significant weight loss, improved mood and better overall health. Losing weight through other means can also be helpful in treating OSA.

Your sex life

Sex enhances quality of life and has an impact on both mental and physical health. While diabetes does not prevent sex, it can significantly influence sexual function and the ability to achieve satisfying and enjoyable sex. The biggest barrier is usually reluctance to share feelings and ask for help. Most people feel uncomfortable disclosing or discussing sexual problems, but there are many effective ways to ensure a healthy and fulfilling sex life if you have diabetes.

Testosterone is a hormone that influences libido, arousal and the number and strength of orgasms in both men and women. Low testosterone levels are more common in people with diabetes, but can be topped up with supplements. Post-menopausal women who need only small doses to restore normal levels may find prohormones such as DHEA effective. If you think you may be low in testosterone, you can take a simple screening questionnaire, followed by blood tests if necessary.

Reduced libido and arousal are the most common sexual issues for diabetic women, usually as a result of changes in body chemistry or physical fatigue, low self-esteem, pain, poor sleep, depression and the strain of chronic illness. Management usually involves treating both chemistry and behaviour. Many sex therapists achieve results simply by improving a couple's communication both in and out of bedroom.

Some women with diabetes may also find vaginal lubrication difficult, making intercourse uncomfortable and climax more difficult. This can be due to damage to the blood vessels and nerves of the pelvis (which can be partly prevented by good diabetes care). Some medications used to treat diabetes can also reduce lubrication. Although common, particularly in ageing women, this need not be a barrier to sexual enjoyment – lubricants, oestrogen-containing creams and sufficient foreplay can all help. Hormone replacement therapy (HRT) is not appropriate for post-menopausal women with diabetes because of the risk of heart disease and clotting.

Erectile dysfunction is a common sexual problem, affecting at least three-quarters of all diabetic men. Coordinated function among nerves and blood vessels and the right mindset are required to maintain an erection, so if any of these components isn't functioning optimally, an erection will fail. Anything that protects your heart (weight loss, glucose control, low cholesterol and blood pressure, increased phy-sical activity, and so on) will protect your penis. A number of very effective treatments are now available, including oral medications, injections, urethral suppositories, vacuum erection devices and penile prostheses. When used in the right setting, each can improve sex and quality of life.

Your mind

We all fear developing dementia as we get older. It can be the end result of a number of different processes that damage the brain and its functions, including poor blood supply or degenerative diseases such as Alzheimer's or Parkinson's. People with diabetes have increased rates of dementia, but as with other complications, good diabetes management with the following will reduce your risks.

1 Keep your arteries open – Anything that protects your heart from damage will also reduce your risk of dementia. Lower your blood pressure, lose weight, improve your glucose and lipid control, stop smoking and exercise regularly.

2 Exercise regularly – Not only does exercise improve physical health, but people who remain fit and active retain their cognitive faculties better.

3 Eat well – Your diet influences your risk of cognitive decline and dementia, largely through its effects on weight, blood pressure and the metabolic control of glucose and lipid levels. Diets high in trans-fats and saturated fats are associated with increased rates of cognitive decline. Foods naturally high in antioxidants may improve cognitive function.

4 Keep your mind active – Use it or lose it. Mental activity maintains mental activity. Any kind of social isolation can lead to stress, depression and mental decline. Join a club or society and stay socially as well as mentally active. The trick is to find something challenging that you can enjoy every day.

Diabetes and vitamin B12 (cyanocobalamin)

Vitamin B12 is important for healthy brain function. Between 5 and 20 per cent of all adults develop B12 deficiency during their lifetime and this risk is increased if you have type 2 diabetes. B12 deficiency is also more common if you are taking the antidiabetic drug metformin or have had bariatric surgery (see below).

B12 is naturally found only in animal products, such as red meat, poultry, fish, eggs and milk, so vegetarians (and particularly vegans) are at increased risk of B12 deficiency. Chronic B12 deficiency is associated with anaemia, fatigue, depression and impaired mental function. Rather than waiting for problems to arise, some specialists recommend that adults with type 2 diabetes take B12 supplements or eat B12-fortified foods. Another alternative is following the high-protein option of the eating plan recommended in this book (see Chapter 2).

Your weight

This book offers a wealth of advice on weight loss through diet and exercise. Some people who are dangerously overweight, however, may need extra help to lose weight, including medication or surgery. Each of these interventions depends on diet and lifestyle changes to be successful, and should never be considered as an alternative to lifestyle changes.

Medications to help weight loss include the following.

- Orlistat – Reduces the absorption of fat from the diet by a third, by inhibiting the enzymes that break down fats in the intestines. By limiting the amount of fat digested, it also reduces the kilojoules obtained from fat. In some people this is enough to cause modest weight reduction but many people cannot tolerate its side effects, including flatulence and oily, loose stools.
- Acarbose and incretin analogues – These drugs used to lower blood glucose levels can also cause significant weight loss (see Chapter 6).

A more effective means of losing weight for people with serious weight problems is surgery (known as bariatric surgery). In many people, the weight loss is so significant that they become free of diabetes. The two most common techniques are:

- gastric banding – This involves placing an adjustable band around the upper part of the stomach, creating a small pouch, which means you eat much less before feeling full.
- gastric bypass surgery – Also creates a small pouch that reduces the amount you can eat at one time, but then bypasses the remainder of the stomach by connecting the small intestine to the new pouch. This involves more invasive, major surgery, but has more significant effects on blood glucose control.

- sleeve gastrectomy – Reduces the size of the stomach to a small tube by cutting most of it away.

Surgery is not without major risks. It should only be considered if you have diabetes and a BMI of greater than 35.

Cancer

Many of the things that make diabetes more likely (such as poor diet, inactivity and obesity) can also increase your risk of developing some cancers. There is much you can do to reduce your risks of both.

1   Give up smoking – Smoking is the leading cause of preventable cancer death. Avoiding cigarette smoke is the most effective way to reduce your risk of cancer. Do what it takes to give up and encourage others to do the same.

2   Participate in cancer screening programs – Early detection is the best opportunity for effective treatment. If you have type 2 diabetes you should strongly consider regular screening for appropriate cancers, including, for women, an annual mammogram from the age of 50, and regular PAP smears every two years from your twenties; and, for men and women, bowel cancer screening from the age of 50. If you are at increased risk (e.g. you have a strong family history of cancer or have had cancer before), you will require more intensive surveillance. Talk to your doctor about the best options for your particular situation.

3   Reduce your weight – At least one in every five cancer deaths is due to excess body fat.

4   Exercise regularly – There are strong links between weight gain, physical inactivity and some forms of cancer. Not only does exercise improve physical health, but people who remain fit and active have a lower risk of some cancers.

5   Eat well – A low-fat diet rich in fresh fruits, vegetables and fibre appears to protect against many forms of cancer, including breast, colon and prostate cancer. People whose diets are high in processed foods have an increased risk of cancer.

6   Limit your alcohol intake – Heavy alcohol use has been linked to some forms of cancer, including breast and colon cancer.

7   Take your medication – Some medications used to treat diabetes may actually reduce your risk of cancer.

8 Rising to the challenge

Lifestyle changes can make a profound difference to your health.

MOST OF US, with or without diabetes, could substantially improve our health and wellbeing with simple lifestyle changes. What and how much we eat and drink, and how much exercise we do can profoundly affect our health. Sometimes these changes require us to adjust aspects of our social activities, leisure pursuits and long-established routines and habits. Although such changes can be very challenging, if you have type 2 diabetes you need to do your best to make them a priority.

> *I cut down on portions. The big thing was realising how much I was eating before.*
> DAVID

> *Anything I'm not supposed to eat, I don't buy it, so it's not in the house. If it's not here, I can't eat it.*
> LENA

> *My palate has significantly changed. The long period of time helped to change my dietary habits. As a result, I continue to feel a sense of flow-on and benefits.*
> ANDY

Anyone can succeed

Over the years we have encountered thousands of people with type 2 diabetes in our clinics and during our research. Their experiences have taught us a number of things, the most important being you can change your weight, wellbeing and health if you have the right guidance and support. The people who have followed the CSIRO four-month type 2 diabetes program have achieved impressive weight loss and corresponding improvements in general health. They say they feel fitter and healthier, and their medical examinations prove it.

With a moderate weight loss of around 10 per cent, most people achieve substantial reductions in blood glucose levels, cholesterol levels and blood pressure. Some people who were on blood-pressure or glucose-lowering medication at the start of the program have been able to reduce their medication. Levels of LDL (bad) cholesterol can drop by 20 per cent. Psychological measures reveal improvements in people's overall quality of life, energy levels and sexual function. They report being less emotionally distressed about their diabetes and often say they feel more positive and better within themselves. Some rediscover activities they had enjoyed in the past but had let slide, while others pursue new activities they had never contemplated before.

Participating in this program gave me back more confidence.
BRETT

I was very excited and keen to go back to my doctor and show what I'd actually achieved by doing this.
SANDRA

The challenges

Maintaining healthy habits without support is challenging. That's why we recommend staying in regular contact with your diabetes care team. The people we spoke to said that the improvements in their health, weight or diabetes symptoms during the program motivated them to keep up the changes once the program was finished.

I was motivated by my weight loss. I wanted to continue to keep the weight off and to control my blood glucose.
AUDREY

I had this great sense of achievement with what I'd done with the exercise. I was keen to keep it going.
MARK

PART 2

Menu plans

Option 1 (6500 kJ), Week 1

ALLOWABLE DAILY SNACKS: 20 g nuts or seeds and 1 reduced-fat dairy snack (suitable for options 1 and 2)

WEEK 1	DAY 1	DAY 2	DAY 3
BREAKFAST	40 g low-GI, high-fibre cereal with 250 ml low-fat/skim milk	40 g oats with 250 ml low-fat/skim milk	40 g low-GI, high-fibre cereal with 125 ml low-fat/skim milk & 15 g dried fruit **MORNING TEA OPTION:** 1 piece fresh fruit
LUNCH	Harissa Chicken with Capsicum & Herb Salad (see p 210) 1 piece fresh fruit **AFTERNOON TEA OPTION:** 30 g dried fruit	Roast pork roll (1 × 80 g wholegrain bread roll with 2 tsp light margarine, 100 g roast pork, 20 g low-fat cheese, ½ cup sliced tomato & red onion, apple sauce & 1 cup salad leaves) **AFTERNOON TEA OPTION:** 1 piece fresh fruit	Spicy Egg Curry with Tomato & Coriander Salad (see p 214) 100 g low-fat/skim yoghurt **AFTERNOON TEA OPTION:** Homemade Tomato Soup (see p 138) with ½ slice multigrain bread & 1 tsp light margarine
DINNER	Veal Steak with Creamy Mushroom Sauce & Spinach (see p 177) 150 g sweet potato **SUPPER OPTION:** 1 slice toasted fruit loaf with 1 tsp light margarine	Grilled Fish with Peach Salsa (see p 188) Asian-style Coleslaw with Mint & Coriander (see p 167) ¼ cup cooked basmati rice	Beef Stir-fry with Mushrooms & Baby Corn (see p 174) ½ cup cooked green leafy vegetables **SUPPER OPTION:** Floating Islands (see p 251)

DAY 4	DAY 5	DAY 6	DAY 7
40 g untoasted muesli with 100 g low-fat/skim yoghurt	2 slices wholegrain toast with 1 tsp light margarine, 2 poached eggs, ½ grilled tomato & ¼ cup mushrooms 150 ml unsweetened fruit juice	Baked Berry Breakfast Pudding (see p 134) **MORNING TEA OPTION:** Golden Pikelets (see p 142)	1 slice wholegrain toast with 1 tsp light margarine & vegemite or jam; 1 slice wholegrain toast with 20 g low-fat cheese, grilled or toasted 150 ml unsweetened fruit juice
Quesadilla (see p 161) 1 cup salad leaves with 2 tsp olive-oil dressing **AFTERNOON TEA OPTION:** 150 g fresh fruit salad with 100 g low-fat-custard	Chicken Caesar Salad (see p 156) 150 ml unsweetened fruit juice **AFTERNOON TEA OPTION:** 1 slice fruit loaf with 1 tsp light margarine	Lentil Stew with Carrot and Zucchini (see p 218) Labne (see p 141) **AFTERNOON TEA OPTION:** 1 piece fresh fruit with 200 g low-fat/skim yoghurt	Barbecued Lamb Skewers with Minted Yoghurt (see p 222) ½ cup cooked couscous **AFTERNOON TEA OPTION:** 1 piece fresh fruit
Miso Salmon with Bean Sprout & Cucumber Salad (see p 187) ½ cup cooked basmati rice **SUPPER OPTION:** 1 piece fresh fruit	Garlic & Pepper Pork with Broccolini & Mushrooms (see p 182) 100 g dry-roasted pumpkin **SUPPER OPTION:** 200 g low-fat/skim yoghurt	Chicken Cacciatore with Zucchini Spaghetti (see p 236) **SUPPER OPTION:** Chocolate Sponge (see p 253) with 100 g low-fat/skim yoghurt	Vegetable & Chickpea Moroccan Stew (see p 236)

Option 1 (6500 kJ), Week 2

WEEK 2	DAY 1	DAY 2	DAY 3
BREAKFAST	40 g oats with 150 ml low-fat/skim milk & 100 g low-fat/skim yoghurt **MORNING TEA OPTION:** 150 g drained tinned fruit in natural juice	2 slices wholegrain toast with 2 tsp light margarine, 2 poached eggs, ½ grilled tomato & ½ cup mushrooms **MORNING TEA OPTION:** 200 g low-fat/skim yoghurt with 30 g sultanas	40 g low-GI, high-fibre cereal with 250 ml low-fat/skim milk **MORNING TEA OPTION:** 1 piece fresh fruit
LUNCH	Pork & Cabbage Rolls (see p 205) 150 ml unsweetened fruit juice **AFTERNOON TEA OPTION:** 200 g low-fat/skim yoghurt	Hot & Sour Fish Soup (see p 160) 1 × 40 g bread roll **AFTERNOON TEA OPTION:** 250 ml low-fat milk or 1 small skim-milk cappuccino or latte	Curried egg roll (1 × 80 g wholegrain roll, 2 hard-boiled eggs mashed with curry powder to taste, 1–2 tsp low-fat mayonnaise & 1 cup salad leaves) **AFTERNOON TEA OPTION:** Asian-style Coleslaw with Mint & Coriander (see p 167)
DINNER	Grilled Tofu Sticks with Asparagus & Cherry Tomato Salad (see p 217) ½ cup cooked basmati rice	Rack of Lamb with Pea & Asparagus Pilaf (see p 234) **SUPPER OPTION:** 150 g drained tinned fruit in natural juice	Braised Beef with Cinnamon & Star Anise (see p 229) ¼ cup cooked basmati rice ¼ cup cooked vegetables **SUPPER OPTION:** Chocolate Pudding (see p 252) with 150 g low-fat vanilla custard

DAY 4	DAY 5	DAY 6	DAY 7
1 toasted English muffin with 2 tsp light margarine & 1 tsp jam 200 g low-fat/skim yoghurt	Baked Berry Breakfast Pudding (see p 134) **MORNING TEA OPTION:** 150 g low-fat/skim yoghurt	40 g low-GI, high-fibre cereal with 250 ml low-fat/skim milk	Stuffed Mushrooms with Roast Tomatoes (see p 124) 150 ml unsweetened fruit juice
Lamb Pie with Mint Yoghurt (see p 153) 150 ml unsweetened fruit juice **AFTERNOON TEA OPTION:** Red Kidney Bean Dip with Crudites (see p 139)	Hearty Bean & Vegetable Soup (see p 192) 1 slice wholegrain bread with 1 tsp light margarine **AFTERNOON TEA OPTION:** 1 piece fresh fruit	Lamb Kofta with Baba Ganoush & Tabbouleh (see p 203) 200 g low-fat/skim yoghurt **AFTERNOON TEA OPTION:** 150 g drained tinned fruit in natural juice	Open Chicken Burger (see p 197) **AFTERNOON TEA OPTION:** 1 piece fresh fruit
Tamarind Fish (see p 193) ½ cup side salad from Free List (see p 20) with oil-free dressing **SUPPER OPTION:** 250 ml low-fat/skim milk	Spanish Chicken & Lemon Beans (see p 180) ½ cup cooked couscous with ½ chopped tomato	Herbed Roast Beef with Cauliflower Mash & Horseradish Sauce (see p 226) 150 g sweet potato **SUPPER OPTION:** 1 piece fresh fruit	Baked Fish Fillet with Capsicum Braise & Roast Tomatoes (see p 240) ½ cup cooked basmati rice **SUPPER OPTION:** 200 g low-fat/skim yoghurt

Option 1 (6500 kJ), Week 3

WEEK 3	DAY 1	DAY 2	DAY 3
BREAKFAST	40 g untoasted muesli with 100 g low-fat/skim yoghurt **MORNING TEA OPTION:** 1 piece fresh fruit	Porridge with Fruit, Vanilla Yoghurt & Slivered Almonds (see p 133)	40 g low-GI, high-fibre cereal with 250 ml low-fat/skim milk **MORNING TEA OPTION:** 1 piece fresh fruit
LUNCH	Tandoori Chicken with Tomato & Cucumber Salad (see p 209) **AFTERNOON TEA OPTION:** 15 g dried fruit	Tuna sandwich (2 slices wholegrain bread with 100 g tinned tuna, 20 g low-fat cheese, 1 cup finely chopped lettuce, tomato & celery)	Pork Sang Choy Bow (see p 154) Aromatic Asian Noodle Soup (see p 150) **AFTERNOON TEA OPTION:** 200 g low-fat/skim yoghurt with 15 g dried fruit
DINNER	Thai-style Yellow Seafood Curry (see p 190) **SUPPER OPTION:** Baked Lime Cheesecake (see p 257)	Individual Cottage Pies with Sweet Potato Topping (see p 200) **SUPPER OPTION:** Cranberry & Cinnamon Poached Pears (see p 254)	Steak Pizzaiola with Watercress & Pear Salad (see p 178) 150 g sweet potato

DAY 4	DAY 5	DAY 6	DAY 7
40 g untoasted muesli with 200 g low-fat/skim yoghurt	40 g low-GI, high-fibre cereal with 250 ml low-fat/skim milk **MORNING TEA OPTION:** 2 wholegrain crispbreads	1 toasted English muffin with 2 tsp light margarine & 1 tsp jam 250 ml low-fat/skim milk or 1 small skim-milk cappuccino or latte	Omelette with Tomato & Fresh Herbs (see p 129) 150 ml unsweetened fruit juice **MORNING TEA OPTION:** 1 slice wholegrain toast with 1 tsp light margarine
Harissa Chicken with Capsicum & Herb Salad (see p 210) 1 slice toasted multigrain bread (as croutons) + 10 g low-fat cheese **AFTERNOON TEA OPTION:** 1 piece fresh fruit	Stuffed Capsicum with Parsley Salad (see p 204) 1 piece fresh fruit **AFTERNOON TEA OPTION:** 1 slice fruit loaf with 1 tsp light margarine	Quesadilla (see p 161) **AFTERNOON TEA OPTION:** 150 g drained tinned fruit in natural juice	Spicy Barbecued Chicken with Green Pawpaw Salad (see p 223) **AFTERNOON TEA OPTION:** 1 slice multigrain bread with ½ tomato & 20 g low-fat cheese, grilled
Fish & Fennel Stew (see p 219) ½ cup side salad from Free List (see p 20) with oil-free dressing **SUPPER OPTION:** 1 piece fresh fruit	Swiss Steak with Celeriac Mash (see p 230) 100 g dry-roasted pumpkin **SUPPER OPTION:** 1 piece fresh fruit	Slow-cooked Lamb with Middle Eastern Spices (see p 233) ½ cup cooked basmati rice **SUPPER OPTION:** 1 piece fresh fruit	Moroccan Fish Tagine with Herbed Couscous (see p 239)

Option 1 (6500 kJ), Week 4

WEEK 4	DAY 1	DAY 2	DAY 3
BREAKFAST	40 g low-GI, high-fibre cereal with 125 ml low-fat/skim milk	40 g oats with 250 ml low-fat/skim milk **MORNING TEA OPTION:** 1 piece fresh fruit	Banana & Blueberry Smoothie (see p 133)
LUNCH	Beef, cheese & tomato toasted sandwich (2 slices wholegrain bread with 2 tsp light margarine, 100 g shaved roast beef, 20 g low-fat cheese & ½ cup sliced tomato) **AFTERNOON TEA OPTION:** 150 g drained tinned fruit in natural juice	Curried egg roll (1 × 80 g wholegrain roll, 2 hard-boiled eggs mashed with curry powder to taste, 1–2 tsp low-fat mayonnaise & 1½ cups salad leaves)	Hearty Bean & Vegetable Soup (see p 192) Feta & Zucchini Frittata (see p 130) **AFTERNOON TEA OPTION:** 1 slice fruit loaf, toasted
DINNER	Chicken Cacciatore with Zucchini Spaghetti (see p 236) 1 slice wholegrain bread **SUPPER OPTION:** 100 g low-fat/skim yoghurt with 150 g fresh mixed berries	Steak Pizzaiola with Watercress & Pear Salad (see p 178) 1 × 40 g multigrain bread roll with 1 tsp light margarine **SUPPER OPTION:** 2 crispbreads plus 20 g low-fat cheese	Crispy-skin Salmon with Rocket & Fennel Salad (see p 245) 1 cup cooked couscous **SUPPER OPTION:** 1 piece fresh fruit

DAY 4	DAY 5	DAY 6	DAY 7
40 g untoasted muesli with 200 g low-fat/skim yoghurt	2 slices wholegrain toast with 1 tsp light margarine, 2 poached eggs, ½ grilled tomato & ¼ cup mushrooms **MORNING TEA OPTION:** 150 ml unsweetened fruit juice	1 toasted English muffin with 2 tsp light margarine & 1 tsp jam 250 ml low-fat/skim milk or 1 small skim-milk cappuccino or latte	Corn Fritters with Fresh Tomato Salsa (see p 126) 150 ml unsweetened fruit juice **MORNING TEA OPTION:** 200 g low-fat/skim yoghurt
Turkey salad roll (1 × 80 g wholegrain bread roll with 10 g 80% reduced-fat Philadelphia cream cheese spread, 150 g roast turkey, cranberry sauce & 1 cup salad leaves) **AFTERNOON TEA OPTION:** 1 piece fresh fruit	Meatballs with Spaghetti (see p 151) 20 g shredded low-fat cheese **AFTERNOON TEA OPTION:** Asian-style Coleslaw with Mint & Coriander (see p 167)	Individual Cottage Pie with Sweet Potato Topping (see p 200) 150 ml unsweetened fruit juice **AFTERNOON TEA OPTION:** 1 piece fresh fruit	Penne with Tuna & Tomato Sauce (see p 155) 20 g shredded low-fat cheese **AFTERNOON TEA OPTION:** 1 piece fresh fruit
Veal Steak with Creamy Mushroom Sauce & Spinach (see p 177) 200 g dry-roasted pumpkin **SUPPER OPTION:** 150 g drained tinned fruit in natural juice	Parmesan Crumbed Chicken with Garlic Mushrooms (see p 206) 100 g sweet potato **SUPPER OPTION:** 1 piece fresh fruit	Baked Ocean Trout with a Creamy Herb Sauce & Watercress Salad (see p 185) 150 g sweet potato **SUPPER OPTION:** 200 g low-fat/skim yoghurt	Barbecued Steak with Green Bean & Tomato Salad (see p 176) ½ cup cooked basmati rice

Option 1 (6500 kJ), Week 5

WEEK 5	DAY 1	DAY 2	DAY 3
BREAKFAST	40 g low-GI, high-fibre cereal with 250 ml low-fat/skim milk **MORNING TEA OPTION:** 100 g low-fat/skim yoghurt with 15 g dried fruit	40 g oats with 250 ml low-fat/skim milk or 1 small skim-milk cappuccino or latte **MORNING TEA OPTION:** 1 piece fresh fruit	Scrambled Tofu with Parsley & Soy (see p 131) 150 ml unsweetened fruit juice **MORNING TEA OPTION:** 200 g low-fat/skim yoghurt
LUNCH	Curried egg roll (1 × 80 g wholegrain bread roll, 2 hard-boiled eggs mashed with curry powder to taste, 1–2 tsp low-fat mayonnaise & 1 cup salad leaves)	Harissa Chicken with Capsicum & Herb Salad (see p 210) 1 slice multigrain toast (as croutons) **AFTERNOON TEA OPTION:** 100 g low-fat/skim yoghurt	Creamy Mushroom Soup (see p 244) 1 slice multigrain toast **AFTERNOON TEA OPTION:** Roast Vegetable Salad (see p 168) with ½ slice multigrain toast (as croutons)
DINNER	Garlic & Pepper Pork with Broccolini & Mushrooms (see p 182) 150 ml unsweetened fruit juice **SUPPER OPTION:** Buttermilk Puddings with Rhubarb & Strawberries (see p 259)	Fish & Fennel Stew (see p 219) ½ cup side salad from Free List (see p 20) with oil-free dressing **SUPPER OPTION:** 1 piece fresh fruit	Grilled Tofu Sticks with Asparagus & Cherry Tomato Salad (see p 217) ½ cup cooked basmati rice **SUPPER OPTION:** 150 g fresh fruit salad with 100 g low-fat/skim yoghurt

DAY 4	DAY 5	DAY 6	DAY 7
1 toasted English muffin with 1 tsp jam 200 g low-fat/skim yoghurt	Porridge with Fruit, Vanilla Yoghurt & Slivered Almonds (see p 133)	Baked Berry Breakfast Pudding (see p 134) **MORNING TEA OPTION:** 150 g low-fat/skim yoghurt	40 g oats with 150 ml low-fat/skim milk, 100 g low-fat/skim vanilla yoghurt & cinnamon to taste
Tuna, avocado & bean salad (100 g tinned tuna, 100 g tinned beans, 40 g avocado & 1 cup salad leaves) 150 ml unsweetened fruit juice **AFTERNOON TEA OPTION:** 4 wholegrain crispbreads with 20 g low-fat cheese	Salmon salad roll (1 × 80 g wholegrain bread roll, 100 g tinned salmon, 1 hard-boiled egg, 40 g low-fat ricotta, ½ cup baby spinach leaves & ½ cup chopped tomato & green beans with 1 tsp oil-free dressing)	Calamari Salad with Coriander & Lime (see p 159) **AFTERNOON TEA OPTION:** 1 × 80 g multigrain bread roll with 20 g low-fat cheese & 40 g avocado	Spicy Egg Curry with Tomato & Coriander Salad (see p 214) **AFTERNOON TEA OPTION:** 250 ml low-fat/skim milk or 1 small skim-milk cappuccino or latte with 1 slice fruit loaf, toasted
Herbed Roast Beef with Cauliflower Mash & Horseradish Sauce (see p 226) 100 g sweet potato **SUPPER OPTION:** 150 g drained tinned fruit in natural juice	Beef Stir-fry with Mushrooms & Baby Corn (see p 174) Greek Salad (see p 171) **SUPPER OPTION:** 1 piece fresh fruit	Lightly Spiced Lamb with Tomato & Spinach (see p 231) 1 cup cooked couscous **SUPPER OPTION:** 150 g drained tinned fruit in natural juice	Swiss Steak with Celeriac Mash (see p 230) **SUPPER OPTION:** Apple & Blackberry Pie (see p 258)

Option 1 (6500 kJ), Week 6

WEEK 6	DAY 1	DAY 2	DAY 3
BREAKFAST	40 g low-GI, high-fibre cereal with 250 ml low-fat/skim milk 1 piece fresh fruit	40 g oats with 250 ml low-fat/skim milk **MORNING TEA OPTION:** 150 ml unsweetened fruit juice	1 slice wholegrain toast with 100 g baked beans & 1 poached egg **MORNING TEA OPTION:** 1 piece fresh fruit
LUNCH	Thai Beef Salad (see p 148) 100 g low-fat custard **AFTERNOON TEA OPTION:** Red Kidney Bean Dip with Crudites (see p 139)	Spanish Chicken & Lemon Beans (see p 180) **AFTERNOON TEA OPTION:** 12 plain rice crackers with 20 g 80% reduced-fat Philadelphia cream cheese	Hot & Sour Fish Soup (see p 160) ½ cup side salad from Free List (see p 20) with 1 tsp olive oil dressing 1 × 80 g multigrain bread roll **AFTERNOON TEA OPTION:** 250 ml low-fat/skim milk or 1 small skim-milk cappuccino or latte
DINNER	Tamarind Fish (see p 193) ¼ cup cooked basmati rice **SUPPER OPTION:** Cranberry & Cinnamon Poached Pears (see p 254)	Slow-cooked Lamb with Middle Eastern Spices (see p 233) ½ cup cooked couscous **SUPPER OPTION:** 1 apple stewed in own juice	Barbecued Steak with Green Bean & Tomato Salad (see p 176) **SUPPER OPTION:** 1 piece fresh fruit with 200 g low-fat/skim yoghurt

DAY 4	DAY 5	DAY 6	DAY 7
40 g untoasted muesli with 200 g low-fat/skim yoghurt 150 ml unsweetened fruit juice	40 g low-GI, high-fibre cereal with 150 ml low-fat/skim milk, 100 g low-fat/skim vanilla yoghurt & 10 g seed mix	40 g low-GI, high-fibre cereal with 250 ml low-fat/skim milk or 1 small skim-milk cappuccino or latte	Feta & Zucchini Frittata (see p 130) 150 ml unsweetened fruit juice
Pork & Cabbage Rolls (see p 205) 1 cup salad leaves with 1 tsp olive-oil dressing **AFTERNOON TEA OPTION:** 30 g dried fruit with 100 g low-fat skim yoghurt	Chicken salad (150 g roast chicken, 50 g chickpeas, 20 g low-fat cheese, 2 cups salad leaves, ½ cup sliced tomato & red onion, & 2 tsp olive-oil dressing) 150 ml unsweetened fruit juice	Slow-cooked Lamb with Middle Eastern Spices (see p 233) 1 cup cooked couscous **AFTERNOON TEA OPTION:** 1 piece fresh fruit	Bean salad (200 g tinned three-bean mix, 20 g low-fat cheese, 1 cup chopped salad vegetables & 1 tsp olive-oil dressing) **AFTERNOON TEA OPTION:** 4 wholegrain crispbreads with Garlicky Mushroom Pate (see p 140)
Miso Salmon with Bean Sprout & Cucumber Salad (see p 187) ¼ cup cooked basmati rice **SUPPER OPTION:** Labne (see p 141) with 100 g low-fat/skim dairy dessert	Fresh Tomato Salsa with Pita Chips (see p 196) Open Chicken Burgers (see p 197) **SUPPER OPTION:** 1 piece fresh fruit	Tandoori Chicken with Tomato & Cucumber Salad (see p 209) **SUPPER OPTION:** 200 g low-fat/skim yoghurt with 150 g fruit stewed in own juice	Hearty Bean & Vegetable Soup (see p 192) **SUPPER OPTION:** 1 piece fresh fruit

Option 2 (6500 kJ), Week 1

ALLOWABLE DAILY SNACKS: 20 g nuts or seeds and 1 reduced-fat dairy snack (suitable for options 1 and 2)

WEEK 1	DAY 1	DAY 2	DAY 3
BREAKFAST	40 g low-GI, high-fibre cereal with 250 ml low-fat/skim milk 1 slice fruit loaf with 1 tsp light margarine	40 g oats with 150 ml low-fat/skim milk, 100 g low-fat/skim natural yoghurt, 15 g sultanas & cinnamon to taste **MORNING TEA OPTION:** 1 piece fresh fruit	40 g low-GI, high-fibre cereal with 250 ml low-fat/skim milk **MORNING TEA OPTION:** 150 ml unsweetened fruit juice
LUNCH	Hot & Sour Fish Soup (see p 160) 1 slice wholegrain toast **AFTERNOON TEA OPTION:** 2 wholegrain crispbreads with 20 g low-fat cheese; 2 wholegrain crispbreads with 40 g avocado	Vegetable Gumbo (see p 165) 1 slice wholegrain toast **AFTERNOON TEA OPTION:** 1 slice multigrain bread with 1 tsp light margarine & Vegemite	Lamb Pie with Mint Yoghurt (see p 153) **AFTERNOON TEA OPTION:** 2 wholegrain crispbreads with 20 g low-fat cheese
DINNER	Veal Steak with Creamy Mushroom Sauce & Spinach (see p 177) **SUPPER OPTION:** Apple & Blackberry Pie (see p 258)	Steak Pizzaiola with Watercress & Pear Salad (see p 178) **SUPPER OPTION:** 1 toasted wholegrain English muffin with 2 slices tomato & 2 slices (40 g) low-fat cheese, grilled	Tamarind Fish (see p 193) ½ cup cooked basmati rice ½ cup cooked vegetables **SUPPER OPTION:** 1 piece fresh fruit

DAY 4	DAY 5	DAY 6	DAY 7
40 g untoasted muesli with 200 g low-fat/skim yoghurt & cinnamon to taste **MORNING TEA OPTION:** 150 ml unsweetened fruit juice	2 slices wholegrain toast with 1 tsp light margarine, 1 poached egg, ½ grilled tomato, 20 g low-fat cheese & ¼ cup grilled mushrooms	Baked Berry Breakfast Pudding (see p 134) **MORNING TEA OPTION:** Golden Pikelets (see p 142) with 200 g low fat/skim strawberry yoghurt	1 slice wholegrain toast with 2 tsp light margarine & Vegemite or 1 tsp jam; 1 slice wholegrain toast with 20 g low-fat cheese, toasted **MORNING TEA OPTION:** 150 ml unsweetened fruit juice
Meatballs with Spaghetti (see p 151) 20 g low-fat cheese, shredded **AFTERNOON TEA OPTION:** 150 g drained tinned fruit in natural juice	Greek Salad (see p 171) 1 × 80 g multigrain bread roll with 1 tsp light margarine 150 ml unsweetened fruit juice **AFTERNOON TEA OPTION:** 1 piece fresh fruit	Homemade Tomato Soup (see p 138) 1 × 40 g multigrain bread roll with 1 tsp light margarine **AFTERNOON TEA OPTION:** 200 g low-fat/skim yoghurt with 150 g fresh or frozen mixed berries	Pork Sang Choy Bow (see p 154) 2 slices wholegrain toast **AFTERNOON TEA OPTION:** 1 piece fresh fruit
Pork & Cabbage Rolls (see p 205) 1 cup cooked couscous with 1 tsp olive oil	Miso Salmon with Bean Sprout & Cucumber Salad (see p 187) 1 slice wholegrain bread topped with 20 g avocado **SUPPER OPTION:** 2 slices fruit loaf, toasted	Individual Cottage Pie with Sweet Potato Topping (see p 200) **SUPPER OPTION:** Couscous salad (1 cup cooked couscous, ½ (70 g) cup sweet corn, & ½ cup chopped capsicum & red onion)	Lentil Stew with Carrot & Zucchini (see p 218) ½ cup cooked basmati rice **SUPPER OPTION:** 200 g low-fat/skim yoghurt

Option 2 (6500 kJ), Week 2

WEEK 2	DAY 1	DAY 2	DAY 3
BREAKFAST	40 g oats with 250 ml low-fat/skim milk **MORNING TEA OPTION:** 1 slice fruit loaf with 2 tsp light margarine	40 g low-GI, high-fibre cereal with 150 ml low-fat/skim milk & 15 g dried fruit	40 g low-GI, high-fibre cereal with 250 ml low-fat/skim milk **MORNING TEA OPTION:** 200 g low-fat/skim yoghurt
LUNCH	Thai Beef Salad (see p 148) 1 slice multigrain bread with 1 tsp light margarine **AFTERNOON TEA OPTION:** 200 g low-fat/skim yoghurt with 1 piece fresh fruit	Creamy Mushroom Soup (see p 244) 1 × 80 g multigrain bread roll with 1 tsp light margarine **AFTERNOON TEA OPTION:** 2 cups side salad from Free List (see p 20) with oil-free dressing	Chicken Caesar Salad (see p 156) 150 ml unsweetened fruit juice **AFTERNOON TEA OPTION:** Blueberry Muffin (see p 144)
DINNER	Braised Beef with Cinnamon & Star Anise (see p 229) 100 g sweet potato & 200 g pumpkin, mashed **SUPPER OPTION:** 150 g drained tinned fruit in natural juice with ½ cup diet jelly	Baked Ocean Trout with a Creamy Herb Sauce & Watercress Salad (see p 185) 100 g sweet potato & 70 g sweet corn **SUPPER OPTION:** Berry & Mango Ice-cream Cake with Chocolate Sauce (see p 248)	Beef Stir-fry with Mushrooms & Baby Corn (see p 174) 1 cup egg noodles 1 cup broccoli &/or cauliflower **SUPPER OPTION:** 1 piece fresh fruit

DAY 4	DAY 5	DAY 6	DAY 7
40 g untoasted muesli with 200 g low-fat/skim yoghurt **MORNING TEA OPTION:** 150 ml unsweetened fruit juice	40 g oats with 150 ml low-fat/skim milk, 100 g low-fat/skim natural yoghurt & cinnamon to taste **MORNING TEA OPTION:** 1 piece fresh fruit	40 g low-GI, high-fibre cereal with 250 ml low-fat/skim milk **MORNING TEA OPTION:** 150 ml unsweetened fruit juice	Stuffed Mushrooms with Roast Tomatoes (see p 124) 150 ml unsweetened fruit juice **MORNING TEA OPTION:** 200 g low-fat/skim yoghurt
Calamari Salad with Coriander & Lime (see p 159) **AFTERNOON TEA OPTION:** 2 slices fruit loaf, toasted	Aromatic Asian Noodle Soup (see p 150) 150 ml unsweetened fruit juice **AFTERNOON TEA OPTION:** 200 g low-fat/skim yoghurt	Greek Salad (see p 171) 1 × 80 g multigrain bread roll with 1 tsp light margarine **AFTERNOON TEA OPTION:** 2 wholegrain crispbreads with Garlicky Mushroom Pate (see p 140)	Homemade Tomato Soup (see p 138) 1 × 80 g multigrain bread roll **AFTERNOON TEA OPTION:** 1 piece fresh fruit
Hearty Bean & Vegetable Soup (see p 192) 1 slice multigrain bread with 1 tsp light margarine **SUPPER OPTION:** 1 piece fresh fruit	Garlic & Pepper Pork with Broccolini & Mushrooms (see p 182) ½ cup cooked basmati rice **SUPPER OPTION:** 1 slice multigrain bread with 1 tsp light margarine & Vegemite	Baked Fish Fillet with Capsicum Braise & Roast Tomatoes (see p 240) 100 g sweet potato & 200 g pumpkin, mashed **SUPPER OPTION:** 100 g low-fat/skim yoghurt with 150 g fresh fruit salad	Grilled Tofu Sticks with Asparagus & Cherry Tomato Salad (see p 217) ¾ cup cooked basmati rice

Option 2 (6500 kJ), Week 3

WEEK 3	DAY 1	DAY 2	DAY 3
BREAKFAST	40 g untoasted muesli with 200 g low-fat/skim yoghurt **MORNING TEA OPTION:** 1 slice fruit loaf with 1 tsp light margarine	Porridge with Fruit, Vanilla Yoghurt & Slivered Almonds (see p 133)	40 g low-GI, high-fibre cereal with 250 ml low-fat/skim milk **MORNING TEA OPTION:** 1 piece fresh fruit
LUNCH	Tuna sandwich (2 slices wholegrain bread with 50 g drained tinned tuna, 20 g low-fat cheese, 1 cup finely chopped lettuce, tomato & celery, & 40 g avocado)	Roast Vegetable Salad (see p 168) 1 piece fresh fruit **AFTERNOON TEA OPTION:** Blueberry Muffin (see p 144)	Thai Beef Salad (see p 148) 1 × 80 g multigrain bread roll with 1 tsp light margarine **AFTERNOON TEA OPTION:** 1 piece fresh fruit
DINNER	Individual Cottage Pie with Sweet Potato Topping (see p 200) **SUPPER OPTION:** Apple & Blackberry Pie (see p 258)	Harissa Chicken with Capsicum & Herb Salad (see p 210) 1½ cups cooked couscous **SUPPER OPTION:** 200 g low-fat/skim yoghurt	Fish & Fennel Stew (see p 219) **SUPPER OPTION:** 4 wholegrain crispbread with 1 slice (20 g) low-fat cheese

DAY 4	DAY 5	DAY 6	DAY 7
40 g untoasted muesli with 200 g low-fat/skim yoghurt	40 g low-GI, high-fibre cereal with 250 ml low-fat/skim milk	40 g low-GI, high-fibre cereal with 250 ml low-fat/skim milk	Omelette with Tomato & Fresh Herbs (see p 129) 2 slices wholegrain toast
MORNING TEA OPTION: 1 piece fresh fruit	**MORNING TEA OPTION:** 1 slice multigrain bread with 1 tsp light margarine & Vegemite	**MORNING TEA OPTION:** 150 ml unsweetened fruit juice	**MORNING TEA OPTION:** 150 ml unsweetened fruit juice
Curried egg sandwich (2 slices wholegrain bread, 1 hard-boiled egg mashed with curry powder to taste, 1–2 tsp low-fat mayonnaise, 1 cup salad leaves, ½ cup sliced cucumber & ½ cup sliced tomato)	Hot & Sour Fish Soup (see p 160) 1 × 80 g wholegrain bread roll 1 piece fresh fruit	Vegetable Gumbo (see p 165) 1 slice toasted pita bread topped with 10 g 80% reduced-fat Philadelphia cream cheese	Zucchini Soup with Fresh Mint (see p 164) 1 × 80 g multigrain bread roll
AFTERNOON TEA OPTION: 1 piece fresh fruit	**AFTERNOON TEA OPTION:** Asian-style Coleslaw with Mint & Coriander (see p 167)	**AFTERNOON TEA OPTION:** 1 piece fresh fruit	**AFTERNOON TEA OPTION:** 4 wholegrain crispbreads with 1 slice (20 g) low-fat cheese
Braised Beef with Cinnamon & Star Anise (see p 229) ½ cup cooked basmati rice	Rack of Lamb with Pea & Asparagus Pilaf (see p 234) 150 ml unsweetened fruit juice	Chicken Cacciatore with Zucchini Spaghetti (see p 236) 1 cup cooked basmati rice	Moroccan Fish Tagine with Herbed Couscous (see p 239)
SUPPER OPTION: 200 g low-fat/skim yoghurt	**SUPPER OPTION:** 4 wholegrain crispbreads with 1 slice (20 g) low-fat cheese	**SUPPER OPTION:** 200 g low-fat/skim yoghurt	**SUPPER OPTION:** 150 g drained tinned fruit in natural juice

Option 2 (6500 kJ), Week 4

WEEK 4	DAY 1	DAY 2	DAY 3
BREAKFAST	40 g low-GI, high-fibre cereal with 250 ml low-fat/skim milk **MORNING TEA OPTION:** 150 ml unsweetened fruit juice	40 g oats with 150 ml low-fat/skim milk, ½ sliced banana & cinnamon to taste	Banana & Blueberry Smoothie (see p 133) **MORNING TEA OPTION:** 2 slices wholegrain toast with 1 tsp light margarine & Vegemite
LUNCH	Greek Salad (see p 171) 1 × 80 g multigrain bread roll with 1 tsp light margarine **AFTERNOON TEA OPTION:** 4 wholegrain crispbreads with 20 g avocado & 1 piece fresh fruit	Eggplant Parmigiana with Fennel Salad (see p 213) 2 wholegrain crispbreads **AFTERNOON TEA OPTION:** 1 slice wholegrain bread with 1 tsp light margarine & Vegemite	Creamy Mushroom Soup (see p 244) 1 × 80 g multigrain bread roll **AFTERNOON TEA OPTION:** 100 g low-fat/skim yoghurt
DINNER	Barbecued Steak with Green Bean & Tomato Salad (see p 176) 100 g sweet potato & 100 g pumpkin, dry-roasted	Grilled Fish with Peach Salsa (see p 188) 1 cup cooked basmati rice	Steak Pizzaiola with Watercress & Pear Salad (see p 178) 1 cup cooked couscous **SUPPER OPTION:** 1 apple stewed in juices with 100 g low-fat/skim vanilla yoghurt

DAY 4	DAY 5	DAY 6	DAY 7
40 g untoasted muesli with 200 g low-fat/skim yoghurt **MORNING TEA OPTION:** 1 piece fresh fruit	2 slices wholegrain toast with 2 tsp light margarine, 2 slices (40 g) low-fat cheese, ½ grilled tomato & ¼ cup grilled mushrooms **MORNING TEA OPTION:** 150 ml unsweetened fruit juice	40 g low-GI, high-fibre cereal with 125 ml low-fat/skim milk 30 g dried fruit	Corn Fritters with Fresh Tomato Salsa (see p 126) 150 ml unsweetened fruit juice **MORNING TEA OPTION:** 1 toasted English muffin with 2 tsp light margarine & 1 tsp jam
Pork Sang Choy Bow (see p 154) ½ cup cooked basmati rice 150 ml unsweetened fruit juice **AFTERNOON TEA OPTION:** 2 wholegrain crispbreads with 1 slice (20 g) low-fat cheese & 1 cup side salad with 1 tsp olive-oil dressing	Tuna sandwich (2 slices wholegrain bread with 50 g drained tinned tuna, 1 cup finely chopped lettuce, tomato & celery, & 2 tsp olive-oil dressing)	Chicken Caesar Salad (see p 156) 20 g shaved reduced-fat parmesan **AFTERNOON TEA OPTION:** Blueberry Muffin (see p 144)	Cauliflower & Broccoli Soup (see p 166) 1 × 80 g multigrain bread roll **AFTERNOON TEA OPTION:** 100 g low-fat/skim yoghurt
Spanish Chicken & Lemon Beans (see p 180) ¼ cup cooked basmati rice	Thai-style Yellow Seafood Curry (see p 190) ½ cup cooked basmati rice **SUPPER OPTION:** 150 g drained tinned fruit in natural juice	Spicy Barbecued Chicken with Green Pawpaw Salad (see p 223) 1 slice wholegrain bread 1 cup side salad from Free List (see p 20) with 10 ml oil-free dressing	Crispy-skin Salmon with Rocket & Fennel Salad (see p 245) 1 cup cooked couscous **SUPPER OPTION:** 150 g drained tinned fruit in natural juice with 150 g low-fat custard

Option 2 (6500 kJ), Week 5

WEEK 5	DAY 1	DAY 2	DAY 3
BREAKFAST	40 g low-GI, high-fibre cereal with 250 ml low-fat/skim milk & 30 g dried fruit **MORNING TEA OPTION:** 1 slice fruit loaf with 1 tsp light margarine	40 g oats with 150 ml low-fat/skim milk & 100 g low-fat/skim vanilla yoghurt **MORNING TEA OPTION:** 1 slice fruit loaf with 1 tsp light margarine	Scrambled Tofu with Parsley & Soy (see p 131) 1 slice toasted wholewheat Mountain Bread 150 ml unsweetened fruit juice **MORNING TEA OPTION:** 1 piece fresh fruit
LUNCH	Roast Vegetable Salad (see p 168) 12 plain rice crackers with Garlicky Mushroom Pate (see p 140) 150 ml unsweetened fruit juice	Lamb Pie with Mint Yoghurt (see p 153) 1 piece fresh fruit 1 slice fruit loaf with 1 tsp light margarine **AFTERNOON TEA OPTION:** 150 g low-fat/skim yoghurt with 15 g dried fruit & 10 g seed mix	Penne with Tuna & Tomato Sauce (see p 155) **AFTERNOON TEA OPTION:** 1 slice multigrain bread with 20 g mashed avocado
DINNER	Baked Ocean Trout with a Creamy Herb Sauce & Watercress Salad (see p 185) 200 g sweet potato **SUPPER OPTION:** 200 g low-fat custard	Pork Medallions with Mustard Sauce & Cabbage & Apple Salad (see p 184) 1 slice wholewheat or rye Mountain Bread with 10 g 80% reduced-fat Philadelphia cream cheese	Eggplant Parmigiana with Fennel Salad (see p 213) 1 × 80 g multigrain bread roll

DAY 4	DAY 5	DAY 6	DAY 7
40 g untoasted muesli with 200 g low-fat/skim yoghurt **MORNING TEA OPTION:** 1 piece fresh fruit	Porridge with Fruit, Vanilla Yoghurt & Slivered Almonds (see p 133) **MORNING TEA OPTION:** 1 slice wholegrain toast with ½ sliced tomato & 10 g low-fat cheese, grilled	40 g untoasted muesli with 200 g low-fat/skim yoghurt **MORNING TEA OPTION:** 1 piece fresh fruit & 1 slice fruit loaf, toasted with 1 tsp light margarine	40 g low-GI, high-fibre cereal with 250 ml low-fat/skim milk **MORNING TEA OPTION:** 1 slice fruit loaf with 1 tsp light margarine
Thai Beef Salad (see p 148) 30 g dried fruit **AFTERNOON TEA OPTION:** 4 wholegrain crispbreads with 1 slice (20 g) low-fat cheese & 40 g avocado	Calamari Salad with Coriander & Lime (see p 159) 1 × 80 g multigrain bread roll	Homemade Tomato Soup (see p 138) 1 × 80 g multigrain bread roll with 1 tsp light margarine **AFTERNOON TEA OPTION:** 1 piece fresh fruit	Vegetable Gumbo (see p 165) 2 slices wholewheat Mountain Bread, toasted **AFTERNOON TEA OPTION:** 150 ml unsweetened fruit juice
Garlic & Pepper Pork with Broccolini & Mushrooms (see p 182) ½ cup cooked basmati rice **SUPPER OPTION:** 1 slice multigrain bread with 1 tsp light margarine & 1 tsp jam or marmalade	Fish & Fennel Stew (see p 219) 150 g drained tinned fruit in natural juice **SUPPER OPTION:** 200 g low-fat/skim yoghurt	Herbed Roast Beef with Cauliflower Mash & Horseradish Sauce (see p 226) 200 g sweet potato 70 g sweet corn **SUPPER OPTION:** 250 ml low-fat custard	Slow-cooked Lamb with Middle Eastern Spices (see p 233) 100 g sweet potato & 200 g pumpkin, roasted with 1 tsp olive oil **SUPPER OPTION:** 200 g low-fat custard with 150 g fresh or frozen mixed berries

Option 2 (6500 kJ), Week 6

WEEK 6	DAY 1	DAY 2	DAY 3
BREAKFAST	40 g low-GI, high-fibre cereal with 250 ml low-fat/skim milk 150 ml unsweetened fruit juice **MORNING TEA OPTION:** 1 piece fresh fruit	40 g oats with 250 ml low-fat/skim milk **MORNING TEA OPTION:** 12 plain rice crackers with 20 g avocado & Garlicky Mushroom Pate (see p 140)	2 slices wholegrain toast with 100 g baked beans & 1 poached egg **MORNING TEA OPTION:** 150 ml unsweetened fruit juice
LUNCH	Roast beef sandwich (2 slices wholegrain bread, 2 tsp light margarine, 50 g lean roast beef, ½ cup sliced cucumber & ½ cup sliced tomato)	Penne with Tuna & Tomato Sauce (see p 155) **AFTERNOON TEA OPTION:** 1 piece fresh fruit	Cauliflower & Broccoli Soup (see p 166) 1 × 80 g multigrain bread roll with 1 tsp light margarine **AFTERNOON TEA OPTION:** 150 g fresh fruit salad with 200 g low-fat/skim yoghurt
DINNER	Lamb Kofta with Baba Ganoush and Tabbouleh ½ cup cooked basmati rice **SUPPER OPTION:** 200 g low-fat/skim dairy dessert	Stuffed Capsicum with Parsley Salad (see p 204) 150 ml unsweetened fruit juice **SUPPER OPTION:** Golden Pikelets (see p 142)	Veal Steak with Creamy Mushroom Sauce & Spinach (see p 177) 200 g dry-roasted sweet potato

DAY 4	DAY 5	DAY 6	DAY 7
40 g untoasted muesli with 200 g low-fat/skim yoghurt **MORNING TEA OPTION:** 1 piece fresh fruit 1 slice fruit loaf, toasted, with 1 tsp light margarine	40 g low-GI, high-fibre cereal with 250 ml low-fat/skim milk **MORNING TEA OPTION:** 1 toasted English muffin with 2 tsp light margarine & 1 tsp jam	Stuffed Mushrooms with Roast Tomatoes (see p 124) 150 ml unsweetened fruit juice **MORNING TEA OPTION:** 1 slice multigrain bread with 20 g avocado	Feta & Zucchini Frittata (see p 130) 150 ml unsweetened fruit juice **MORNING TEA OPTION:** 1 slice fruit loaf, toasted
Roast Vegetable Salad (see p 168) 4 wholegrain crispbreads with 20 g ricotta cheese **AFTERNOON TEA OPTION:** 150 ml unsweetened fruit juice	Calamari Salad with Coriander & Lime (see p 159) 1 slice multigrain bread with 1 tsp light margarine **AFTERNOON TEA OPTION:** 4 wholegrain crispbreads with 1 slice (20 g) low-fat cheese	Tuna sandwich (2 slices wholegrain bread with 50 g drained tinned tuna, 20 g low-fat ricotta cheese, & 1 cup finely chopped lettuce, tomato & celery)	Homemade Tomato Soup (see p 138) 2 slices wholegrain bread **AFTERNOON TEA OPTION:** 1 toasted English muffin with 20 g low-fat cheese
Miso Salmon with Bean Sprout & Cucumber Salad (see p 187) 1 × 80 g wholegrain bread roll	Fresh Tomato Salsa with Pita Chips (see p 196) Open Chicken Burger (see p 197) 150 ml unsweetened fruit juice **SUPPER OPTION:** 1 baked apple	Vegetable & Chickpea Moroccan Stew (see p 237) **SUPPER OPTION:** 1 piece fresh fruit	Garlic and Pepper Pork with Broccolini and Mushrooms (see p 182) **SUPPER OPTION:** 1 piece fresh fruit

PART 3

Recipes

Breakfasts

Stuffed mushrooms with roast tomatoes

Begin the day with a savoury treat. If you have access to freshly grown herbs in your backyard or on your balcony, using them in this recipe lifts the flavour.

Serves 4
Prep time
10 minutes
Cooking time
25 minutes
1 serve =
2 units bread
1 unit dairy
2 units vegetables
1 unit fats

400 g large flat or portobello mushrooms
1 tablespoon olive oil
2 spring onions, finely chopped
2 cloves garlic, crushed
1 cup (50 g) baby spinach leaves, shredded
80 g low-fat ricotta
3 tablespoons chopped flat-leaf parsley
freshly ground black pepper, to taste
300 g cherry truss tomatoes
olive oil spray
1 tablespoon balsamic vinegar
8 slices low-GI wholegrain toast

1 Preheat the oven to 180°C. Line a large baking tray with baking paper.

2 Remove the stalks from the mushrooms. Arrange the mushroom caps on the baking tray, topside down, and then finely chop the stalks.

3 Heat the olive oil in a frying pan over medium heat. Add the spring onion, garlic and chopped mushroom stalks and fry for 2–3 minutes or until cooked through. Add the spinach and continue to cook, stirring, until all the liquid has evaporated. Remove from the heat and stir in the ricotta and parsley. Season with black pepper.

4 Spoon the spinach and ricotta mixture into the mushroom caps. Place the tomatoes on the tray alongside the stuffed mushrooms, and spray both with olive oil.

5 Bake for 15 minutes or until the mushrooms are cooked. Drizzle the tomatoes with the balsamic vinegar. Divide the mushrooms and tomatoes among four plates and serve with wholegrain toast.

*You can vary the herbs in the mushroom stuffing — try adding some thyme leaves to the mix or replacing the parsley with basil.

Corn fritters with fresh tomato salsa

These fritters make a great addition to a communal breakfast table.
The whole family will enjoy them.

Serves 4
Prep time
20 minutes
Cooking time
10 minutes
1 serve =
½ unit protein
1 unit bread
1 unit vegetables
1 unit fats

1 red capsicum (pepper),
   seeded and finely diced
1 cup (150 g) corn kernels
2 spring onions, finely chopped
1 tablespoon chopped flat-leaf
   parsley
1 teaspoon Cajun spice mix
   (optional)
4 eggs, lightly beaten
¼ cup (125 ml) low-fat milk
3 tablespoons wholemeal flour
½ teaspoon baking powder
1 tablespoon olive oil

Tomato salsa
2 tomatoes, finely diced
2 spring onions, thinly sliced
1 tablespoon roughly chopped
   flat-leaf parsley
2 tablespoons lemon juice

1 Combine the capsicum, corn, spring onion, parsley and spice mix (if using) in a large bowl. Stir in the egg and milk, then add the flour and baking powder and mix until smooth.

2 To make the tomato salsa, combine all the ingredients in a bowl and set aside.

3 Heat a non-stick frying pan over medium heat and add a teaspoon of the oil. Working in batches, add 1 heaped tablespoon of batter per fritter to the pan and fry for 2–3 minutes each side or until cooked through. Repeat with the remaining batter, adding a little oil to the pan as necessary. You should be able to make 12–16 fritters.

4 Serve the fritters topped with the fresh tomato salsa.

* Try different spices, such as curry powder or Moroccan spices, in place of the Cajun spice mix.

* You can use ready-made salt-reduced salsa to save preparation time.
* The corn and capsicum in the fritters can be replaced with diced cooked vegetables of your choice.

* The filling for the omelette can be varied. Try mushrooms, roasted capsicum (pepper), spinach and ricotta, or any leftover vegetables you have in the fridge.

Omelettes with tomato and fresh herbs

These omelettes can be rolled and then wrapped up in baking paper or foil and taken out the door with you for a breakfast on the run.

Serves 4

Prep time
15 minutes

Cooking time
15 minutes

1 serve =
1 unit protein
1 unit dairy
1 unit vegetables
1 unit fats

1 tablespoon olive oil
4 spring onions, finely chopped
4 tomatoes, diced
8 eggs, lightly beaten
4 tablespoons chopped herbs,
    such as flat-leaf parsley,
    basil or chives
4 tablespoons grated
    low-fat cheese
salt-reduced tomato salsa or
    ketchup, to serve (optional)

1 Heat 2 teaspoons of the oil in a 20 cm non-stick frying pan over medium heat. Add the spring onion and tomato and fry, stirring, for 3–4 minutes or until starting to soften. Remove from the pan and set aside. Wipe out the pan with a paper towel.

2 Heat ½ teaspoon oil in the pan, add a quarter of the beaten egg and cook, stirring, for 1 minute until starting to set. Continue to cook for 1–2 minutes until just set on top, then spoon a quarter of the tomato mixture, herbs and grated cheese over half the omelette and fold the other side over. Slide onto a plate. Repeat with the remaining ingredients to make 4 omelettes in total. Serve immediately with salsa or ketchup, if using.

* For a sweet version, add a little Splenda or other powdered sweetener to the egg mix and fill with berries or stewed fruit.

Feta and zucchini frittata

This is a great recipe for mornings where you have the luxury of a little more time –
a lovely addition to a weekend brunch. Alternatively, you could make a batch on a
Sunday night and reheat it for a rushed, but nutritious Monday breakfast.

Serves 4
Prep time
10 minutes
Cooking time
30 minutes
1 serve =
1 unit protein
1 unit dairy
1 unit vegetables
1 unit fats

1 tablespoon olive oil
1 small onion, finely chopped
2 large zucchini (courgettes),
   thinly sliced
½ teaspoon dried oregano
freshly ground black pepper
8 eggs, lightly whisked
½ cup (125 ml) low-fat milk
80 g low-fat feta, crumbled
3 tablespoons grated parmesan
lemon wedges, to serve

1 Preheat the oven to 180°C. Heat the oil in a 20 cm non-stick, ovenproof frying pan over medium heat. Add the onion and cook until softened, then add the zucchini and continue cooking until the zucchini is translucent. Stir in the oregano and season with pepper. Reduce the heat to low.

2 Combine the eggs and milk. Pour into the pan and sprinkle over the feta. Cook gently for 3–4 minutes or until the base is just set. Sprinkle with the parmesan and transfer to the oven.

3 Bake for 15–20 minutes or until set and golden on top. Allow to cool for 10 minutes, then serve with lemon wedges.

* The zucchini can easily be replaced by other vegetables, such as mushrooms or asparagus.
* Any leftovers make a great lunch served with a salad the next day.
* Feta cheese is not very high in calcium, so be sure to supplement your diet with low-fat dairy products to meet your daily calcium requirements.

Scrambled tofu with parsley and soy

Vegetarians and tofu-lovers will enjoy this topping on toast of a morning,
as a nice replacement for scrambled eggs.

Serves 4

Prep time

10 minutes

Cooking time

5 minutes

1 serve =

1 unit protein

1 unit bread

½ unit fats

2 teaspoons olive oil

2 spring onions, finely chopped

2 tablespoons finely chopped
   flat-leaf parsley

2–3 teaspoons salt-reduced
   soy sauce

500 g firm tofu, crumbled

freshly ground black pepper

4 slices low-GI wholegrain toast

1 Heat the oil in a frying pan over medium heat, add the spring onion and fry for 2 minutes or until softened. Add the parsley, soy sauce and tofu and cook, stirring gently, for 3 minutes or until heated through. Be careful not to overcook.

2 Season to taste with black pepper and serve with toast.

* To add extra flavour, add some chopped mushrooms to the pan with the spring onion.
* To boost your vegetable intake, try serving the tofu with wilted spinach and grilled tomatoes.

* Try different low-fat yoghurt flavours and fruit combinations to suit your taste. Matching flavours can work really well, like pairing berry yoghurt with fresh berries, or apricot yoghurt with fresh apricot and peach slices.

Porridge with fruit, vanilla yoghurt and slivered almonds

This porridge is a warming and filling beginning to the day, particularly on cold mornings.

Serves 4
Prep time
5 minutes
Cooking time
10 minutes
1 serve =
2 units bread
½ unit dairy
1 unit fruit
1 unit fats

1½ cups (160 g) wholegrain oats
1 cup (250 ml) low-fat milk
80 g chopped dried fruit,
    such as cranberries, apricots
    or pears
pinch of ground cinnamon
200 g low-fat vanilla yoghurt
2 serves fresh fruit of choice,
    such as strawberries,
    blueberries or pears
4 tablespoons slivered almonds

1 Combine the oats, milk, dried fruit and cinnamon in a saucepan and bring to a simmer over low heat. Cook, stirring, for 5–10 minutes or until the oats have softened and the liquid has been absorbed. Add a little water if the porridge is too thick.

2 Meanwhile, combine the yoghurt and fresh fruit in a bowl.

3 Spoon the porridge into four bowls and top with the fruit and yoghurt mix. Sprinkle with the almonds and serve.

Banana and blueberry smoothies

These smoothies can be whizzed together in no time at all. If you're really in a rush, you could pour the smoothies into lidded travel mugs and take them with you to drink on your way to work or school.

Serves 2
Prep time
5 minutes
Cooking time
nil
1 serve =
1 unit bread
1 unit dairy
1 unit fruit

1 firm banana
150 g blueberries
1 cup (250 ml) low-fat milk
200 g low-fat vanilla or
    berry yoghurt
1 tablespoon honey or Splenda
    or other powdered sweetener

1 Combine all the ingredients in a blender or food processor and blend until smooth. Pour into two glasses and serve immediately.

* You can use fresh or frozen blueberries in this smoothie. Using frozen berries gives an extra icy chill.
* The banana can be replaced with peach or mango and the blueberries with strawberries.

Baked berry breakfast puddings

When you're getting bored with the usual morning drudge, why not try one of these puddings for something a little different?

Serves 4
Prep time
15 minutes
Cooking time
30 minutes
1 serve =
½ unit protein
1 unit bread
¼ unit dairy
1 unit fruit

olive oil spray
4 slices low-GI wholegrain bread,
   torn into large pieces
1 cup (150 g) blueberries,
   fresh or frozen
1 cup (125 g) raspberries,
   fresh or frozen
4 eggs
1 cup (250 ml) skim milk
2 tablespoons Splenda or other
   powdered sweetener
2 teaspoons grated orange zest
icing sugar, to dust (optional)

1 Preheat the oven to 180°C.

2 Spray 4 × 1 cup (250 ml) ovenproof dishes with olive oil. Layer the bread and berries in each dish.

3 Whisk together the eggs, milk, sweetener and orange zest in a large bowl. Divide the egg mixture among the dishes and then place the puddings in a baking dish. Pour enough boiling water into the dish to come halfway up the sides of the dishes.

4 Bake for 25–30 minutes or until set. Allow to cool for 10 minutes, then dust with icing sugar (if using) and serve.

* These puddings can be prepared and cooked the day before and then warmed through when you're ready to eat them.
* You can make one big breakfast pudding to share instead of individual dishes.

* Try other fruits such as cherries or peaches. Tinned fruit in natural juice (drained) is also a suitable substitute for the berries.

Snacks

* **Free** To make this a Free List soup, omit the olive oil and milk and place all the ingredients except the basil in the saucepan and simmer for 30 minutes. Remove from the heat, then puree and serve with fresh basil leaves.
* When tomatoes are in season in the summertime, take advantage of their freshness and make the soup with 1 kg peeled fresh tomatoes in place of the tinned tomatoes, and increase the cooking time to 30 minutes.
* For extra flavour, add 1 teaspoon curry powder or other spices (such as Moroccan, Cajun or an Italian herb mix) to the soup when adding the onion.

Homemade tomato soup

This soup is a very warming snack on a cold, rainy day, but it could also be served chilled during a hot summer. Serve with a slice of low-GI bread for a satisfying lunch (remember to add 1 unit bread to your nutritional count).

Serves 4
Prep time
15 minutes
Cooking time
30 minutes
1 serve =
1½ units
vegetables
1 unit fats

1 tablespoon olive oil
1 onion, finely chopped
2 cloves garlic, crushed
1 carrot, finely diced
2 × 400 g tins diced tomatoes
3 cups (750 ml) salt-reduced
  chicken stock
½ cup (125 ml) low-fat milk
  (optional)
freshly ground black pepper
fresh basil leaves, to garnish

1 Heat the oil in a saucepan. Add the onion, garlic and carrot and cook, stirring, for 5 minutes or until starting to soften.

2 Add the tomato and stock and bring to the boil, then reduce the heat and simmer for 20 minutes or until the vegetables are soft.

3 Remove from the heat and puree roughly with a stick blender or transfer to a food processor and blend. Combine the puree and milk, if using, in the saucepan and gently heat through. Season to taste with pepper and serve garnished with basil leaves.

Red kidney bean dip with crudites

This dip is very versatile and is delicious spread over low-GI crispbread or bread.

Serves 4
Prep time
15 minutes
Cooking time
nil
1 serve =
1 unit protein
1 unit bread
1 unit vegetables

1 × 400 g tin kidney beans, drained and rinsed
2 cloves garlic, crushed
½ teaspoon Tabasco
2 teaspoons ground cumin
1 tablespoon fat-free mayonnaise
1 tablespoon tomato ketchup
2 tablespoons lemon juice
2 cups (350–400 g) vegetable sticks, such as carrot, celery, cucumber and zucchini (courgette)

1 Combine the beans, garlic, Tabasco, cumin, mayonnaise, ketchup and lemon juice in a food processor and process until smooth. Spoon into a bowl and serve with vegetable sticks for dipping.

* Cover any leftovers with plastic wrap and store in the fridge for up to 4 days.
* You could replace the kidney beans with tinned chickpeas or white beans.

Garlicky mushroom pate

This recipe is also lovely made with Swiss brown mushrooms and works well served as a dip with vegetable sticks.

Serves 4
Prep time
15 minutes, plus cooling time
Cooking time
10 minutes
1 serve =
1 unit vegetables
½ unit fats

2 teaspoons olive oil
500 g button mushrooms,
 cut into 1 cm pieces
4 spring onions, chopped
5 cloves garlic, crushed
1 tablespoon lemon juice
1 teaspoon thyme leaves
1 teaspoon tomato paste (puree)
¼ teaspoon Tabasco
1 tablespoon finely chopped
 flat-leaf parsley (optional)

1 Heat the oil in a frying pan over medium heat. Add the mushroom, spring onion and garlic and cook over medium heat, stirring, for 5 minutes or until the mushroom is cooked and most of the liquid has evaporated.

2 Place the mushroom mixture in a food processor with the lemon juice, thyme, tomato paste and Tabasco and puree until smooth (add a little water or vegetable stock if necessary). Stir in the parsley, if using.

3 Spoon into a small bowl, then cover and refrigerate until cool. See notes below for serving suggestions.

* Use as a spread on low-GI bread or crispbread, topped with sliced tomato.
* Spread on slices of cucumber and garnish with parsley leaves or sliced olives to serve as finger food with drinks.

Labne

This recipe needs to be started a couple of days in advance, so plan ahead.
The labne make great nibblies to pass around when having friends over on
the weekend or on a special occasion.

Serves 4

Prep time

15 minutes, plus
refrigeration time

Cooking time

nil

1 serve =

1 unit bread

½ unit dairy

400 g low-fat natural yoghurt
4 tablespoons chopped fresh
   herbs, such as flat-leaf parsley,
   thyme, basil or rosemary
2 low-GI crispbreads,
   broken into pieces

1 Spoon the yoghurt into a sieve lined with
   muslin. Place over a bowl, then cover and
   refrigerate for 48 hours.

2 Roll tablespoons of the yoghurt mixture into
   balls, then roll in the chopped herbs to coat.
   Serve immediately with the crispbread pieces
   or refrigerate for later.

* You may like to add some
  freshly ground black pepper,
  spices or chilli to the
  herbs for a more intensely
  flavoured coating.
* The labne could also be served
  alongside a savoury salad.

Golden pikelets

This recipe may make more pikelets than you need, but they freeze well (see note adjacent), and make good lunchbox fillers.

* Serve with sugar-free fruit spread or sliced fresh fruit and low-fat yoghurt or low-fat ricotta.
* Any leftover pikelets can be frozen for up to 1 month. To defrost, thaw at room temperature then warm in the microwave and serve.

Serves 8
(makes 16)
Prep time
15 minutes
Cooking time
15 minutes
1 serve =
1¼ units bread

½ cup (75 g) wholemeal flour
½ cup (75 g) plain flour
1 teaspoon baking powder
3 tablespoons quick-cooking oats
2 teaspoons Splenda or other
   powdered sweetener
¼ teaspoon ground cinnamon
1 egg, lightly beaten
1 cup (250 ml) low-fat milk
1 teaspoon vanilla extract
olive oil spray

1 Combine the flours, baking powder, oats, sweetener and cinnamon in a large mixing bowl and make a well in the centre. Add the egg, milk and vanilla and whisk to combine. Set aside to rest for 10 minutes.

2 Heat a large non-stick frying pan over medium heat and spray with olive oil. Spoon 1 tablespoon of batter per pikelet into the pan, tilt to spread slightly and cook for about 2 minutes until bubbles appear on the surface. Turn over and cook for 1 minute or until cooked through. Remove from the pan and keep warm while you repeat with the remaining batter to make 16 pikelets.

Moroccan fruit salad

Whip together this delicious summery snack when entertaining company or for a little luxury on your own.

Serves 4
Prep time
15 minutes, plus
refrigeration time
Cooking time
nil
1 serve =
1 unit fruit

1 orange, segmented,
  any excess juice reserved
1 pink grapefruit, segmented,
  any excess juice reserved
1 slice rockmelon, cubed
1 pear, cored and cubed
mint leaves, to garnish

Dressing
1 tablespoon Splenda or
  other powdered sweetener
½ teaspoon ground cinnamon
1 tablespoon lemon juice
2 teaspoons orange blossom
  water (optional)

1 Combine the fruit in a shallow dish.

2 Place all the dressing ingredients in a small bowl with any reserved juice and stir until the sweetener has dissolved. Pour over the fruit. Refrigerate for at least 1 hour, then serve chilled in individual glasses or bowls, garnished with mint leaves.

* Chopped watermelon, sliced apple, figs and grapes also go well in this salad.
* Orange blossom water is traditionally used in Middle-Eastern cooking and is available in gourmet food stores and supermarkets. It has a strong flavour so be careful not to use too much. You could substitute it with rosewater, if liked.
* A generous dollop of low-fat yoghurt is delicious with this, and is a helpful way to increase your dairy intake for the day.

Blueberry muffins

If you're looking for good lunchbox fillers, then these muffins are ideal.

Serves 8
(makes 16)

Prep time

10 minutes

Cooking time

15 minutes

1 serve =

1¼ units bread

1 cup (150 g) wholemeal flour

2 teaspoons baking powder

2 tablespoons Splenda or other powdered sweetener

2 eggs, lightly beaten

1 teaspoon vanilla extract

½ teaspoon grated lime zest (optional)

½ cup (125 ml) buttermilk

½ cup (75 g) blueberries or other berries of choice

1 Preheat the oven to 180°C. Grease or line 16 mini-muffin holes with paper patty cases.

2 Combine the flour, baking powder and sweetener in a large mixing bowl. Whisk together the eggs, vanilla, lime zest and buttermilk in a separate bowl, then add to the dry ingredients and stir until just combined. Add the berries and mix gently.

3 Spoon the batter into the muffin holes and bake for 12–15 minutes or until they spring back when pressed and a cake skewer comes out clean. Cool in the tin for 5 minutes, then transfer to a wire rack to cool completely.

✳ For a lighter muffin, you can replace half the wholemeal flour with plain flour.

✳ Be careful not to overmix the batter — otherwise, the muffins may become tough.

* Frozen berries are fine but don't thaw them before adding them to the batter as they will be too soggy. You could also use other fruit, such as diced apple or pear.

Lunches and light meals

Thai beef salad

When you buy a whole bunch of coriander, reserve the roots and stems you won't be using in this recipe. They are very flavoursome and can be chopped and stored in zip-lock bags in the freezer to be incorporated into stir-fries and curries when you need them.

Serves 4
Prep time
15 minutes
Cooking time
6 minutes
1 serve =
½ unit protein
2 units vegetables

200 g lean thick steak, such as rump, sirloin or New York cut
olive oil spray
1 small red (Spanish) onion, thinly sliced
1 Lebanese (small) cucumber, halved and thinly sliced
1 red capsicum (pepper), seeded and thinly sliced
250 g cherry tomatoes, halved
½ cup (15 g) coriander leaves
½ cup (10 g) mint leaves
¼ (150 g) Chinese cabbage, finely shredded

Dressing
1 clove garlic, crushed
1–2 chillies, seeded and finely chopped
1 tablespoon fish sauce
2 tablespoons lime juice
½ teaspoon Splenda or powdered sweetener

1 Heat a grill plate or non-stick frying pan over medium–high heat. Spray the steak with olive oil and cook for 3 minutes on each side, or until cooked to your liking. Set aside to cool, then slice thinly.

2 Meanwhile, combine all the dressing ingredients and set aside.

3 Place the onion, cucumber, capsicum, tomato, coriander and mint in a large bowl. Add half of the dressing and toss to combine. Spread out the cabbage on a large serving plate. Arrange the salad on top of the cabbage, top with the steak, drizzle with the remaining dressing and serve.

* **Free** Add some bean sprouts and shredded carrot to the salad for extra crunch and omit the beef — then you will have a filling, Free List lunch.

* The beef could be replaced with grilled seafood, such as prawns or sliced squid hoods, or sliced grilled chicken breast fillet.

Aromatic Asian noodle soup

Hot chicken soup has long been thought of as a good pick-me-up for those who are ill and stuck in bed. Even if there is no proven medicinal value, this soup is still very nutritious and tasty.

Serves 4
Prep time
15 minutes
Cooking time
20 minutes
1 serve =
½ unit protein
1 unit bread
1 unit vegetables

1.5 litres salt-reduced
  chicken stock
3 slices ginger
2 cloves garlic, crushed
1½ tablespoons salt-reduced
  soy sauce
200 g chicken breast fillets,
  sliced
1 carrot, julienned
100 g shiitake mushrooms,
  stems discarded and
  caps chopped
2 baby bok choy, cut into quarters
¼ teaspoon ground white pepper
160 g cooked rice vermicelli
50 g bean sprouts
2 spring onions, sliced
coriander leaves, Thai basil
  leaves and sliced chilli,
  to serve

1 Place the chicken stock, ginger, garlic and soy sauce in a large saucepan and bring to the boil. Reduce the heat and simmer for 5 minutes.

2 Add the chicken, carrot and mushroom and cook for a further 10 minutes. Add the bok choy and white pepper to the broth (the bok choy will wilt straight away). Lift out and discard the ginger slices.

3 Divide the vermicelli noodles among four bowls and ladle the soup over the top. Finish with the bean sprouts, spring onion, herbs and chilli, to taste.

* **Free** For a Free List soup, omit the chicken and vermicelli, and instead add some baby corn, snowpeas (mange-tout) and shredded Chinese cabbage with the mushrooms and carrots, to fill out the meal.

* The chicken could be replaced with tofu for a vegetarian option, or for a meat-lover's version use beef and beef stock instead of the chicken breast and chicken stock.

Meatballs with spaghetti

This dish works really well served with a fresh green salad dressed in balsamic vinegar, which will up your vegetable intake as well as bring colour to the table and variety to the palate.

Serves 4

Prep time

15 minutes

Cooking time

25 minutes

1 serve =

½ unit protein

2 units bread

1 unit vegetables

1 unit fats

4 cups (600 g) cooked spaghetti, to serve

3 tablespoons chopped flat-leaf parsley or basil

Meatballs

200 g lean minced beef

½ small onion, grated or finely chopped

1 clove garlic, crushed

½ teaspoon dried oregano

2 tablespoons chopped flat-leaf parsley

Tomato sauce *Free*

1 tablespoon olive oil

½ onion, finely chopped

2 cloves garlic, crushed

1 × 400 g tin diced tomatoes

1 teaspoon dried oregano

½ cup (125 ml) salt-reduced beef stock or water

2 teaspoons balsamic vinegar

1 To make the meatballs, combine all the ingredients in a bowl. Using wet hands, roll teaspoons of the mixture into balls. Set aside.

2 To prepare the sauce, heat the oil in a frying pan over medium heat and cook the onion and garlic, stirring, for 5 minutes or until softened. Add the tomato, oregano, stock and balsamic vinegar and bring to the boil. Reduce the heat and simmer for 10 minutes. Add the meatballs to the pan and simmer for a further 10 minutes or until the sauce has thickened and the meatballs are cooked through.

3 To serve, divide the cooked spaghetti among four pasta bowls, top with a portion of meatballs and tomato sauce and sprinkle with the parsley or basil.

* For different-flavoured meatballs, try replacing the oregano with dried Italian herbs or Moroccan spice mix.
* This is delicious served with a sprinkling of parmesan or pecorino cheese — but don't forget to factor this into your daily nutritional intake.
* Chicken meatballs can be made by substituting the beef with lean minced chicken.

* You can spoon any filling
you like into the bread cups —
try a bolognese sauce or
some chilli beef.

Lamb pies with mint yoghurt

If you're a garlic fan and love Greek-style food, try adding a large clove
of crushed garlic to the mint yoghurt for an extra kick of flavour.

Serves 4

Prep time

15 minutes

Cooking time

40 minutes

1 serve =

½ unit protein

1 unit bread

¼ unit dairy

3 units vegetables

½ unit fats

1 tablespoon olive oil
1 onion, finely diced
1 clove garlic, crushed
200 g lean minced lamb
½ teaspoon ground cinnamon
1 teaspoon ground coriander
1 teaspoon ground cumin
½ teaspoon chilli powder
   (optional)
1 × 400 g tin diced tomatoes
3 tablespoons chopped coriander
   leaves
freshly ground black pepper,
   to taste
4 pieces wholemeal Mountain
   Bread
olive oil spray

Mint yoghurt
200 g low-fat natural yoghurt
1 Lebanese (small) cucumber,
   finely diced
1 tablespoon lemon juice
2 tablespoons chopped mint

Salad *Free*
2 cups (80 g) salad leaves
250 g cherry tomatoes, halved
2 tablespoons roughly torn mint
1 tablespoon lemon juice

1 Heat the oil in a small frying pan over
   medium heat and cook the onion and garlic
   for 5 minutes or until the onion is soft. Add
   the lamb, cinnamon, ground coriander, cumin
   and chilli powder and cook, stirring to break
   the mince up, for 5 minutes or until browned.
   Add the tomato and simmer for 25 minutes,
   then stir through the coriander leaves and
   some black pepper.

2 Meanwhile, to make the mint yoghurt,
   combine all the ingredients in a bowl.

3 To make the salad, place all the salad leaves,
   tomato and mint in a serving bowl and gently
   toss. Drizzle with the lemon juice.

4 Preheat the oven to 180°C. Trim the corners
   off each piece of mountain bread to make rough
   circles and gently press each one into a 1 cup
   (250 ml) capacity ovenproof ramekin or Texas
   muffin pan and spray lightly with olive oil.
   Bake for 4–5 minutes or until crisp.

5 To serve, spoon the lamb mixture into the four
   hot bread cups, top with a dollop of the mint
   yoghurt and serve with the salad alongside.

Pork sang choy bow

This is a really fun meal and finger food to share with friends over a casual lunch. To add to the experience, you could serve the sang choy bow with little dipping plates of salt-reduced soy sauce garnished with freshly sliced red chilli.

Serves 4

Prep time
15 minutes, plus soaking time

Cooking time
10 minutes

1 serve =
½ unit protein
1 unit vegetables
1 unit fats

8 iceberg lettuce leaves
1 tablespoon vegetable oil
2 teaspoons grated ginger
1 clove garlic, crushed
½ small onion, finely chopped
200 g lean minced pork
1 stick celery, finely diced
75 g water chestnuts, drained and chopped
4 shiitake mushrooms, stems discarded and caps chopped
2 tablespoons Chinese Shaoxing rice wine
1 tablespoon salt-reduced soy sauce
2 teaspoons oyster sauce
3 tablespoons finely sliced spring onion
coriander leaves, to garnish

1 Soak the lettuce leaves in cold water for 30 minutes, then drain well.

2 Heat the oil in a small wok or frying pan over high heat. Add the ginger, garlic, onion and pork and cook, stirring, for 4–5 minutes or until the pork is browned. Add the celery, water chestnut and mushroom and cook for another 2 minutes. Stir in the rice wine, soy sauce and oyster sauce and cook for 1 minute, then add the spring onion.

3 Spoon the pork mixture into the lettuce cups, garnish with coriander leaves and serve.

* To make chicken sang choy bow, use lean minced chicken in place of the pork, or try chopped peeled and deveined prawns as a substitute to make seafood sang choy bow.

Penne with tuna and tomato sauce

A simple pasta dish, yet very filling, this meal benefits from a scattering of sliced, pitted black olives if you have some on hand.

Serves 4

Prep time

10 minutes

Cooking time

20 minutes

1 serve =

½ unit protein

2 units bread

3 units vegetables

1 unit fats

200 g penne pasta

1 tablespoon olive oil

½ onion, finely chopped

2 cloves garlic, crushed

½–1 teaspoon dried chilli flakes

1 × 700 g jar chunky salt-reduced tomato passata *or* 700 g plain tomato pasta sauce

200 g tinned tuna in springwater, drained

4 tablespoons chopped flat-leaf parsley

4 cups (300 g) green salad dressed with fat-free vinaigrette, to serve

1 Bring a saucepan of water to the boil and cook the pasta according to the packet instructions. Drain and keep warm.

2 Meanwhile, heat the oil in a frying pan over medium heat. Add the onion and garlic and cook for 5 minutes or until softened. Add the chilli flakes and passata or pasta sauce and simmer for 5–10 minutes or until the sauce begins to thicken.

3 Stir in the tuna and cook for a further 1–2 minutes or until the tuna is warmed through. Add the warm pasta to the sauce and toss to combine. Sprinkle with the parsley and serve with a portion of dressed salad to the side.

✳ Any other type of cooked seafood, such as grilled white fish fillet or sliced squid hoods, can be added to the sauce instead of the tuna. Alternatively, add raw seafood to the pan at the same stage as adding the passata.

✳ Fresh basil makes a fragrant garnish in place of the parsley.

Chicken Caesar salad

This recipe is prepared with a foolproof method to make your own tangy mayonnaise in a jar. It's very simple and can be used as a dressing for many a plain salad.

Serves 4

Prep time
15 minutes

Cooking time
15 minutes

1 serve =
½ unit protein
½ unit bread
½ unit dairy
1 unit vegetables
1 unit fats

2 slices low-GI wholegrain bread, crusts removed, cut into cubes
olive oil spray
1 clove garlic
2 baby cos lettuces, leaves separated and roughly torn
150 g cooked chicken breast, roughly shredded
40 g shaved parmesan

Dressing
1 egg, at room temperature
2 teaspoons olive oil
¼ cup (60 ml) fat-free French salad dressing
1 teaspoon Dijon mustard
freshly ground black pepper, to taste

1 Preheat the oven to 180°C. Line a baking tray with baking paper.

2 Place the bread cubes on the baking tray and spray them with olive oil. Bake for 15 minutes or until crisp.

3 Meanwhile, to make the dressing, bring a small saucepan of water to the boil. Add the egg and cook for 1 minute. Crack the egg open and scoop the contents into a glass jar with a lid. Add the olive oil, salad dressing and mustard, secure the lid and shake until combined and thick. Season with black pepper and set aside.

4 Halve the garlic clove and rub the cut sides over the inside of four bowls. Divide the lettuce among the bowls, followed by the chicken, then pour over the dressing. Toss gently to combine. Sprinkle with the croutons and parmesan and serve immediately.

* Minus the chicken, this salad is a nice side dish served with grilled pork or beef.

* Pregnant women can avoid the raw egg in the dressing by replacing the egg and olive oil with 2 tablespoons egg-free, fat-free mayonnaise.

* For a little more heat, toss 1–2 chopped red chillies with the oil and squid at the first step.

Calamari salad with coriander and lime

This is perfect for a summer lunch and combines the strong tastes of coriander, garlic, lime and chilli to give the dish a distinctly fresh and Asian flavour.

Serves 4
Prep time
15 minutes
Cooking time
10 minutes
1 serve =
½ unit protein
3 units vegetables
½ unit fats

200 g squid hoods, cleaned
2 teaspoons olive oil
2 tablespoons chopped coriander, plus extra leaves to serve
1 clove garlic, crushed
2½ tablespoons lime juice
2 teaspoons sweet chilli sauce
freshly ground black pepper, to taste
lemon wedges, to serve

Salad *Free*
4 cups (300 g) salad leaves
1 red (Spanish) onion, thinly sliced
1 Lebanese (small) cucumber, halved and thinly sliced
250 g cherry tomatoes, halved

1 Cut the squid hoods down one side and open out flat. Score the inside in a criss-cross pattern and cut into 5 cm pieces. Toss with the oil in a bowl.

2 Combine the coriander, garlic, lime juice, sweet chili sauce and pepper in a large bowl to make a dressing for the cooked squid.

3 Heat a grill plate or frying pan over high heat. Add the squid and cook for 2–3 minutes or until cooked through (you may need to do this in batches). As soon as it is ready, add the squid to the bowl with the dressing and toss to combine.

4 Place the salad ingredients on a serving platter or divide among individual plates and top with the dressed squid. Garnish with extra coriander leaves and serve with lemon wedges.

* This salad works well with many other types of seafood — prawns are particularly good, or try a combination of seafood.

Hot and sour fish soup

Lemongrass hails from South and South-East Asia. In India it is used for medicinal purposes and in perfume-making, and elsewhere it is commonly used in cooking. The white stem is too hard to eat, but here, where it is bruised and added to the soup while cooking, it provides a sharp and citron-y flavour.

Serves 4

Prep time
10 minutes

Cooking time
20 minutes

1 serve =
½ unit protein
1½ units vegetables

1 litre salt-reduced chicken stock
1 × 3 cm piece ginger, sliced
2 stalks lemongrass,
    white part only, bruised
1 clove garlic, crushed
4 kaffir lime leaves
1 large tomato, diced
200 g firm fish fillets,
    skin and bones removed,
    cut into 2 cm pieces
1 cup (90 g) button mushrooms,
    quartered
2 tablespoons lime juice
1 tablespoon fish sauce
2 baby bok choy, chopped
pinch of Splenda or other
    powdered sweetener (optional)
sambal oelek, to taste
2 cups (150 g) bean sprouts
½ cup (15 g) coriander leaves
lime wedges, to serve

1 Place the stock, ginger, lemongrass, garlic and lime leaves in a large saucepan and bring to the boil over high heat. Reduce the heat and simmer gently for 5 minutes.

2 Add the tomato, fish, mushroom, lime juice, fish sauce, bok choy and sweetener (if using) and simmer for a further 5 minutes or until the fish is just cooked. Discard the ginger and lemongrass.

3 Ladle the fish, vegetables and broth into four deep bowls. Stir through the sambal oelek to taste, top with the bean sprouts and coriander and serve with lime wedges.

✱ This soup could be made with prawns or tofu instead of fish.
✱ Experiment with other fresh herbs — Thai basil and mint could be used instead of or in addition to the coriander.
✱ Sambal oelek is a chilli paste traditionally used in Malaysian and Indonesian cooking. You can find it in the international aisle of your supermarket or in Asian supermarkets.
✱ **Free** To make this a Free List meal, omit the fish.

Quesadillas

Enjoy dreaming of sunny Mexico while munching on this lunch, which is ready before you can say 'quesadilla!' It's bound to become a favourite with the kids, and is a simple recipe they can learn to master too.

Serves 4
Prep time
5 minutes
Cooking time
5 minutes
1 serve =
1 unit protein
1 unit bread
1 unit dairy
2½ units vegetables
1 unit fats

olive oil spray
4 low-GI tortillas or 4 sheets low-GI
   Mountain Bread

Bean and salsa option
1 × 400 tin kidney beans,
   rinsed and drained, ½ mashed,
   ½ left whole
1 cup (260 g) ready-made
   salt-reduced salsa
4 cups (300 g) baby spinach leaves

Tomato and capsicum option
80 g grated low-fat cheese,
   such as cheddar
4 spring onions, sliced
3 tomatoes, thinly sliced
150 g roast capsicum
   (drained of any oil)

1 Heat a frying pan over low–medium heat or preheat a sandwich press, and spray with olive oil.

2 Lay 4 tortilla or Mountain Bread halves on your work surface and top each with a quarter of the filling ingredients of your choice. Sandwich the remaining tortilla or Mountain Bread halves on top.

3 Cook the quesadillas in the pan for 2–3 minutes on each side or until golden. Alternatively, place them on the sandwich press, lower the top and cook for 3–4 minutes or until golden. Serve immediately.

* A ready-made, jarred variety of roast capsicum (pepper) or a homemade version can be used for the tomato and capsicum filling. Just be wary of lots of added oils and fats in any ready-made version.
* Lean grilled chicken fillet, sliced, with avocado and fat-free mayonnaise also makes a tasty filling option.

Soups
and salads

* This soup can also be served chilled on a hot summer's day.
* **Free** To make this a Free List soup, omit the oil — place the onion, garlic, zucchini (courgette) and stock in a saucepan and simmer for 20 minutes, then puree and serve with the mint.

Zucchini soup with fresh mint

The mint garnish adds a wonderful freshness to this soup, but you could use fresh flat-leaf parsley, basil or oregano in its place.

Serves 4

Prep time

10 minutes

Cooking time

30 minutes

1 serve =

1 unit vegetables

1 unit fats

1 tablespoon olive oil
1 onion, finely chopped
2 cloves garlic, crushed
800 g zucchini (courgettes), sliced
1 litre salt-reduced chicken or vegetable stock
1 tablespoon chopped mint

1 Heat the oil in a medium saucepan over medium heat, add the onion and garlic and cook for 5 minutes or until the onion is soft. Add the zucchini and fry for 2–3 minutes. Pour in the stock and bring to the boil, then reduce the heat and simmer for 20 minutes.

2 Remove from the heat and puree with a stick blender (or transfer to a food processor). Serve sprinkled with chopped mint.

* **Free** To make this a Free List soup, omit the oil and flour. Place all the ingredients except the spinach and parsley in a large saucepan over medium heat and simmer for 20 minutes. Add the spinach and stir until wilted. Serve sprinkled with parsley.

Vegetable gumbo

This is full of aromatic herbs and spices, so it smells wonderful when cooking. It can be served on its own or over a bed of brown rice for a lunch option with carbs.

Serves 4
Prep time
15 minutes
Cooking time
30 minutes
1 serve =
1½ units vegetables
1 unit fats

1 tablespoon olive oil
1 tablespoon plain flour
1 onion, finely chopped
2 cloves garlic, crushed
2 sticks celery, diced
1 green capsicum (pepper), diced
1 zucchini (courgette), diced
1 teaspoon ground cumin
1 teaspoon smoked paprika
1 teaspoon cayenne pepper
½ teaspoon dried thyme
1 × 400 g tin diced tomatoes
1 cup (250 ml) salt-reduced chicken or vegetable stock
1 tablespoon Worcestershire sauce
2 cups (90 g) baby spinach leaves
½ cup (15 g) flat-leaf parsley

1 Heat the oil in a large saucepan over medium heat. Add the flour and mix to a paste then cook, stirring, until it turns a dark gold colour. Add the onion, garlic, celery and capsicum and stir to combine. Cook for 2–3 minutes or until the vegetables start to soften.

2 Stir in the zucchini, herbs and spices, then the tomato, stock and Worcestershire sauce and simmer for 20 minutes. Add the spinach and stir through until wilted. Serve sprinkled with parsley.

* Serve with Tabasco sauce if you like a little heat with your meal.
* Diced fresh tomatoes may be used in place of tinned, if preferred.

Cauliflower and broccoli soup

Cauliflower and broccoli are part of the cruciferous vegetable family, all of whose members are known to be rich in beta-carotene, vitamins B1 and C, folate, calcium, iron, potassium and fibre – so there are definite benefits to enjoying this soup! It can be made entirely with cauliflower, if preferred, for a creamy white soup.

Serves 4
Prep time
15 minutes
Cooking time
40 minutes
1 serve =
¼ unit dairy
1½ units vegetables
1 unit fats

1 tablespoon olive oil
1 onion, finely chopped
1 garlic clove, crushed
½ small (500 g) cauliflower, roughly chopped
1 head (250 g) broccoli, roughly chopped
1 litre salt-reduced chicken or vegetable stock
1 cup (250 ml) low-fat milk
freshly ground black pepper

1 Heat the oil in a large saucepan over medium heat. Add the onion and garlic and cook for 5 minutes or until the onion is soft.

2 Add the cauliflower, broccoli and stock and bring to the boil. Reduce the heat and simmer for 20–25 minutes or until the vegetables are very soft. Remove from the heat and puree with a stick blender or transfer to a food processor and blend.

3 Combine the puree and milk in the pan and gently heat through. Season to taste with pepper and serve.

* A sprinkling of grated cheese is delicious served over this soup — just remember to count the dairy and fat units.

* 1 teaspoon of curry powder (or more to taste) can be added with the onions for a curried-soup flavour.

* **Free** To make this a Free List soup, omit the oil and replace the milk with 1 cup (250 ml) extra stock or water — place all the ingredients in a saucepan and simmer for 20–25 minutes, then puree and serve.

Asian-style coleslaw with mint and coriander *Free*

This salad is full of flavour and colour, and is Free List and guilt-free too. You could add shredded chicken, pork or cooked prawns for a more substantial meal with protein content, and/or some cooked rice noodles for added bread content, or simply enjoy it just as it is.

Serves 4
Prep time
20 minutes
Cooking time
nil
1 serve =
1½ units vegetables

2 cups (160 g) finely shredded cabbage
2 cups (160 g) finely shredded red cabbage
1 red (Spanish) onion, finely sliced
1 carrot, coarsely grated
3 tablespoons finely shredded mint, plus extra mint leaves to serve
coriander leaves, to serve

Dressing
4 tablespoons lime juice
1 tablespoon fish sauce
1 clove garlic, crushed
1 long red chilli, finely sliced
½ teaspoon Splenda or other powdered sweetener

1 Combine all the dressing ingredients in a screw-top jar or in a bowl. Set aside.

2 Place all the salad ingredients in a large bowl. Add the dressing and toss well to combine. Sprinkle with coriander and extra mint leaves and serve.

✱ Bean sprouts, and cucumber cut into batons, make nice additions or substitutes for any of the vegetables. Chinese cabbage also works well in place of either of the varieties of cabbage.

Roast vegetable salad

This is a very warming and colourful salad. If you don't have the listed vegetables on hand, they can be substituted with others, such as sweet potato, eggplant (aubergine) or choko.

Serves 4
Prep time
15 minutes
Cooking time
45 minutes
1 serve =
½ unit bread
3 units vegetables
1 unit fats

4 pickling onions, peeled
300 g pumpkin, cut into
    3 cm pieces
1 bulb fennel, quartered
1 red capsicum (pepper),
    seeded and quartered
3 zucchini (courgettes),
    cut into thick slices
olive oil spray
150 g truss cherry tomatoes
4 cups (300 g) rocket leaves

Herb dressing
1 tablespoon olive oil
1 tablespoon balsamic vinegar
    or lemon juice
1 clove garlic, crushed
1 tablespoon chopped parsley
    or thyme

1 Preheat the oven to 200°C.

2 Combine the dressing ingredients in a screw-top jar or in a bowl. Set aside.

3 Arrange the onions, pumpkin, fennel, capsicum and zucchini in a large baking dish and spray with olive oil. Bake for 25 minutes, then turn them over. Add the tomatoes, spray with olive oil and bake for a further 20 minutes or until the vegetables are tender and lightly golden.

4 Pour the dressing over the vegetables and toss gently to combine.

5 Arrange the rocket on a serving platter or divide among individual plates, then top with the roast vegetables and serve.

★ **Free** To make this a Free List salad, omit the oil from the dressing.

* Add chickpeas to the vegetables when they come out of the oven if you wish to increase your bread count.
* A sprinkling of low-fat feta or ricotta makes a delicious topping just before serving.

Greek salad

This salad is delicious on its own, but is also a wonderful accompaniment to barbecued lamb or other grilled meat.

Serves 4
Prep time
15 minutes
Cooking time
nil
1 serve =
1 unit dairy
2½ units vegetables
1 unit fats

6 tomatoes, diced
2 Lebanese (small) cucumbers, diced
1 red (Spanish) onion, sliced
80 g kalamata olives, drained and pitted
1 teaspoon chopped oregano
160 g low-fat feta, roughly crumbled
freshly ground black pepper
4 cups (300 g) cos lettuce
oregano or flat-leaf parsley leaves, to serve

Dressing
1 tablespoon olive oil
2 tablespoons lemon juice

1 Combine the dressing ingredients in a screw-top jar or in a bowl.

2 Place the tomato, cucumber, onion, olives, oregano and feta in a large bowl. Add the dressing and some pepper and gently toss to combine.

3 Arrange the lettuce on a serving platter or on individual plates and top with the salad. Garnish with oregano or parsley leaves and serve

✻ **Free** To make this a Free List salad, omit the feta and the oil from the dressing.

Weeknight dinners

Beef stir-fry with mushrooms and baby corn

This stir-fry is open to the ingredients you have in your crisper, but it is nice to use Asian mushrooms such as shiitake, enoki or oyster. You can buy mixed packs of these in the greengrocer section of your supermarket

Serves 4
Prep time
15 minutes
Cooking time
15 minutes
1 serve =
1 unit protein
1 unit bread
1 unit vegetables
1 unit fats

400 g lean beef (eye or scotch fillet), thinly sliced
½ teaspoon Chinese five-spice powder
80 g egg noodles
1 tablespoon vegetable oil
1 onion, thinly sliced
1 clove garlic, sliced
2 teaspoons grated ginger
1 red capsicum (pepper), sliced
125 g fresh baby corn, halved
100 g mushrooms, such as shiitake or button, sliced
100 g snowpeas (mange-tout), trimmed
½ cup (125 ml) salt-reduced beef stock
1 tablespoon oyster sauce
1 teaspoon sugar
1 tablespoon Chinese Shaoxing rice wine
1 teaspoon cornflour
sliced spring onion or coriander leaves, to serve

1 Combine the beef and five-spice powder in a bowl and set aside.

2 Prepare the egg noodles according to the packet instructions, drain and set aside.

3 Heat the oil in a wok or large frying pan over high heat. Add the beef in batches and cook, stirring, for 3–4 minutes or until browned on both sides. Remove and set aside. Add the onion, garlic and ginger to the pan and cook for 1 minute until fragrant, then add the capsicum, corn, mushrooms and snowpeas and stir-fry for 2 minutes.

4 Return the beef to the pan, then stir in the stock, oyster sauce, sugar and rice wine and bring to the boil. Blend the cornflour with 1 tablespoon water, then add to the sauce and stir until thickened. Add the noodles and toss to combine.

5 Serve immediately, garnished with spring onion or coriander leaves.

* **Free** To make this dish a Free List meal, omit the beef and the egg noodles, and replace the sugar with powdered sweetener. Serve as a vegetarian stir-fry in a bowl.

* This could be prepared with any tender sliced meat, such as lamb, pork or chicken.
* If you like it hot, add some sliced chilli or chilli sauce when adding the stock.

Barbecued steak with green bean and tomato salad

Giving the steak the chance to marinate overnight intensifies the flavour of this meal. Watch your cooking time – it's important not to overcook the steak so that it is tender.

Serves 4
Prep time
15 minutes, plus
marinating time
Cooking time
10 minutes
1 serve =
1½ units protein
3 units vegetables
1 unit fats

1 × 600 g skirt steak
1 clove garlic, crushed
2 teaspoons olive oil
1 tablespoon balsamic vinegar
1 tablespoon Worcestershire sauce
2 teaspoons thyme leaves or
   1 teaspoon dried thyme
freshly ground black pepper

Green bean and tomato salad
400 g green beans, trimmed
250 g grape tomatoes, quartered
½ red (Spanish) onion, thinly sliced
2 teaspoons olive oil
1 tablespoon balsamic or
   red wine vinegar
1 clove garlic, crushed
2 teaspoons Dijon mustard
½ cup (40 g) basil or flat-leaf
   parsley leaves

1 Score both sides of the steak in a diamond pattern using a sharp knife. Take care as you do this – the cuts should only be about 2 mm deep. Combine the garlic, oil, vinegar, Worcestershire sauce and thyme in a ceramic dish. Add the steak and turn to coat, then cover and marinate in the fridge overnight.

2 Preheat a barbecue or heavy-based frying pan until very hot. Remove the steak from the marinade and pat dry with a paper towel. Season with pepper and cook on the barbecue or in the pan for 3–4 minutes on each side (it should be cooked to medium). Transfer to a plate, then cover and leave to rest for 10 minutes.

3 Meanwhile, to make the salad, bring a large saucepan of water to the boil. Add the beans and cook for 1 minute. Drain and rinse under cold water to stop the cooking process, then drain again and combine with the tomato and onion. Place the remaining ingredients in a bowl and mix to make a dressing. Pour over the salad and toss to coat.

4 Slice the steak thinly and serve with the salad.

* Other cuts of steak, such as rump or sirloin, may be used. The skirt cut is not quite as tender (which is why it should only be cooked to medium) but often has a superior flavour.

* It is important to rest the steak before slicing it to serve, to ensure it stays nice and juicy.

Veal steak with creamy mushroom sauce and spinach

This is quite a quick meal to prepare, but make sure you're keeping an eye on all the different components of the dish as they bubble away on the stovetop. The results are well worth the attention.

Serves 4

Prep time

10 minutes

Cooking time

15 minutes

1 serve =

1 unit protein

½ unit dairy

4 units vegetables

1 unit fats

1 tablespoon olive oil

2 cloves garlic, crushed

1 cup (250 ml) low-fat evaporated milk

2 tablespoons Worcestershire sauce

100 g button or small Swiss brown mushrooms, sliced

1 tablespoon chopped flat-leaf parsley

400 g thin veal steaks

olive oil spray

4 cups (200 g) baby spinach leaves

2 carrots, sliced, steamed

2 cups (170 g) broccoli florets, steamed

1   Heat 1 teaspoon of the oil in a small saucepan over low heat. Add half the garlic and cook gently for 1 minute. Pour in the evaporated milk and Worcestershire sauce and bring to a simmer. Cook for 5 minutes or until slightly reduced.

2   Meanwhile, heat the remaining oil in a frying pan over medium heat. Add the mushrooms and cook, stirring, for 5 minutes or until golden. Remove the mushrooms from the pan and then stir them through the creamy sauce along with the parsley.

3   Increase the heat of the frying pan to high. Spray the veal steaks with olive oil and place in the hot frying pan. Cook for 1 minute on each side, then remove from the pan and keep warm. Reduce the heat to medium. Add the spinach leaves and remaining garlic to the frying pan and cook for 2 minutes or until the spinach is wilted.

4   Divide the steaks, spinach, carrot and broccoli among four plates. Spoon the mushroom sauce over the steaks and serve.

✱ You can make this meal with grilled chicken breast fillets, beef steaks or pork cutlets instead of veal — just remember to monitor the cooking time to ensure the meat is cooked through.

Steak pizzaiola with watercress and pear salad

As the name suggests, this recipe of Neapolitan origin combines all the great flavours of pizza – tomato, garlic, olives, basil – with a juicy steak to create an irresistible dish.

Serves 4
Prep time
15 minutes
Cooking time
20 minutes
1 serve =
1½ units protein
½ unit fruit
3½ units vegetables
1½ units fats

3 teaspoons olive oil
3 cloves garlic, crushed
6 tomatoes, peeled,
    seeded and diced
1 teaspoon dried oregano
freshly ground black pepper
4 × 150 g thick steaks
    (eye fillet or New York cut)
olive oil spray
3 tablespoons torn basil leaves
4 black olives, pitted and sliced

**Watercress and
pear salad** *Free*
150 g watercress, leaves only
½ red (Spanish) onion, thinly sliced
2 pears, thinly sliced
1 tablespoon white balsamic
    vinegar
2 teaspoons seeded mustard
1 teaspoon olive oil

1 Heat the oil in a saucepan over medium heat and add the garlic. Cook gently for 1 minute. Add the tomato and oregano and cook over low heat, stirring every couple of minutes, for 10 minutes or until a thick sauce is formed. You may need to add a little water if the mixture gets too dry. Season with black pepper.

2 Meanwhile, to prepare the salad, toss the watercress leaves, onion and pear in a large bowl. Combine the vinegar, mustard and oil in a small screw-top jar. Set aside until you are almost ready to serve.

3 Heat a grill plate or heavy-based frying pan over medium–high heat. Spray the steaks with olive oil and cook for 3 minutes on each side or until cooked to your liking. Cover and leave to rest for 10 minutes.

4 Pour the dressing over the salad and toss to coat. Divide the salad and steaks among four plates. Add the basil to the tomato sauce and spoon it over the steaks. Garnish with the sliced olives and serve.

* For the best result, bring the steaks to room temperature before you cook them.

* White balsamic vinegar
  is available in the condiments
  aisle at your supermarket.
  It is milder than regular
  balsamic and a good
  ingredient to use in
  light salad dressings.

Spanish chicken and lemon beans

The delicious combination of spices and herbs (paprika, cinnamon, thyme and parsley) gives this dish a real richness and depth. It's a good idea to keep your spice cupboard stocked up, as the addition of a few choice spices can make a couple of simple and cheap ingredients, like a tin of tomatoes and a few chicken thighs, into a great meal.

Serves 4

Prep time
15 minutes

Cooking time
35 minutes

1 serve =
1 unit protein
1 unit bread
2½ units vegetables
1½ units fats

1 tablespoon olive oil
400 g skinless chicken legs
1 onion, peeled and sliced
3 cloves garlic, sliced
2 red capsicums (peppers), seeded and sliced
1 tablespoon sweet paprika
1 × 400 g tin diced tomatoes
2 dried bay leaves
3 sprigs thyme
1 stick cinnamon
¾ cup (185 ml) salt-reduced chicken stock
2 tablespoons sherry vinegar
2 tablespoons chopped parsley
1 cup (200 g) cooked basmati rice

Lemon beans
4 cups (440 g) green beans
2 tablespoons lemon juice
20 g toasted slivered almonds

1   Heat the oil in a large frying pan over medium heat. Add the chicken and brown on all sides. Remove from the pan and set aside. Add the onion, garlic and capsicum and cook, stirring, for 5–10 minutes or until softened. Add the paprika and stir to combine.

2   Add the tomato, bay leaves, thyme, cinnamon, stock, vinegar and reserved chicken to the pan and bring to the boil. Reduce the heat, cover and simmer for 25 minutes or until the chicken is cooked and the sauce has thickened. If the sauce has not thickened, you may need to uncover the pan for the last 5 minutes of cooking. Remove the cinnamon stick and bay leaves when the dish has finished cooking. Sprinkle over the parsley.

3   To prepare the beans, steam them for 3–4 minutes or until cooked to your liking. Toss with the lemon juice and almonds and serve alongside the chicken with the rice.

* For variety, instead of serving the chicken with rice, you could serve it with toasted Mountain Bread cut into wedges. This is perfect for scooping up the sauce.

Garlic and pepper pork with broccolini and mushrooms

Enjoy a quick trip to Thailand at the dinner table with this simple stir-fry dish.

Serves 4
Prep time
10 minutes
Cooking time
10 minutes
1 serve =
1 unit protein
1 unit bread
3 units vegetables
1 unit fats

1 tablespoon fish sauce
2 teaspoons oyster sauce
1 teaspoon brown sugar
½ cup (125 ml) salt-reduced chicken stock
1 tablespoon vegetable oil
3 cloves garlic, crushed
1 red chilli, seeded and sliced (optional)
400 g pork fillet, thinly sliced
½ teaspoon coarsely ground black pepper
200 g broccolini, halved lengthways
400 g button mushrooms, halved
1 teaspoon cornflour
1 cup (200 g) cooked basmati rice
3 tablespoons Thai basil leaves

1   Combine the fish sauce, oyster sauce, sugar and stock in a jug or bowl and set aside.

2   Heat the oil in a large frying pan or wok over high heat and cook the garlic and chilli (if using) for 30 seconds. Add the pork and pepper and stir-fry for 2–3 minutes or until the pork is browned. (You may need to do this in batches.) Remove the pork from the pan.

3   Add the broccolini and mushroom to the pan and stir fry for 1–2 minutes or until the vegetables start to become tender. Pour in the sauce mixture and simmer for 1 minute. Mix the cornflour with 1 tablespoon water, smoothing out any lumps. Add this to the pan with the pork and stir until the sauce has thickened and the pork is heated through.

4   Divide the rice and stir-fry among four bowls, garnish with the basil leaves and serve.

* Replace the pork with chicken, beef or lamb.
* If Thai basil leaves are unavailable, use ordinary basil leaves.

* Feel free to add more vegetables or vary the vegetable combination used. For example, try adding beans, cauliflower or capsicum (pepper).

Pork medallions with mustard sauce and cabbage and apple salad

Reminiscent of a hearty German or Austrian winter meal, this dish has flavours that work perfectly together. It will fill you up to satisfaction.

Serves 4

Prep time

15 minutes

Cooking time

5 minutes

1 serve =

1 unit protein

½ unit fruit

1 unit vegetables

400 g pork fillet,
   cut into 2 cm slices
olive oil spray

Mustard sauce

2 teaspoons seeded mustard

1 tablespoon lemon juice

1 clove garlic, crushed

3 tablespoons low-fat natural
   yoghurt

Cabbage and apple salad

4 cups (320 g) finely shredded
   red cabbage

2 apples, cored and finely
   julienned

½ red (Spanish) onion, finely sliced

3 tablespoons low-fat natural
   yoghurt

1 tablespoon sherry vinegar

¼ teaspoon Splenda or other
   powdered sweetener

1 To make the salad, combine the cabbage, apple and onion in a large bowl. Mix together the yoghurt, vinegar and sweetener in a small bowl, then add to the salad. Mix well and set aside.

2 To make the mustard sauce, combine all the ingredients. Set aside.

3 Preheat a grill plate or heavy-based frying pan over medium heat. Spray the pork slices with olive oil, place in the pan and cook for 2–3 minutes on each side or until just cooked.

4 Serve the pork topped with the sauce, alongside the salad.

* Take care not to overcook the pork — it is fine for it to be slightly pink in the centre.
* You could use lean pork chops instead of pork fillet.

Baked ocean trout with a creamy herb sauce and watercress salad

A very simple-to-prepare dish, and yet the flavours are very sophisticated. The dill is a stand-out in the herb sauce and marries perfectly with the trout.

Serves 4

Prep time

15 minutes

Cooking time

20 minutes

1 serve =

1½ unit protein

1 unit vegetables

½ unit fats

4 × 150 g ocean trout fillets, skin and bones removed

Herb sauce

2 tablespoons fat-free mayonnaise

2 tablespoons low-fat natural yoghurt

2 teaspoons lemon juice

½ clove garlic, crushed

2 teaspoons finely chopped chives

2 teaspoons finely chopped dill

Watercress salad

1 bunch (350 g) watercress, leaves picked

1 Lebanese (small) cucumber, seeded and thinly sliced

4 radishes, thinly sliced

1 tablespoon chopped dill

2 teaspoons olive oil

2 tablespoons lemon juice

1 teaspoon Dijon mustard

1 Preheat the oven to 140°C.

2 Place the trout fillets on a baking tray lined with baking paper and bake for 20 minutes.

3 Meanwhile, to make the herb sauce, combine all the ingredients in a small bowl.

4 To make the salad, place the watercress, cucumber, radish and dill in a large bowl and gently toss to combine. Whisk together the oil, lemon juice and mustard to create a dressing, then pour over the salad.

5 Divide the baked trout fillets among four plates, drizzle with the herb sauce and serve with watercress salad.

✳ For variety, the cooked trout fillets can be broken into chunks and tossed through the salad with the herb sauce drizzled over the top.

* White fish fillets, such as snapper, blue eye cod or ling, also work well in this recipe.

Miso salmon with bean sprout and cucumber salad

This fresh and easy meal is a tribute to Japanese cuisine. Enjoy exploring the different flavours and crispy textures while taking in a healthy dose of omega-3s through the fish.

Serves 4
Prep time
15 minutes
Cooking time
10 minutes
1 serve =
1½ units protein
1 unit vegetables

olive oil spray
1 tablespoon miso paste
1 tablespoon mirin
4 × 150 g salmon fillets,
    skin and bones removed
lime wedges, to serve

Bean sprout and cucumber salad Free
1 cup (80 g) bean sprouts, trimmed
1 carrot, cut into matchsticks
1 cucumber, cut into matchsticks
3 cm piece ginger, cut into
    matchsticks
½ cup (15 g) coriander leaves
½ cup (10 g) mint leaves

Lime and mirin dressing
1 tablespoon lime juice
1 tablespoon mirin
1 teaspoon soy sauce
½ teaspoon sesame oil

1 Heat a grill plate or non-stick frying pan over medium heat and spray with olive oil.

2 Combine the miso and mirin in a bowl and brush over both sides of the salmon. Grill the salmon for 3 minutes on each side or until cooked to your liking.

3 Combine all the salad ingredients in a large bowl. Mix the dressing ingredients in a small bowl or shake together in a screw-top jar, then pour over the salad.

4 Serve the salmon alongside or on top of the salad, with the lime wedges.

✳ Mirin is a sweet rice vinegar and miso is a fermented soybean paste. Both ingredients are commonly used in Japanese cooking and are available in the Asian section of your supermarket or in Asian food stores.

✳ Free To make the lime and mirin dressing Free List, omit the sesame oil.

Grilled fish with peach salsa

The salsa combines the natural sweetness of a juicy fruit with the tanginess of lime juice and a kick of heat from the fresh chilli. Not only can it be used with this grilled fish, but it also makes a nice accompaniment to barbecued prawns or grilled chicken.

Serves 4

Prep time

15 minutes

Cooking time

10 minutes

1 serve =

1½ units protein

1 unit fruit

2½ units vegetables

1 unit fats

4 × 150 g thick white fish fillets, skin and bones removed
olive oil spray
4 cups (200 g) baby salad leaves
250 g cherry tomatoes, halved

Peach salsa

4 peaches or nectarines, diced
120 g avocado, diced
1 red (Spanish) onion, diced
1–2 red chillies, seeded and finely diced
2 tablespoons lime juice
½ cup (15 g) coriander leaves

1 Place all the ingredients for the peach salsa in a large bowl and gently toss to combine. Set aside.

2 Heat a grill plate or large non-stick frying pan over medium heat. Spray the fish fillets with olive oil and cook for 3–4 minutes on each side or until just cooked through.

3 Spoon the salsa onto serving plates and top with the fish. Serve with the baby salad leaves and tomato halves to the side.

* If fresh peaches or nectarines aren't available, use drained peaches in natural juice.
* If preferred, the fish could also be baked in a preheated 180°C oven for 15–20 minutes.

* You can make
  a delicious mango
  salsa by replacing
  the peaches with
  mangoes.

Thai-style yellow seafood curry

Rather than heading to your local Thai takeaway when craving a yummy curry, why not whip this one up yourself? You'll have peace of mind knowing what has gone into your meal, as well as satisfying your tummy and taste buds.

Serves 4
Prep time
20 minutes
Cooking time
20 minutes
1 serve =
1 unit protein
1 unit bread
3 units vegetables

3 cups (750 ml) salt-reduced chicken stock
2 cups (280 g) snake beans, trimmed and sliced
1 zucchini (courgette), halved and sliced
1 red capsicum (pepper), seeded and sliced
200 g squid hoods, cleaned and cut into 5 cm pieces
200 g peeled and deveined uncooked prawns
½ cup (125 ml) coconut-flavoured low-fat evaporated milk
1 tablespoon fish sauce
2 teaspoons Splenda or other powdered sweetener
1–2 tablespoons lime juice
1 cup (200 g) cooked basmati rice
coriander leaves, to serve

Yellow curry paste
2 stalks lemongrass, white part only, sliced
5 cm piece ginger, finely grated
3 cloves garlic, roughly chopped
5 red Asian shallots, roughly chopped
1 teaspoon dried chilli flakes
1 teaspoon ground turmeric
1 teaspoon ground cumin
1 teaspoon ground coriander

1. Combine all the curry paste ingredients in a food processor, adding a little water if necessary to form a coarse paste.

2. Put ¾ of the paste in a saucepan and cook gently for 1–2 minutes until fragrant. Pour the chicken stock into the saucepan, bring to a simmer and simmer for 10 minutes. Add the beans, zucchini and capsicum and cook for 5 minutes, then add the squid and prawns and simmer for a further 5 minutes or until the seafood is just cooked.

3. Stir in the evaporated milk, fish sauce, sweetener and lime juice and simmer to heat through. Serve the curry with the rice and a sprinkling of coriander leaves.

* You can replace the prawns and squid with white fish fillets if you like.
* This recipe makes a little more curry paste than required for the recipe, so store the leftovers in a jar in the fridge for up to 4–5 days and use to flavour a simple stir-fry. If you prefer a hotter curry, use all of the paste.

*You can use any type of tinned beans or chickpeas for this recipe.
*This soup tastes even better the next day as the flavours have had time to intensify overnight. Any leftovers make the perfect packed lunch.

Hearty bean and vegetable soup

Silverbeet (Swiss chard) can often be confused with spinach as they are similar in appearance, both having large green leaves and white-ish stalks. Silverbeet is native to the Mediterranean and is available all year round at the supermarket. Take care to select those with crisp, fresh leaves and creamy white stalks – avoid wilted stems or leaves.

Serves 4
Prep time
20 minutes
Cooking time
25 minutes
1 serve =
1 unit protein
2 units bread
1 unit dairy
2 units vegetables
1 unit fats

400 g tin borlotti or cannellini beans, rinsed and drained
1 tablespoon olive oil
1 onion, finely chopped
2 cloves garlic, crushed
1 teaspoon chopped thyme
2 sticks celery, sliced
2 carrots, diced
2 tomatoes, diced
pinch of dried chilli flakes, or more to taste
1 litre salt-reduced vegetable stock
300 g silverbeet (Swiss chard), leaves only, chopped
balsamic vinegar, to serve
freshly ground black pepper

1 Mash 260 g of the beans. Set aside.

2 Heat the oil in a large saucepan over medium heat. Add the onion, garlic, thyme, celery and carrot and cook, stirring, for 5 minutes or until starting to soften.

3 Add the tomato and chilli and cook for another 2–3 minutes, then add the stock, silverbeet and pureed beans. Bring to the boil, then reduce the heat and simmer for 10 minutes. Stir in the remaining beans and cook for a few minutes until heated through.

4 To serve, ladle the soup into deep bowls, drizzle with a little balsamic vinegar and sprinkle with pepper.

Tamarind fish

Tamarind concentrate is a popular souring ingredient in Indian cooking. It is available in the Asian food section of your supermarket or at Asian stores.

Serves 4
Prep time
15 minutes
Cooking time
15 minutes
1 serve =
1 unit protein
1 unit bread
1 unit vegetables
1 unit fats

1 tablespoon vegetable oil
1 red (Spanish) onion, finely diced
3 cloves garlic, crushed
1 stalk lemongrass, white part only, finely chopped
1 teaspoon ground turmeric
2 red chillies, seeded and finely chopped
4 tablespoons tamarind liquid concentrate
1 tablespoon fish sauce
2 teaspoons Splenda or other powdered sweetener
400 g firm white fish fillets, chopped into chunks
1 cup (200 g) cooked basmati rice
2 cups (300 g) steamed or stir-fried green vegetables, to serve

1 Heat the oil in a saucepan or wok over medium heat. Add the onion, garlic and lemongrass and cook for 3–4 minutes or until the onion is starting to colour. Add the turmeric and chilli and cook for a further 30 seconds.

2 Stir in the tamarind, fish sauce, sweetener and ½ cup (125 ml) water and bring to a simmer. Simmer for 4–5 minutes, then add the fish and simmer for a further 4–5 minutes or until the fish is cooked through. Serve with the rice and vegetables.

* If preferred, the fish fillets can be replaced with other seafood, such as prawns or mussels.

Casual night
in with friends

MENU

* Fresh tomato salsa
  with pita chips

* Open chicken burgers

* Berry and mango
  ice-cream cake with
  chocolate sauce

Fresh tomato salsa with pita chips

Ditch the traditional shop-bought tomato ketchup and salsa for this homemade version instead. Not only is it a lovely dipping sauce, it also works well spooned over grilled fish or chicken.

Serves 4
Prep time
15 minutes
Cooking time
15 minutes
1 serve =
1 unit bread
1 unit vegetables

4 pieces wholemeal Mountain Bread
olive oil spray

Fresh tomato salsa
4 tomatoes, finely diced
1 small red (Spanish) onion, finely chopped
1 clove garlic, crushed
½–1 teaspoon Tabasco sauce (optional)
3 tablespoons lime juice
3 tablespoons chopped coriander
½ teaspoon ground coriander
½ teaspoon ground cumin

1 Preheat the oven to 200°C. Cut the bread into biscuit-sized triangles and spread out on two baking trays. Spray with olive oil and bake for 5 minutes or until crisp.

2 To make the salsa, combine all the ingredients in a bowl and set aside for 10–15 minutes to allow the flavours to infuse. Serve the salsa with the chips for dipping.

✳ For extra flavour, sprinkle some dried herbs or paprika over the mountain bread before baking.
✳ Vary the flavours in the salsa according to what you have on hand. For example, replace the coriander with basil or parsley, and add some diced capsicum (pepper).

Open chicken burgers

Another fun meal and delicious alternative to eating out.

Serves 4

Prep time
15 minutes

Cooking time
5 minutes

1 serve =
1 unit protein
1 unit bread
1½ units vegetables
1 unit fats

olive oil spray
400 g lean minced chicken
2 spring onions, finely chopped
1 small zucchini (courgette), grated
1 egg
2 teaspoons grated lemon zest
3 teaspoons piri-piri seasoning
2 low-GI bread rolls, cut in half
8 oak lettuce leaves
2 tomatoes, sliced
1 Lebanese (small) cucumber, sliced
120 g avocado, sliced
½ cup (130 g) store-bought tomato salsa or Fresh Tomato Salsa (see opposite)
chilli sauce or fat-free mayonnaise, to serve (optional)

1 Preheat a grill plate or non-stick frying pan to medium and spray with olive oil.

2 Place the minced chicken, spring onion, zucchini, egg, lemon zest and piri-piri seasoning in a bowl and mix well. Using wet hands, form into four 1 cm-thick patties. Grill or fry for 2–3 minutes on each side or until cooked through.

3 Divide the bread roll halves among four plates and top with the lettuce, tomato, cucumber, avocado, chicken patties and a dollop of salsa. Serve with chilli sauce or mayonnaise, if desired.

✳ Another way to make these burgers is to replace the patties with chicken breast fillet that has been coated with piri-piri seasoning, then grilled and sliced.

✳ Try different seasoning mixes: Cajun, Moroccan and Italian blends all work well, or just use chilli flakes.

For dessert, see page 248 for the
Berry and mango ice-cream cake with chocolate sauce
recipe.

Dinners on a shoestring

Individual cottage pies with sweet potato topping

This is classic comfort food the whole family will enjoy on a cosy night in.

Serves 4
Prep time
20 minutes
Cooking time
1 hour
1 serve =
1 unit protein
1 unit bread
4 units vegetables
1 unit fats

1 tablespoon olive oil
1 onion, finely chopped
2 cloves garlic, crushed
400 g lean minced beef
2 carrots, finely diced
1 stick celery, finely diced
2 tablespoons tomato paste
  (puree)
1½ cups (375 ml) salt-reduced
  beef stock
1 tablespoon Worcestershire sauce
1 teaspoon dried basil
1 cup (120–160 g) fresh or frozen
  peas *or* 1 cup (120 g) green
  beans, cut into 1 cm pieces
2 teaspoons cornflour
400 g sweet potato,
  cut into chunks
1 tablespoon low-fat milk
freshly ground black pepper
olive oil spray
2 cups (120 g) steamed broccoli
  or green beans

1 Preheat the oven to 180°C.

2 Heat the oil in a saucepan over medium heat. Add the onion and garlic and cook, stirring, for 5 minutes or until starting to soften.

3 Add the beef and cook until browned, breaking up any lumps. Add the carrot, celery, tomato paste, stock, Worcestershire sauce, basil and peas or beans. Bring to a simmer and cook for 20 minutes or until the vegetables are soft. Mix the cornflour with a little water and add to the pan, stirring until thickened.

4 Meanwhile, place the sweet potato in a saucepan with just enough water to cover. Bring to the boil, then reduce the heat and simmer for 15–20 minutes or until cooked through. Drain well, then mash with the milk and season with pepper.

5 Spoon the meat mixture into four ovenproof dishes and top with the sweet potato. Spray with olive oil and bake for 20–30 minutes or until lightly golden. Serve with the steamed greens.

* Curry powder can be added with the beef for added depth of flavour, or replace the basil with Italian herbs or oregano.

* This is also delicious made using lean minced beef, or a combination of minced beef and pork, in place of the lamb. Alternatively, just grill some lamb fillets or backstraps and serve with the baba ganoush and tabbouleh.

Lamb kofta with baba ganoush and tabbouleh

Inspired by flavours from the Middle East, this meal is great to serve up at a weekend barbecue and won't cost you a fortune.

Serves 4
Prep time
30 minutes
Cooking time
30 minutes
1 serve =
1 unit protein
1 unit bread
3 units vegetables
2 units fats

350 g lean minced lamb
1 small onion, finely chopped
2 cloves garlic, crushed
1 teaspoon sweet paprika
1 teaspoon ground cumin
3 tablespoons finely chopped
   flat-leaf parsley
1 egg, beaten
olive oil spray
4 pieces wholemeal flatbread

Baba ganoush
1 large eggplant (aubergine)
1 clove garlic
1 tablespoon tahini
1–2 tablespoons lemon juice

Tabbouleh
2 tablespoons bulgur
1 bunch (150 g) flat-leaf parsley,
   finely chopped
½ bunch (50 g) mint,
   finely chopped
3 tomatoes, diced
3 spring onions, finely chopped
2 tablespoons lemon juice
2 teaspoons olive oil

1. To prepare the baba ganoush, grill the eggplant on a barbecue or grill plate for 20 minutes or until the skin is blackened. (Alternatively, bake it in a preheated 200°C oven.) When cool enough to handle, remove the skin and mash the flesh or process in a food processor to form a coarse puree. Place in a bowl with the remaining ingredients and mix well. Set aside.

2. Meanwhile, to make the tabbouleh, pour boiling water over the bulgur and soak for 15 minutes. Drain and cool, then combine with the remaining ingredients. Set aside.

3. Combine the lamb, onion, garlic, paprika, cumin, parsley and egg in a bowl. With wet hands, form into eight log shapes and thread onto skewers.

4. Preheat a barbecue grill plate or place a heavy-based frying pan over medium heat. Spray with olive oil, then add the kofta and cook for 2–3 minutes on all sides until cooked through.

5. Serve the kofta with the baba ganoush, tabbouleh and flatbread.

* The bread can be used to wrap the meat and vegetables or as a scoop.

Stuffed capsicums with parsley salad

Capsicums (peppers) come in many shapes, sizes and colours. Red capsicums are used here, but you could use whatever is available or preferred.

Serves 4
Prep time
20 minutes
Cooking time
1 hour
1 serve =
1 unit protein
½ unit bread
1 unit dairy
2 units vegetables
1½ units fats

1 tablespoon olive oil
1 onion, finely chopped
2 cloves garlic, crushed
400 g lean minced lamb
1 tablespoon Moroccan spice mix
3 tablespoons tomato paste (puree)
½ cup (100 g) cooked basmati rice
2 tablespoons chopped
    flat-leaf parsley
2 tablespoons chopped coriander
¾ cup (195 g) salt-reduced
    tomato passata
½ cup (125 ml) salt-reduced
    beef stock
1 teaspoon Tabasco (optional)
2 large red capsicums (peppers),
    halved lengthways, seeds
    and membrane removed
80 g low-fat feta, crumbled

Parsley salad
1 cup (40 g) tightly packed
    flat-leaf parsley leaves, torn
½ cup (10 g) mint leaves, torn
2 tomatoes, diced
3 spring onions, finely sliced
2 tablespoons lemon juice
2 teaspoons olive oil

1 Preheat the oven to 180°C.

2 Heat the oil in a frying pan over medium heat. Add the onion and garlic and cook for 5 minutes until softened. Add the lamb and cook for 4–5 minutes or until browned, breaking up any lumps. Stir in the spice mix and tomato paste and cook for 1 minute. Add the rice and herbs and mix well, then remove the pan from the heat.

3 Pour the passata, stock and Tabasco into a baking dish just large enough to hold the capsicum halves in a single layer. Fill the capsicum halves with the lamb mixture and place in the baking dish. Cover tightly with foil and bake for 45 minutes.

4 To prepare the salad, combine all the ingredients in a large bowl.

5 Sprinkle the feta over the stuffed capsicums and serve with the cooking liquid and parsley salad.

✱ This mixture also makes a nice stuffing for large zucchini (courgettes) or tomatoes.
✱ You could replace the lamb with beef, pork or chicken if preferred, and vary the spices — try Cajun spice mix or curry powder.

Pork and cabbage rolls

The combination of pork and cabbage make a perfect match –
they are a very popular mix of ingredients in Central and Eastern Europe.

Serves 4
Prep time
20 minutes
Cooking time
1½ hours
1 serve =
1 unit protein
1 unit bread
5 units vegetables

8 large Savoy cabbage leaves
4 slices day-old low-GI bread
400 g lean minced pork
1 onion, finely chopped
3 cloves garlic, crushed
3 tablespoons chopped
flat-leaf parsley
2 teaspoons chopped fresh thyme
or 1 teaspoon dried thyme
½ teaspoon sweet paprika
½ teaspoon caraway seeds
2 cups (520 g) salt-reduced
tomato passata
1 cup (250 ml) salt-reduced
beef stock
cauliflower mash (see page 226),
to serve
2 cups (240 g) steamed
green beans

1   Preheat the oven to 180°C.

2   Blanch the cabbage leaves in boiling water
for 2–3 minutes, then remove any hard stem
or core.

3   Break the bread into chunks. Place in a food
processor and process to create fine breadcrumbs.
Combine the breadcrumbs, pork, onion, garlic,
parsley and thyme in a bowl.

4   Place one-eighth of the pork mixture on each
cabbage leaf and roll up, bringing in the sides.
Place in an ovenproof dish, seam-side down,
just large enough to fit the rolls in a single layer.

5   Combine the passata and stock and pour over
the rolls. Cover the dish tightly with foil and
bake for 1½ hours.

6   Serve with the cauliflower mash and
steamed beans.

* You could use any combination of
lean mince – chicken, veal, lamb
or beef – for this.
* You can make these and then freeze
them (defrost in the fridge overnight)
or they keep well in the fridge for
reheating and eating the next day –
perfect for a work lunch.

Parmesan crumbed chicken with garlic mushrooms

Rather than ordering the usual rubbery chicken schnitzel from your local pub or bistro, why not enjoy this fresh, homemade version instead? You could even dress it up and serve it at a dinner party.

Serves 4
Prep time
20 minutes
Cooking time
20 minutes
1 serve =
1 unit protein
1 unit bread
3 units vegetables
1½ units fats

4 slices day-old low-GI bread
2 eggs
1 tablespoon low-fat milk
1 tablespoon plain flour
3 tablespoons grated parmesan
2 tablespoons finely chopped
    flat-leaf parsley
400 g chicken breast fillets,
    cut into 4 × 2 cm-thick pieces
4 cups (300 g) rocket leaves
    or green salad

Garlic mushrooms Free
8 large flat mushrooms
2 teaspoons olive oil
4 cloves garlic, crushed
½ teaspoon fresh thyme leaves
freshly ground black pepper

Tomato and capsicum sauce
1 × 400 g tin diced tomatoes
2 teaspoons olive oil
1 onion, finely chopped
1 red capsicum (pepper),
    seeded and finely chopped
2 cloves garlic, crushed
pinch of Splenda or other
    powdered sweetener

1 Preheat the oven to 200°C. Line two baking trays with baking paper.

2 Break the bread into chunks. Place in a food processor and process to create fine breadcrumbs.

3 Combine the eggs, milk and flour in a small bowl and mix until smooth. Combine the breadcrumbs, parmesan and parsley in another bowl. Dip the chicken pieces into the egg mix and then into the crumb mix. Place on one of the prepared trays.

4 To prepare the mushrooms, place the mushrooms on the other tray and sprinkle with the oil, garlic and thyme. Season to taste with pepper. Place both trays in the oven and bake for 20 minutes or until the chicken is golden and cooked through and the mushrooms are tender.

5 Meanwhile, combine all the sauce ingredients in a small saucepan over medium heat and bring to the boil. Reduce the heat and simmer for 15–20 minutes.

6 Place one piece of chicken and two mushrooms on each plate and spoon over the tomato and capsicum sauce. Serve immediately alongside the rocket or green salad.

* Any leftover pieces of crumbed chicken can be used to make a sandwich the next day, with low-GI bread and lots of green salad.
* Cook extra mushrooms to enjoy later at room temperature as a snack.

* You could cook the chicken on the barbecue for an extra smoky flavour, or replace the chicken with turkey tenderloins for something different.

Tandoori chicken with tomato and cucumber salad

This is a much healthier version than any tandoori chicken dish you will find at your local Indian takeaway or restaurant. You can rest easy knowing what has gone into your meal – the convenience versions have lots of hidden fats, salts and sugars.

Serves 4

Prep time
20 minutes, plus marinating time

Cooking time
15 minutes

1 serve =
1 unit protein
1 unit bread
¼ unit dairy
1½ units vegetables
½ unit fat

2 tablespoons tandoori paste
4 tablespoons low-fat natural yoghurt
400 g skinless chicken thigh fillets, cut into large pieces
olive oil spray
1 cup (200 g) cooked basmati rice
¾ cup (210 g) low-fat natural yoghurt

Tomato and cucumber salad
1 onion, finely chopped
4 tomatoes, diced
1 cucumber, diced
3 tablespoons lime juice
½ teaspoon Splenda or other powdered sweetener
3 tablespoons coriander and mint leaves, roughly chopped

1 Mix the tandoori paste and yoghurt in a glass or ceramic bowl. Add the chicken pieces and make sure they are well coated, then cover and marinate in the fridge for at least 2 hours.

2 Preheat the oven to 220°C. Spray a rack with olive oil and place it over a baking tray. Place the chicken pieces on the rack and bake for 10–15 minutes or until cooked through.

3 Meanwhile, to make the salad, combine the onion, tomato and cucumber in a large bowl. Place the lime juice and sweetener in a small bowl and stir to dissolve the sweetener. Drizzle the dressing over the vegetables, add the coriander and mint leaves and gently toss.

4 Serve the chicken with the rice, yoghurt and tomato and cucumber salad.

* Any leftovers would be good in a low-GI wrap for lunch the next day.

Harissa chicken with capsicum and herb salad

Harissa is a hot, spicy red paste served traditionally in North Africa in countries like Tunisia, Morocco, Algeria and Libya, often with bread for dipping. It is a wonderful accompaniment to lamb shanks with couscous and works really well here with chicken.

Serves 4
Prep time
20 minutes, plus marinating time
Cooking time
5 minutes
1 serve =
1½ units protein
½ unit dairy
1½ units vegetables
2 units fats

1 teaspoon ground cumin
1 teaspoon ground coriander
5 red chillies, roughly chopped
2 cloves garlic, roughly chopped
1 tablespoon olive oil
1 tablespoon lemon juice
2 × 300 g chicken breast fillets, sliced in half horizontally to make 4 pieces
minted yoghurt (see page 222), to serve

Capsicum and herb salad

1 red (Spanish) onion, chopped
1 red capsicum (pepper), seeded and diced
1 green capsicum (pepper), seeded and diced
2 sticks celery, thinly sliced
1 cup (20 g) flat-leaf parsley leaves
1 cup (20 g) mint leaves
1 tablespoon olive oil
1 tablespoon lemon juice (or to taste)
freshly ground black pepper

1 Combine the cumin, coriander, chilli, garlic, oil and lemon juice in a small food processor and blend to a paste. Place in a large glass or ceramic bowl with the chicken and turn to coat well. Cover and marinate in the fridge for at least 2 hours or preferably overnight.

2 To make the salad, place the onion, capsicum, celery, parsley and mint in a bowl. Add the oil and lemon juice and season with pepper. Toss to combine.

3 Heat a barbecue grill plate or heavy-based frying pan over medium heat and cook the chicken for 2–3 minutes on each side or until just cooked through.

4 Serve the harissa chicken with the mint yoghurt and capsicum and herb salad.

* You could dice the chicken before adding it to the marinade and thread onto skewers.
* This marinade is also suitable for fish — but only marinate it for half an hour.

* If you're not up for a
very hot meal, remove
the seeds from the
chillies and use only
the chilli flesh.

* This can be eaten hot or at room temperature.

Eggplant parmigiana with fennel salad

Eggplants (aubergines) get a bad wrap from many people, but this versatile vegetable (well, technically a fruit because it is seeded) is a really handy ingredient to have at the ready. It can be served many ways – roasted, chargrilled, stewed, baked or sauteed – and can bulk out many a meal without negatively affecting your daily nutritional intake. Eggplants are the star of this recipe.

Serves 4
Prep time
20 minutes
Cooking time
45 minutes
1 serve =
2½ units dairy
4 units vegetables
2 units fats

3 small eggplants (aubergines), sliced
olive oil spray
1 tablespoon olive oil
1 onion, finely chopped
2 cloves garlic, crushed
¼–½ teaspoon dried chilli flakes
700 g salt-reduced tomato passata
¼ teaspoon Splenda or other powdered sweetener
160 g low-fat ricotta
½ cup (15 g) basil leaves, torn
½ cup (40 g) grated parmesan

Fennel salad
4 cups (300 g) salad leaves
1 small bulb fennel, thinly sliced
balsamic vinegar, to serve

1 Preheat the oven to 180°C. Heat a grill plate or heavy-based frying pan over medium heat.

2 Spray the eggplant slices with olive oil and grill in batches for 2 minutes on each side or until well coloured.

3 Heat the oil in a frying pan and fry the onion and garlic for 5 minutes or until soft. Add the chilli, passata and sweetener and simmer for 5 minutes.

4 Arrange half the eggplant slices in the base of a 20 × 30 cm baking dish and sprinkle with half the ricotta and basil. Pour over half of the tomato sauce and repeat with the remaining eggplant, ricotta, basil and tomato sauce. Sprinkle with the parmesan and bake for 30 minutes. Leave to sit for 10 minutes before slicing to allow the juices to be absorbed.

5 Meanwhile, make the fennel salad. Combine the salad leaves and fennel in a bowl and drizzle with balsamic vinegar. Serve with the eggplant parmigiana.

Spicy egg curry with tomato and coriander salad

If you love a nice curried-egg sandwich, then you will love this dish.
It combines all of those great flavours, but in a lighter, healthier way.

Serves 4
Prep time
15 minutes
Cooking time
40 minutes
1 serve =
1 unit protein
1 unit bread
½ unit dairy
2½ units vegetables
1 unit fats

1 tablespoon vegetable oil
1 onion, sliced
2 cloves garlic, crushed
1 teaspoon chilli powder
1 teaspoon turmeric
2 teaspoons ground coriander
1 teaspoon ground cumin
¼ teaspoon ground ginger
1 × 400 g tin diced tomatoes
1 dried bay leaf
1 cinnamon stick
1 cup (250 ml) coconut-flavoured
  low-fat evaporated milk
1 tablespoon lime juice
8 hard-boiled eggs, halved
1 cup (200 g) cooked basmati rice

Tomato and coriander salad
1 red (Spanish) onion, diced
2 tomatoes, diced
½ green capsicum (pepper), diced
2 tablespoons coriander leaves
2 tablespoons lime juice

1 Heat the oil in a saucepan and fry the onion for 5 minutes or until softened. Add the garlic, chilli powder, turmeric, coriander, cumin, ginger and 1 tablespoon water and cook for 3–4 minutes or until fragrant. Add a little more water if the spices start to stick or burn.

2 Add the tomato, bay leaf, cinnamon and 1 cup (250 ml) water and simmer gently for 20 minutes. Pour in the coconut milk and simmer for another 10 minutes. Add the lime juice.

3 To make the salad, combine all the ingredients in a bowl.

4 Serve the curry with the boiled eggs, rice and tomato and coriander salad.

✳ This flavoursome dish could be served with a meat or vegetable curry as part of an Indian banquet.

* You could omit the eggs and just cook vegetables in this sauce. It could also be used to poach fish.

* Ensure the tofu is
well drained before
grilling — it will 'spit'
and not grill well
if it is wet.

Grilled tofu sticks with asparagus and cherry tomato salad

For something a little different and meat-free, try this quick-to-prepare meal. The flavours of fresh ginger, garlic, and that Japanese favourite, mirin, add a depth and delicious quality to the tofu.

Serves 4
Prep time
10 minutes
Cooking time
10 minutes
1 serve =
1½ units protein
2 units vegetables
3 units fats

2 tablespoons light soy sauce
2 tablespoons mirin
1 clove garlic, crushed
½ teaspoon grated ginger
1 teaspoon sesame oil
750 g firm tofu, well drained
  and cut into 12 pieces

Asparagus and cherry tomato salad
4 cups (300 g) salad leaves
1 bunch (170 g) asparagus,
  blanched and cut into
  3 cm lengths
1 Lebanese (small) cucumber,
  halved and sliced
250 g cherry tomatoes, halved
60 g avocado, sliced

1 Preheat the griller to high. Combine the soy, mirin, garlic, ginger and sesame oil in a bowl, then brush over the tofu sticks. Grill the tofu sticks for 2–3 minutes on each side or until light golden in colour.

2 Arrange all the salad ingredients on serving plates. Top with the grilled tofu and drizzle with any remaining soy mixture. Serve immediately.

Lentil stew with carrot and zucchini

What a colourful dish this is, and vegetarian too. It's adaptable and can be served in several ways, not just as a soup (see tip for suggestions).

Serves 4

Prep time
20 minutes

Cooking time
55 minutes

1 serve =
1 unit protein
1 unit bread
½ unit dairy
4½ units vegetables
1½ units fats

1 tablespoon olive oil
1 large onion, diced
3 cloves garlic, crushed
2 sticks celery, sliced
2 carrots, diced
2 zucchini (courgettes), sliced
200 g brown lentils
1 teaspoon dried oregano
4 tomatoes, diced
2 tablespoons tomato paste (puree)
3½ cups (875 ml) salt-reduced vegetable or chicken stock or water
1 tablespoon balsamic vinegar
freshly ground black pepper
3 tablespoons chopped flat-leaf parsley
40 g shaved or grated parmesan

1 Heat the oil in a large saucepan. Add the onion and garlic and fry for 5 minutes or until the onion is softened. Add the celery, carrot and zucchini and cook, stirring, for 2–3 minutes.

2 Stir in the lentils, oregano, tomato, tomato paste and stock or water and simmer, covered, for 45 minutes or until the lentils are tender.

3 Add the balsamic vinegar and season to taste with pepper. Spoon into four bowls, sprinkle with the parsley and parmesan and serve.

* This is a good base recipe to work from. You can add whatever vegetables you like to the sauce and serve with grilled meat or fish, or enjoy it as is with low-GI bread or rice.
* This will freeze well so cook up a double batch and store some away for another night.

Fish and fennel stew

This is a simple yet classic hearty meal for a summer or winter night.
The aniseed-like flavour of the fennel works beautifully with the fish,
and leaves a fresh, uplifting aftertaste in the mouth.

Serves 4
Prep time
15 minutes
Cooking time
35 minutes
1 serve =
1 unit protein
2 units bread
4 units vegetables
1 unit fats

1 tablespoon olive oil
1 onion, finely chopped
3 cloves garlic, crushed
1 bulb fennel, diced
6 tomatoes, diced
1–2 red chillies, seeded
    and finely chopped
2 sprigs thyme
2 bay leaves
1½ cups (375 ml) fish stock
½ teaspoon paprika
400 g firm white fish fillets,
    chopped into chunks
3 tablespoons chopped
    flat-leaf parsley
4 low-GI wholegrain bread rolls

1 Heat the oil in a saucepan over medium heat. Add the onion, garlic, fennel and tomato and cook for 5 minutes or until they start to soften. Add the chilli, thyme, bay leaves, stock and paprika and bring to the boil. Reduce the heat and simmer for 20 minutes.

2 Add the fish to the stew and simmer for 5–10 minutes or until the fish is cooked through. Sprinkle with the parsley and serve with the bread rolls.

* A combination of prawns, mussels and/or squid can be used in place of the fish fillets for a more diverse stew.
* The stew base can be prepared ahead of time and stored in the fridge or freezer; however, once the seafood is added it is best eaten straight away.

Weekend barbecue picnic

MENU

* Labne

* Barbecued lamb skewers with minted yoghurt

* Spicy chicken with green pawpaw salad

* Lime cheescake

For the starter, see page 141 for the Labne recipe.

Barbecued lamb skewers with minted yoghurt

Enjoy a chat with friends in the sun or a casual game of cricket while these flavoursome lamb skewers sizzle away on the barbecue.

Serves 4

Prep time

20 minutes, plus marinating time

Cooking time

25 minutes

1 serve =

1½ units protein

½ unit dairy

3½ units vegetables

1 unit fats

1 tablespoon olive oil
2 teaspoons ground cumin
2 teaspoons sweet paprika
2 cloves garlic, crushed
1 tablespoon lemon juice
1 tablespoon chopped mint
1 tablespoon chopped
   flat-leaf parsley
600 g lean lamb, diced
2 eggplants (aubergines),
   sliced into 1 cm thick rounds
olive oil spray
4 tomatoes, sliced
4 cups (300 g) salad leaves,
   dressed with lemon juice

Minted yoghurt
400 g low-fat natural yoghurt
4 tablespoons chopped mint
1 clove garlic, crushed

* Lamb backstrap is one of the best cuts to use for this recipe.
* If using bamboo skewers, be sure to soak them in water for 30 minutes before threading the lamb, to prevent scorching during cooking.

1 Combine the oil, cumin, paprika, garlic, lemon juice, mint and parsley in a bowl, add the lamb and toss well to coat. Cover and marinate for at least 1 hour or in the refrigerator overnight.

2 To make the minted yoghurt, combine all the ingredients in a small bowl. Set aside.

3 Preheat the oven to 200°C. Line two baking trays with baking paper.

4 Spray the eggplant rounds with olive oil and place them on one of the baking trays. Bake for 10–15 minutes, then turn them over. Place the tomato slices on the second tray. Return both trays to the oven and bake for 10–15 minutes.

5 Meanwhile, thread the lamb onto skewers to make 8 large or 12 small kebabs. Preheat a grill plate or heavy-based frying pan over medium heat. Add the skewers and cook for 2–3 minutes on each side or until cooked to your liking.

6 Arrange the eggplant and tomato slices on serving plates. Place the lamb skewers on top, drizzle with the minted yoghurt and serve with the salad leaves.

Spicy chicken with green pawpaw salad

Serves 4
Prep time
25 minutes, plus
marinating time
Cooking time
30 minutes
1 serve =
1 unit protein
1 unit bread
1 unit fruit
1½ units vegetables
½ unit fats

600 g skinless chicken thigh fillets
1 cup (200 g) cooked basmati rice

Marinade

1 stalk lemongrass, white part
only, roughly chopped
5 cloves garlic, peeled
1 teaspoon ground white pepper
2 tablespoons chopped coriander
stems and leaves
2 teaspoons brown sugar
1 tablespoon fish sauce

Tangy lime dressing

2 cloves garlic, crushed
3 tablespoons lime juice
2 teaspoons fish sauce
1 teaspoon brown sugar
1 red chilli, seeded and
finely chopped

Green pawpaw salad

1 small green pawpaw or
cooking mango, peeled,
seeded and grated
1 carrot, grated
1 cup (125 g) green beans,
cut into 2 cm pieces
2 tomatoes, diced
2 red Asian shallots, thinly sliced
½ cup (30 g) coriander leaves
½ cup (20 g) mint leaves
20 g unsalted peanuts,
roughly chopped

1 Place all the marinade ingredients in a small food processor and process to form a paste. Rub the paste over the chicken pieces, then cover and refrigerate for at least 2 hours or overnight.

2 Preheat a barbecue grill plate to hot. Grill the chicken for 5 minutes on each side or until cooked through.

3 Combine the dressing ingredients in a screw-top jar or a bowl.

4 Just before the chicken is ready, prepare the salad. Combine all the ingredients (except the peanuts) in a large bowl. Add the dressing and toss to combine, then sprinkle with the peanuts. Serve immediately with the chicken and rice.

* If you don't have a barbecue, preheat the oven to 210°C. Place the chicken pieces on a baking tray and bake for 20–25 minutes or until cooked through.
* **Free** To make the salad a Free List meal, replace the pawpaw or mango with 1 extra carrot or ¼ (150 g) red cabbage and omit the peanuts.
* You can use the marinade to make lemongrass and coriander chicken kebabs. Simply marinate diced chicken, thread onto skewers and grill on the barbecue.

For dessert, see page 257 for the Baked lime cheesecake recipe.

Weekend cooking

Herbed roast beef with cauliflower mash and horseradish sauce

Definitely to be served on a special occasion, or simply an occasion where you need to feel special – there is nothing more comforting than some tender roast beef and mash.

Serves 4
Prep time
20 minutes
Cooking time
45 minutes
1 serve =

1½ units protein
4½ units vegetables
1 unit fats

1 tablespoon olive oil
1 × 600 g eye fillet
½ cup (30 g) chopped fresh herbs
(a mixture of parsley, thyme,
basil and/or rosemary)
2 cloves garlic, crushed
freshly ground black pepper
500 g cherry truss tomatoes
1 bunch (170 g) asparagus,
steamed
150 g green beans, steamed

Cauliflower mash
600 g cauliflower, cut into florets
1 clove garlic, crushed
2 tablespoons low-fat milk

Horseradish sauce
½ cup (140 g) low-fat
natural yoghurt
1 tablespoon horseradish cream
1 clove garlic, crushed

1 Preheat the oven to 200°C.

2 Heat the oil in a heavy-based frying pan and cook the beef over high heat, turning, for 4–5 minutes until seared on all sides. Spread the herbs, the garlic and some pepper on a sheet of baking paper. Roll the beef in the herb mixture until evenly coated, then transfer to a roasting tin. Roast for 35 minutes to cook it medium–rare, or longer until cooked to your liking. Add the tomatoes for the last 20 minutes of roasting. Allow to meat to rest for 15 minutes before serving.

3 Meanwhile, to make the mash, place the cauliflower in a saucepan of water and bring to the boil. Cook for 15 minutes or until tender. Drain well. Blend in a food processor with the garlic and as much milk as necessary to make a smooth puree.

4 To make the horseradish sauce, combine all the ingredients in a bowl.

5 Slice the beef and divide among four serving plates. Spoon the sauce over the top and serve with the tomatoes, cauliflower mash, asparagus and green beans.

* It is important that the beef rests for at least 15 minutes to ensure it remains juicy. Don't be tempted to slice it straight away.

* The eye fillet could
  be replaced with sirloin
  or you could even use
  thick steaks, but be
  mindful that the cooking
  time will be less.

* This recipe freezes well, so you can make a double batch and freeze half for later.

Braised beef with cinnamon and star anise

Popular in Chinese, Indian and Vietnamese cooking, the small, star-shaped spice star anise gives off a heavenly scent during cooking. Along with cinnamon, it makes this perfect for an elegant occasion.

Serves 4
Prep time
20 minutes, plus marinating time
Cooking time
1 hour 15 minutes
1 serve =
1 unit protein
1 unit bread
3 units vegetables
1 unit fats

400 g lean stewing beef, diced
1 tablespoon fish sauce
2 teaspoons brown sugar
1 tablespoon vegetable oil
1 onion, chopped
2 cloves garlic, sliced
4 cm piece ginger, grated
1 stalk lemongrass, white part only, finely chopped
2 carrots, sliced
3 tablespoons tomato paste (puree)
1 tablespoon salt-reduced soy sauce
2 star anise
1 cinnamon stick
4 dried chillies (or to taste)
2 cups (500 ml) salt-reduced beef stock
1 tablespoon cornflour
coriander leaves, to serve
4 cups (150 g) Asian greens, steamed
1 cup (200 g) cooked basmati rice

1 Combine the beef, fish sauce and sugar in a bowl and leave to marinate for at least 30 minutes or overnight.

2 Heat the oil in a heavy-based saucepan over medium–high heat, then add the beef and brown on all sides. Remove and set aside. Add the onion, garlic, ginger and lemongrass to the pan and cook for 5 minutes or until the onion is softened.

3 Return the meat to the pan with the carrot, tomato paste, soy sauce, spices, chillies and stock. Bring to a simmer, then cover and cook for 1 hour or until the meat is very tender.

4 Mix the cornflour with 2 tablespoons of water and add to the saucepan, stirring until the sauce has thickened. Sprinkle with coriander leaves and serve with the steamed Asian greens and rice.

✱ If you prefer, the green vegetables can be added to the pan for the last few minutes of cooking.

Swiss steak with celeriac mash

Don't be deterred by the rather ugly, knobby appearance of the humble celeriac. It transforms into a delicious, silky mash that complements this steak well. You'll find it somewhere between the celery, turnips and swedes at the greengrocer or fresh-food section of the supermarket. If you like, add 2 chopped red chillies and a dash of Tabasco to give some heat to the dish.

Serves 4
Prep time
20 minutes
Cooking time
1 hour 40 minutes
1 serve =
1½ units protein
4 units vegetables
1 unit fats

2 teaspoons plain flour
600 g × 2 cm-thick stewing
   steak, cut into 4 pieces
1 tablespoon olive oil
1 onion, sliced
2 cloves garlic, crushed
1 carrot, thinly sliced
1 stick celery, thinly sliced
1 dried bay leaf
2 cups (520 g) salt-reduced
   tomato passata
1 tablespoon Worcestershire sauce
½ cup (125 ml) salt-reduced beef
   stock or water
2 tablespoons chopped
   parsley or basil
4 cups (600 g) steamed
   vegetables, such as broccoli,
   green beans and/or squash

Celeriac mash
2 cups (285 g) diced celeriac
2 tablespoons low-fat milk

1 Preheat the oven to 150°C.

2 Rub the flour over the steak. Heat the oil in a frying pan over medium heat and brown the meat for 1–2 minutes on each side. Remove and set aside. Add the onion, garlic, carrot, celery and bay leaf to the pan and cook for 5 minutes or until starting to soften. Stir through the passata and bring to a simmer.

3 Place the vegetables, passata and meat in a 1.5 litre ovenproof dish. Pour over the Worcestershire sauce and stock or water. Cover tightly and bake for 1½ hours or until the meat is very tender. Remove the bay leaf just before serving.

4 Meanwhile, to make the celeriac mash, place the celeriac in a saucepan with enough water to cover. Bring to the boil, then reduce the heat and simmer for 20 minutes or until very soft. Drain well and process in a food processor with enough milk to make a smooth puree.

5 To serve, divide the celeriac mash among four plates. Slice the steak and arrange on top of the mash. Spoon over the steak cooking liquid, sprinkle with the parsley or basil and serve with the steamed vegetables.

* The tomato passata could be substituted with a 400 g tin salt-reduced condensed tomato soup and ½ cup (125 ml) water.

Lightly spiced lamb with tomato and spinach

This is a simple but rewarding meal with little preparation time. Allow it to simmer away on the stovetop while you enjoy a small glass of wine and discuss the past week with a loved one.

Serves 4

Prep time
15 minutes

Cooking time
1 hour

1 serve =
1½ units protein
2½ units vegetables
1 unit fats

250 g spinach leaves, roughly chopped
1 tablespoon vegetable oil
1 onion, sliced
600 g lean lamb, diced
3 cloves garlic, crushed
1 teaspoon grated ginger
1 teaspoon chilli powder
2 teaspoons garam masala
2 tomatoes, diced
1 cup (250 ml) salt-reduced beef stock or water
1 red capsicum (pepper), seeded and diced
1 tablespoon lemon juice
3 tablespoons chopped coriander

1 Cook the spinach in a large saucepan with 3 tablespoons water for 4–5 minutes until wilted. Drain well and chop finely.

2 Heat the oil in a saucepan over medium heat and cook the onion for 5 minutes or until soft and golden. Add the lamb and cook, stirring, for 2–3 minutes or until browned all over. Add the garlic, ginger, chilli powder and garam masala and stir to coat the lamb in the spices. Add the tomato and stock or water, then cover and simmer for 30 minutes.

3 Stir in the spinach and simmer for a further 15 minutes or until the lamb is tender and the sauce has thickened. Add the capsicum, lemon juice and coriander and cook for 2–3 minutes. Spoon into shallow bowls and serve.

* You could use a 250 g packet of frozen spinach in place of the fresh.
* To increase the spiciness of this meal, add ½–1 tablespoon cayenne pepper or extra chilli powder with the garlic and ginger.

*You could use diced stewing beef instead of lamb and vary the mix of vegetables — try pumpkin, sweet potato or green beans.

Slow-cooked lamb with Middle Eastern spices

When slow-cooked, the cheapest, gristliest cut of meat can become very tender and soak in any delicious flavours it is cooked in – on this occasion, the heady spices cumin, ginger and paprika.

Serves 4

Prep time

20 minutes, plus marinating time

Cooking time

2 hours 15 minutes

1 serve =

1½ units protein

4 units vegetables

1 unit fats

1 red (Spanish) onion, grated
2 cloves garlic, crushed
½ cup (15 g) coriander leaves, chopped
1 teaspoon ground cumin
1 teaspoon ground ginger
1 teaspoon paprika
600 g boneless lamb shoulder, trimmed of fat and cut into 3 cm cubes
1 tablespoon olive oil
1 × 400 g tin diced tomatoes
1 eggplant (aubergine), diced
1 cup (250 ml) salt-reduced beef stock
2 zucchini (courgettes), thickly sliced
1 red capsicum (pepper), seeded and sliced
½ cup (80 g) green peas
3 tablespoons chopped flat-leaf parsley
3 tablespoons chopped mint
lemon wedges, to serve

1 Combine the onion, garlic, coriander, cumin, ginger and paprika in a bowl. Rub the mixture over the lamb, then cover and leave to marinate for at least 2 hours or overnight.

2 Preheat the oven to 160°C.

3 Heat the oil in a large, heavy-based frying pan or flameproof casserole dish and brown the meat for 1–2 minutes on all sides. Add the tomato, eggplant and stock and bring to a simmer. If using a frying pan, transfer the mixture to a casserole dish, then place in the oven and cook for 1½ hours until the lamb is very tender.

4 Add the zucchini, capsicum and peas, then return the dish to the oven for a further 30 minutes.

5 Divide the lamb and vegetables among four plates, sprinkle with the parsley and mint and serve with lemon wedges.

* This can also be cooked on the stovetop over very low heat.

Rack of lamb with pea and asparagus pilaf

For a little decadence and touch of class, indulge in this combination of lamb, vegies and rice.

Serves 4

Prep time
15 minutes

Cooking time
25 minutes, plus resting time

1 serve =
1 unit protein
1 unit bread
1 unit dairy
2 units vegetables
2 units fats

2 × 350 g lamb racks, trimmed of fat
2 cloves garlic, peeled and cut into slivers
2 rosemary sprigs, cut into 2 cm pieces
4 tablespoons lemon juice
olive oil spray
3 tablespoons chopped mint
20 g parmesan, grated
4 cups (300 g) salad greens, dressed with oil-free vinaigrette or balsamic vinegar

Pea and asparagus pilaf
1 tablespoon olive oil
½ onion, finely chopped
1 clove garlic, crushed
1 stick celery, finely diced
½ cup (80 g) arborio rice
1 cup (250 ml) salt-reduced chicken stock
1 bunch (170 g) asparagus, cut into 5 mm slices
1½ cups (200 g) frozen green peas, thawed

1 Preheat the oven to 190°C.

2 Cut slits in the lamb racks using a sharp knife and insert the garlic slivers and rosemary pieces. Drizzle with the lemon juice and then spray with olive oil. Heat a large, heavy-based frying pan over medium heat and sear the lamb for 2–3 minutes on all sides. Transfer to a roasting tin and roast for 20 minutes or until cooked to your liking. Cover and rest for 15 minutes.

3 Meanwhile, to make the pilaf, heat the olive oil in a saucepan over medium heat. Add the onion, garlic and celery and fry for 3–4 minutes until softened. Add the rice and stir until well coated in the oil. Add the stock and bring to a simmer. Reduce the heat to low, cover and cook gently for 15 minutes, adding the asparagus and peas for the last 5 minutes. All liquid should have been absorbed. Remove from the heat and leave the rice covered for 5–10 minutes before serving.

4 To serve, slice the lamb racks. Divide the pilaf among 4 plates, garnish with the mint and parmesan, then top with the lamb. Serve with dressed salad greens.

* You can use grilled lamb cutlets or backstraps in place of the lamb racks.

* For the pilaf, try adding your choice of freshly chopped herbs, such as basil or parsley, and vary the vegetables according to your taste.

Chicken cacciatore with zucchini spaghetti

The zucchini (courgette) 'spaghetti' in this recipe is a clever way to serve the meal without carbs. It's also a great option for feeding veggie-fussy kids.

Serves 4
Prep time
20 minutes
Cooking time
50 minutes
1 serve =
1½ units protein
4 units vegetables
1 unit fats

1 tablespoon olive oil
1 kg skinless chicken pieces
  on the bone
1 onion, diced
3 cloves garlic, crushed
1 stick celery, thinly sliced
1 carrot, diced
½ cup (125 ml) salt-reduced
  chicken stock
1 cup (90 g) button mushrooms
1 × 800 g tin diced tomatoes
1 tablespoon balsamic vinegar
2 dried bay leaves
1 teaspoon dried oregano
2 large zucchini (courgettes)
2 tablespoons chopped basil
  or flat-leaf parsley

1 Heat the oil in a large, heavy-based saucepan over medium–high heat. Add half the chicken pieces and cook for 3–4 minutes until browned all over. Remove and repeat with the remaining chicken. Set aside.

2 Add the onion, garlic, celery and carrot to the pan and cook, stirring, for 5 minutes or until the onion is soft. Add the stock, mushrooms, tomato, vinegar, bay leaves and oregano and bring to the boil, then reduce the heat and simmer for 30 minutes or until the chicken is cooked through and the sauce has thickened. You may need to turn the chicken from time to time.

3 While the chicken is cooking, cut the zucchini into thin matchsticks (a mandolin is ideal for doing this). Place in a bowl. Just before serving, pour boiling water over the zucchini and leave for 30 seconds. Drain well and divide among four plates.

4 Spoon the chicken and sauce over the zucchini spaghetti, sprinkle with the fresh herbs and serve.

* This chicken cacciatore freezes well, so why not make a double batch?
* Chicken on the bone gives a better flavour, but if you prefer you can use 600 g skinless thigh fillets instead.

Vegetable and chickpea Moroccan stew

This is a wholesome and hearty stew packed with the goodness of a variety of vegetables and spices. You'll find it very filling and satisfying.

Serves 4
Prep time
10 minutes
Cooking time
50 minutes
1 serve =
1 unit protein
2 units bread
2½ units vegetables
2 units fats

2 tablespoons olive oil
2 onions, peeled and sliced
4 cloves garlic, crushed
2 teaspoons grated ginger
1 teaspoon cumin seeds
1 teaspoon hot paprika
½ teaspoon freshly ground black pepper
½ teaspoon ground cinnamon
4 large carrots, peeled and cut into chunks
1 red capsicum (pepper), seeded and diced
2 zucchini (courgettes), cut into large chunks
2 × 400 g tins chickpeas, rinsed and drained
1 × 400 g tin diced tomatoes
1 strip lemon zest
2 cups (500 ml) salt-reduced vegetable or chicken stock
100 g broccoli, broken into florets
100 g green beans, trimmed and cut into 5 cm pieces
1 tablespoon honey
½ cup (15 g) coriander leaves

Herbed couscous
80 g couscous
1 tablespoon chopped coriander
1 tablespoon chopped mint

1 Heat the oil in a large, heavy-based saucepan over medium heat. Add the onion, garlic and ginger and cook for 3–4 minutes or until soft. Add the cumin, paprika, pepper and cinnamon and cook, stirring, for 1 minute or until fragrant.

2 Add the carrot, capsicum and zucchini and stir to combine with the spices. Add the chickpeas, tomato, lemon zest and stock. Bring to a simmer, cover and cook for 30 minutes.

3 Add the broccoli and green beans and cook for a further 10 minutes or until the vegetables are tender. Stir through the honey and sprinkle with the coriander.

4 Prepare the couscous according to the packet instructions and then combine with the coriander and mint. Serve alongside the stew.

* This stew could be prepared in an ovenproof dish and cooked in a moderate oven.
* Vary the vegetables or replace the chickpeas with beans.

Moroccan fish tagine with herbed couscous

A tagine is both a delicious Moroccan stew and the terracotta dish with a conical-shaped lid that it is cooked and served in. To dazzle dinner party guests, you could purchase a tagine dish at a chef's warehouse or supply shop and serve up your tasty stew in it, placing it in the centre of the table for all to dip into.

Serves 4
Prep time
15 minutes, plus marinating time
Cooking time
40 minutes
1 serve =
1 unit protein
2 units bread
2½ units vegetables
1½ units fats

400 g firm white fish fillets, skin and bones removed, cut into pieces
1 tablespoon olive oil
1 red (Spanish) onion, thinly sliced
1 red capsicum (pepper), seeded and thinly sliced
1 stick celery, thinly sliced
1 teaspoon ground cumin
1 red chilli, seeded and finely chopped
1 × 440 g tin diced tomatoes
½ cup (125 ml) salt-reduced fish, chicken or vegetable stock
grated zest of ½ lemon
3 tablespoons chopped coriander

Moroccan marinade
2 teaspoons olive oil
3 cloves garlic, crushed
1 tablespoon lemon juice
½ teaspoon ground cumin
4 tablespoons finely chopped coriander

Herbed couscous
160 g couscous
3 tablespoons chopped herbs, such as flat-leaf parsley, mint and coriander

1 Combine all the marinade ingredients in a bowl, then add the fish pieces and toss to coat. Cover and marinate in the refrigerator for 30 minutes.

2 Heat the oil in a saucepan. Add the onion, capsicum and celery and cook, stirring, for 3–4 minutes or until soft. Stir in the cumin, chilli, tomato, stock and lemon zest and simmer for 20 minutes or until the tomato has broken down. Add the fish and simmer for a further 10 minutes or until the fish is cooked through.

3 For the herbed couscous, prepare the couscous according to the packet instructions, then mix through the herbs.

4 Stir the coriander through the tagine and serve with the herbed couscous.

* The fish can be replaced with any seafood — try prawns, calamari or a marinara mix.
* Experiment with different herbs — add mint instead of coriander to the fish. Some finely grated lemon or lime zest is also nice in the couscous.

Baked fish fillets with capsicum braise and roast tomatoes

Cooking with capsicums (peppers) in three different colours creates an impressive rainbow on the plate. The sweetness of the capsicum and paprika offsets the fish nicely.

Serves 4

Prep time
20 minutes

Cooking time
30 minutes

1 serve =
1½ units protein
3 units vegetables
1½ units fats

1½ tablespoons olive oil
1 red (Spanish) onion, sliced
1 red capsicum (pepper),
   seeded and sliced
1 yellow capsicum (pepper),
   seeded and sliced
1 green capsicum (pepper),
   seeded and sliced
3 cloves garlic, crushed
1 teaspoon sweet paprika
1 cup (260 g) salt-reduced
   tomato passata
½ cup (125 ml) salt-reduced
   fish or vegetable stock
2 teaspoons sherry vinegar
½ teaspoon Splenda or other
   powdered sweetener
4 × 150 g firm white fish fillets,
   skin and bones removed
freshly ground black pepper
1 punnet (250 g) cherry tomatoes
olive oil spray
shredded basil leaves, to serve

1 Preheat the oven to 190°C. Line a baking tray with baking paper.

2 Heat 1 tablespoon of the oil in a saucepan over medium heat. Add the onion and red, yellow and green capsicum and cook, stirring, for 10 minutes or until softened. Stir in the garlic and paprika, then add the passata and stock and bring to the boil. Reduce the heat and simmer for 15–20 minutes or until thickened and reduced. Stir in the vinegar and sweetener.

3 Meanwhile, brush the fish with the remaining oil and season with pepper. Place on the prepared baking tray. Spray the tomatoes with olive oil and place on the tray with the fish. Bake for 15–20 minutes or until the fish is just cooked.

4 Divide the capsicum braise and roast tomatoes among four plates and place the fish fillets on top. Sprinkle with the shredded basil and serve.

* If you like, add the fish directly to the sauce and simmer, covered, for the last 10 minutes of cooking. The fish can also be pan-fried instead of baked.

* The green and
yellow capsicums
(peppers) can be
replaced with red
if you prefer the
sweeter flavour that
red capsicums offer.

Dinner party

MENU

* Creamy mushroom soup

* Crispy-skin salmon with rocket and fennel salad

* Floating islands

Creamy mushroom soup

You can vary the mix of mushrooms you use for this soup to suit your taste – for example, button mushrooms are lighter in colour and flavour than field mushrooms.

Serves 4
Prep time
10 minutes
Cooking time
25 minutes
1 serve =
½ unit dairy
2 units vegetables
½ unit fats

2 teaspoons olive oil
1 onion, chopped
1 clove garlic, crushed
2 sprigs thyme
600 g mushrooms (mixed or a combination), chopped
2 cups (500 ml) salt-reduced chicken stock
2 cups (500 ml) low-fat milk
freshly ground black pepper
1 tablespoon chopped chives or other herbs of choice

1 Heat the oil in a large saucepan over medium heat. Add the onion, garlic and thyme and cook for 2–3 minutes or until the onion is softened.

2 Add the mushroom and stock and simmer for 20 minutes. Remove from the heat, discard the thyme and add the milk, then puree with a stick blender, or in a food processor or blender. Season well with pepper and serve garnished with the chives.

* For a more textured soup, puree only three-quarters of the soup, then stir through the reserved mushroom mixture and serve.
* For a more intense mushroom flavour, soak 10 g dried porcini mushrooms in water for 1 hour and add to the soup with the fresh mushrooms.

Crispy-skin salmon with rocket and fennel salad

If you are worried about the fat content of this recipe, don't be deterred. Although more oil than usual is used in the frying pan to cook the salmon, it is only there to crisp the skin of the fish.

Serves 4
Prep time
10 minutes
Cooking time
5 minutes
1 serve =
1 unit protein
2 units vegetables
1 unit fats

4 × 100 g salmon fillets, skin on, bones removed
2 teaspoons Cajun spice mix
2 tablespoons olive oil
lemon wedges, to serve

Rocket and fennel salad Free
4 cups (200 g) baby rocket leaves
1 cup (30 g) flat-leaf parsley
1 large bulb fennel, thinly sliced
4 tablespoons mint leaves, roughly torn
1 tablespoon red wine vinegar
1½ tablespoons lemon juice
freshly ground black pepper

1 Pat the salmon fillets dry with paper towel, then sprinkle the Cajun spice mix over the skinless side of the fillets.

2 Heat the oil in a large non-stick frying pan until just smoking. Add the fish fillets, skin-side down, and cook for 3 minutes. Do not move them during this time. Turn the fish over and cook for an additional 2 minutes or until cooked to your liking. (For best results, the salmon should be pink in the middle.)

3 Meanwhile, to make the salad, combine the rocket, parsley, fennel and mint in a bowl. Pour the vinegar and lemon juice over the salad and toss to coat. Season with pepper.

4 Serve the salmon fillets and salad with lemon wedges.

* This recipe is also suitable for white fish fillets, such as snapper, with the skin still on.

* When shopping for fresh salmon or other fish, look for fish that is firm; don't buy if it appears waterlogged.

For dessert, see page 251 for the **Floating islands** recipe.

Desserts

Berry and mango ice-cream cake with chocolate sauce

Hot days and balmy nights often call for ice-cream. This fruity ice-cream cake will definitely be a hit for such times.

Serves 8
Prep time
15 minutes, plus
freezing time
Cooking time
5 minutes
1 serve =
1 unit bread
1½ units dairy
1½ units fruit
1 unit fats

1 litre fat-reduced, sugar-free ice-cream, softened
1 cup (125 g) mixed berries (fresh, or frozen and partially thawed), roughly mashed
1 mango, peeled and pureed
4 cups (500 g) mixed berries, extra

Chocolate sauce
4 tablespoons cocoa powder
1 tablespoon Splenda or other powdered sweetener
2 teaspoons cornflour

1 To prepare the chocolate sauce, combine the cocoa powder and sweetener in a small saucepan with ¾ cup (185 ml) water, whisking until smooth. Bring to a simmer over medium heat. Combine the cornflour with 3 tablespoons water in a small bowl and slowly add to the cocoa mixture, stirring constantly until thickened. Set aside to cool.

2 Line a 1.5 litre loaf tin with plastic wrap.

3 Place the softened ice-cream and berries in a large bowl and gently mix together. Spoon into the prepared tin. Dollop the mango puree over the top and, using a skewer or knife, gently swirl through the ice-cream mix. Smooth the top, then cover and freeze for 2–3 hours or until firm. Remove from the freezer 10 minutes before serving.

4 Slice the cake and serve with the chocolate sauce and extra berries.

* The chocolate sauce will keep in the fridge for a week. It can also be spooned over poached fruit. If you would like to thin the consistency, add a little hot water.

* Try substituting the berries and mango with other fruits, such as peach puree, or try adding chopped nuts (but don't forget to add these to your daily nutritional allowance).

* You could make lots of small 'islands' by using two smaller spoons to shape the meringue mixture into oval shapes and then lower into the simmering water.

Floating islands

In France, these clever desserts are know as îles flottantes. They can be quite impressive to serve when you have people around, but don't be intimidated – they are very achievable.

Serves 4
Prep time
20 minutes
Cooking time
10 minutes
1 serve =
½ unit protein
½ unit bread
1 unit dairy
½ unit fruit

300 g fresh, or frozen and
    thawed, raspberries
3 tablespoons Splenda or other
    powdered sweetener
4 egg whites
400 ml low-fat custard

* Other fruit purees can be used as a topping for this dessert — try mangoes or mixed berries.

1 Puree the raspberries and 1 tablespoon of the sweetener in a food processor, adding a little water if necessary to form a puree. Pass the puree through a sieve to remove the seeds.

2 Place the egg whites in a clean, dry mixing bowl and beat using an electric mixer until soft peaks form. Add the remaining sweetener, 1 teaspoon at a time, and whisk until thick and glossy.

3 Half-fill a deep frying pan with water and bring to a simmer. Using a large spoon, scoop one-eighth of the egg-white mix into an oval shape and then add to the water (you will need to do this in batches). Cook gently for 2–3 minutes, turning halfway through. Remove from the water with a slotted spoon and drain on a clean tea towel. You should be able to make eight 'islands'.

4 Spoon the custard into four shallow bowls. Float the soft meringues in the custard and drizzle with the raspberry puree.

* Sugar-free chocolate is available in the health-food section of major supermarkets. There are often orange-flavoured varieties available, which would work well in this recipe as a substitute for the plain dark chocolate.
* To add more colour, try garnishing the puddings with a mixture of orange and ruby grapefruit segments.

Chocolate puddings

While chocolate puddings are traditionally quite rich and heavy, these deliver on taste and decadence without weighing you down. They also benefit from the citrus-y flavour of the orange, which cuts through the bitterness of the dark chocolate.

Serves 4

Prep time
10 minutes

Cooking time
30 minutes

1 serve =

½ unit protein
¼ unit dairy
¼ unit fruit
3 units fats

4 eggs
1 teaspoon cornflour
1 tablespoon Splenda or other powdered sweetener
1 cup (250 ml) low-fat milk
65 g sugar-free dark chocolate, chopped
1 orange, peeled and sliced
½ teaspoon cocoa powder, for dusting

1 Preheat the oven to 170°C.

2 Place the eggs, cornflour and sweetener in a mixing bowl and whisk until combined.

3 Pour the milk into a small saucepan and heat over low heat until almost simmering. Remove the pan from the heat, add the chocolate and stir until melted and smooth. Whisk into the egg mixture until well combined.

4 Pour the batter into 4 × ¾ cup (185 ml) ovenproof dishes and place in a small roasting tin. Pour enough hot water into the tin to come halfway up the sides of the dishes, then bake for 25 minutes or until just set. Cool. Serve topped with the orange slices and very lightly dusted with the cocoa.

Chocolate sponge

This is a really lovely cake to have in your cooking repertoire – a great option
as a birthday or celebration cake that you can enjoy without worrying about
your nutritional intake. The cake can be diced and used to make a quick trifle:
set it in sugar-free jelly with fruit and top with low-fat custard.

Serves 8
Prep time
20 minutes
Cooking time
8 minutes
1 serve =
½ unit protein
1½ units bread
½ unit dairy
1 unit fats

4 eggs
½ cup (110 g) Splenda or other
    powdered sweetener
4 tablespoons cocoa powder
½ cup (75 g) plain flour
4 tablespoons sugar-free fruit
    spread
150 g flavoured Frûche or low-fat
    fromage frais
icing sugar, to dust

1 Preheat the oven to 180°C. Line the base of
   two 18 cm square cake tins with baking paper.

2 Place the eggs and sweetener in the bowl of
   an electric mixer and beat at high speed for
   10 minutes or until thick and pale.

3 Sift the cocoa and flour together, then sift again
   over the egg mixture. Using a large metal spoon,
   gently fold the cocoa and flour through until just
   combined. Spoon the batter into the prepared
   tins, smooth the top and bake for 7–8 minutes
   or until just firm. Allow the cakes to cool in the
   tins for 5 minutes, then turn out onto a wire
   rack to cool completely.

4 Spread the fruit spread over one of the cakes,
   followed by the fromage frais. Place the second
   cake on top and dust with icing sugar.

* To make a black forest sponge,
add some pitted cherries to the
filling or serve them alongside a slice
of sponge. Be mindful of your fruit
intake with this addition.

Cranberry and cinnamon poached pears

These look beautiful and very impressive served at the end of a dinner party.
The cinnamon produces delicious smells while the pears bubble away.

Serves 4
Prep time
10 minutes
Cooking time
25 minutes
1 serve =
½ unit dairy
1¼ units fruit

4 firm pears, peeled
2 cups (500 ml) light
   cranberry juice
1 cinnamon stick
1 vanilla bean, split
2–3 strips orange zest
   (1 cm wide)
200 g low-fat vanilla yoghurt

1 Place the pears in a saucepan just large enough to fit them in a single layer. Add the juice, cinnamon, vanilla and orange zest. Cover with a round of baking paper and bring to the boil over medium heat.

2 Reduce the heat and simmer the pears for 20 minutes or until they are tender. If the liquid does not cover the pears you may need to turn them occasionally. Remove the pan from the heat and leave the pears to cool in the poaching liquid.

3 Serve the pears warm or at room temperature with the vanilla yoghurt, drizzled with a little of the poaching liquid.

* Try replacing the cranberry juice with apple juice for a different flavour.

* You can also poach peaches or apricots using the same method. They may not need as long to cook, so check them regularly for tenderness while poaching.

* To make lemon cheesecake, simply replace the lime zest with lemon zest. Or leave the zest out altogether and replace with 1 teaspoon coconut or almond essence.

Baked lime cheesecake

Traditional cheesecakes are very high in fat and sugar, and therefore perilous for anyone trying to watch their health. However, our version eliminates a lot of that by using low-fat versions of the dairy ingredients, and sweetener in place of sugar. So relax and enjoy.

Serves 10
Prep time
10 minutes
Cooking time
50 minutes
1 serve =
½ unit protein
½ unit bread
1½ units dairy
½ unit fruit
1 unit fats

250 g low-fat ricotta
220 g extra-light (less than 5% fat) cream cheese
250 g low-fat vanilla yoghurt
3 tablespoons cornflour
2 eggs
finely grated zest of 1 lime
½ cup (110 g) Splenda or other powdered sweetener
4 cups (600–800 g) mixed fruit

1 Preheat the oven to 160°C. Line the base of a 20 cm springform tin with baking paper.

2 Combine the ricotta, cream cheese, yoghurt, cornflour, eggs, zest and sweetener in the bowl of an electric mixer and beat at medium speed until smooth.

3 Pour the batter into the prepared tin and bake for 50 minutes or until set. Turn the oven off and leave the cheesecake to cool in the oven for 30 minutes. Run a knife around the edge to loosen, then set aside to cool completely. Serve with the mixed fruit.

* Extra-light cream cheese is available in tubs from the dairy aisle in supermarkets.

Apple and blackberry pie

If you feel like a dose of classic comfort food but are conscious of your diet, look no further. This recipe will warm you up, satisfy sweet cravings and fill your home with reassuring fruity fragrances.

Serves 4
Prep time
15 minutes
Cooking time
35 minutes
1 serve =
1 unit bread
2 units fruit

4 medium Granny Smith apples, peeled, cored and thickly sliced
2 tablespoons Splenda or other powdered sweetener
½ teaspoon ground cinnamon, plus extra for dusting
½ teaspoon vanilla extract
150 g blackberries
8 sheets filo pastry
olive oil spray
icing sugar, for dusting

1 Preheat the oven to 180°C.

2 Place the apple, sweetener, cinnamon and vanilla in a saucepan with 2 tablespoons water. Cook over medium heat for 10 minutes or until the apples are just beginning to soften. Add the blackberries and cook for a further 5 minutes. Spoon into a 1 litre pie or ovenproof dish.

3 Scrunch each sheet of filo pastry and place over the fruit to cover. Spray with olive oil and bake for 20 minutes or until golden.

4 Dust with icing sugar and cinnamon and serve hot.

* Blueberries or cranberries work well as a substitute for the blackberries.
* If you have any dairy allowance remaining for the day, serve the pie with low-fat, sugar-free custard.

Buttermilk puddings with rhubarb and strawberries

Rhubarb and strawberries work really well together and produce beautiful, jewel-like shades of pink and red when cooked. They can also be very easy to grow in the garden if you have a bit of a green thumb – what better idea than to grow your own fruit and make healthy desserts from it?

Serves 4

Prep time

15 minutes, plus
refrigeration time

Cooking time

20 minutes

1 serve =

¼ unit protein

½ unit dairy

½ unit fruit

1 unit vegetables

½ unit fats

½ cup (125 ml) low-fat milk
4 tablespoons Splenda or other
   powdered sweetener
2½ teaspoons powdered gelatine
1½ cups (375 ml) buttermilk
1 teaspoon vanilla extract
4 cups (300 g) chopped rhubarb
1 punnet (250 g) strawberries,
   hulled and halved if large

1 Place the milk and 3 tablespoons of the sweetener in a small saucepan and cook over low heat until the sweetener has dissolved and the mixture is just coming to a simmer. Remove from the heat.

2 Pour 1 tablespoon hot water into a cup, sprinkle over the gelatine and mix together. Pour half the warm milk into a small heatproof jug and add the gelatine mixture. Stand the jug in a saucepan of simmering water and stir until the gelatine has dissolved. Pour the gelatine mixture into the remaining warm milk and mix well to combine. Stir in the buttermilk and vanilla.

3 Pour the mixture into four 1 cup (250 ml) glasses and refrigerate for 3 hours or until set.

4 Place the rhubarb, the remaining sweetener and 4 tablespoons water in a saucepan over medium heat. Bring to the boil, then reduce the heat and simmer, stirring occasionally, for 10 minutes or until just tender. Stir in the strawberries and cook for a further minute or until the strawberries are just beginning to soften. Remove from the heat and set aside to cool.

5 Spoon the rhubarb mixture over the puddings and serve.

* The puddings can also be served with fresh berries or diced fresh fruit of your choice.
* For a different look, you can set the puddings in dariole moulds. Turn them out when set and serve them as panna cotta – perfect for dinner parties.

A total care checklist

DAY-TO-DAY DIABETES MANAGEMENT involves thinking about what you eat and when, monitoring your blood glucose levels and following a management plan. Keeping a close check on key aspects of your health and wellbeing is one of the best ways to stay well. Talk to your diabetes care team about which aspects of your health need the most care and attention. A standard diabetes care checklist will probably go something like this.

Everyday diabetes care checklist

☐ Vision – Make note of any change in vision in either or both eyes.

☐ Feet – Inspect both feet, including the heels, the soles and between the toes. Wash feet daily. Check shoes for any stones, twigs or other sharp objects. Never go barefoot.

☐ Glucose – Monitor your blood glucose levels to keep them as close to healthy levels as possible.

☐ Medication – Organise your pills, how many to take and when.

☐ Injection sites – If you need insulin, check each injection site regularly and rotate the site to ensure consistent glucose control.

☐ Activity – Incorporate at least 30 minutes of moderate-intensity physical activity into at least five days a week, including resistance and aerobic exercise.

☐ Nutrition – Eat healthy nutritious foods.

Regular diabetes checkups

People with diabetes should see their doctor at least every six months. Keep your own appointment records in a diary to stay up to date. At each visit your doctor will usually assess the following.

- ☐ Glucose control – your average control, as indicated by your A1C and your frequency of highs (hyperglycaemia) and lows (hypoglycaemia).

- ☐ Blood pressure – taken lying and standing; ask if you have experienced symptoms of low blood pressure, such as dizziness, fainting or fatigue.

- ☐ Foot health – to check for sensation loss, injury or redness.

- ☐ Weight control – your weight and waist circumference, your progress with weight loss or maintenance.

- ☐ Medications – take all your medicines with you so you can discuss what you take when and how, what you do if you forget, and any side effects.

- ☐ Physical activity – to check you're getting as much activity as you can.

- ☐ Referral – perhaps to a specialist (endocrinologist, ophthalmologist, cardiologist or vascular surgeon) or to an allied health professional (a diabetes educator, dietitian or podiatrist).

Occasional diabetes checkups

At some appointments, your doctor will also assess the following.

- ☐ Cholesterol and triglyceride levels – usually with a fasting blood test.

- ☐ Kidney function – usually with urine and blood tests, at least once a year.

- ☐ Eye health – checks of visual acuity with letter charts, checks for signs of cataracts and for retinal health, at least once a year.

- ☐ Immunisation status – People with type 2 diabetes have an increased risk from infections: you will need an annual influenza vaccine, the pneumococcal vaccine (an initial dose plus a booster more than three years later) and a tetanus booster once every ten years.

- ☐ Cancer screening – People with type 2 diabetes have an increased risk of some cancers.

- ☐ Diet assessment – to ensure you're eating as well as you can.

- ☐ Driving safety assessment – to check for any risks factors for car accidents.

- ☐ Sexual function assessment – to ensure your complete health and wellbeing.

- ☐ Mental health assessment – to check for depression and other mental illnesses.

Other health services

The comprehensive management of type 2 diabetes usually means regularly seeing a range of other health professionals. These might include the following.

- ☐ Optometrist or ophthalmologist – at least once a year, even if your vision is normal, more frequently if you have increased risk of eye complications.

- ☐ Podiatrist – for a complete foot examination.

- ☐ Pharmacist – to explain how medicines work and review your medicines with your doctor (which is useful once a year); can also help organise your medicines, so you always take the right ones at the right time.

- ☐ Dietitian – to help you choose the best food to eat to lose weight or maintain your weight.

- ☐ Diabetes educator – to provide you, your family and your carers with the information, knowledge, skills, motivation and confidence to manage your condition and make decisions about your care and treatment.

- ☐ Dentist – at least once a year, to prevent gum disease and tooth decay.

- ☐ Hospital diabetes program – The Hospital Admission Risk Program (HARP), for example, provides outpatient care and support.

- ☐ Community diabetes program – Most capital cities and major regional centres have community programs such as support groups, education sessions and supermarket tours.

- ☐ Fitness centre or exercise professional – to help you stay active.

- ☐ Weight-loss program – to help you lose weight and keep it off.

- ☐ Quit-smoking program – to help you quit.

Resources

THERE IS PLENTY of information on the internet and in books and magazines to help you learn more about diabetes. Here are some recommended resources to start with.

National diabetes organisations

Diabetes Australia

diabetesaustralia.com.au, 1300 136 588

A national organisation providing support for people with diabetes. The National Diabetes Service Scheme (NDSS) is operated by Diabetes Australia and provides practical assistance, information and subsidised products for all people with diabetes (ndss.com.au). The Diabetes Australia website has a range of diabetes fact sheets in English and other languages – look in the 'Living with Diabetes' and 'Resources' sections. The website also has details of the state- and territory-based organisations that can provide further resources and local information.

Baker IDI Heart and Diabetes Institute

bakeridi.edu.au, (03) 8532 1800

A medical research and clinical services organisation that provides diabetes care and education in Melbourne. The website has extensive material for people with diabetes, including information about healthy eating, caring for yourself, and about diabetes complications. See the 'Education Services' section of the website.

Juvenile Diabetes Research Foundation

jdrf.org.au; offices in many capital cities

This organisation is committed to improving the lives of the type 1 diabetes community. It keeps people with the condition informed about the latest developments in type 1 diabetes research. It also provides a range of support services to help those who have been recently diagnosed through to those managing life with type 1 diabetes. The website provides fact sheets with everything you need to know about the condition. The Juvenile Diabetes Research Foundation also raises funds for research into a cure for type 1 diabetes.

Other national organisations

National Heart Foundation of Australia

heartfoundation.org.au, 1300 362 787

The website provides information on healthy eating, including understanding dietary fats and cholesterol and interpreting food labels. Check the recipe finder for healthy, nutritious meal ideas. The website has information on physical activity options in your local community, including Heart Foundation Walking Groups and the Heart Moves program, a low- to moderate-intensity program designed for people who haven't exercised for a while and suitable for people with diabetes. It includes resistance training, and activities to improve flexibility, coordination and functional movement.

Federal Department of Health and Ageing

health.gov.au, 1800 020 103

The department's A Healthy Active Australia website (healthyactive.gov.au) provides tools and strategies for weight loss. It includes physical activity guidelines for all ages.

Kidney Health Australia

www.kidney.org.au

The website contains health fact sheets and many resources for people with kidney disease and for those wishing to care for their kidney health.

State government programs

You can also try your state government's health website. Here are some examples, but check the 'Your Government' section of the *White Pages* for more.

Go for Your Life (Vic)

goforyourlife.vic.gov.au

A range of resources on healthy eating, including recipes, and a community directory to access local physical activity options in Victoria.

Better Health Channel (Vic)

betterhealth.vic.gov.au

Information on a range of chronic conditions. The diabetes information includes healthy eating, physical activity, diabetes complications, food quizzes and recipes.

Live Life Well (NSW)

livelifewell.nsw.gov.au/livelifewell

Basic information on quitting smoking, being active, healthy eating and stress management, as well as diabetes-prevention programs, including Prevent Diabetes Live Life Well (click on 'Live Life Well Initiatives in NSW').

Be Active (SA and WA)

SA: beactive.com.au; WA: beactive.wa.gov.au

Information on physical activity and options in your local community, including exercise tips, programs and events.

Getting Moving Tasmania (Tas)

getmoving.tas.gov.au

Local physical activity options in Tasmania, including walking groups. Also includes tips on increasing physical activity and leading an active lifestyle.

Physical activity

Try your local community centre, recreation centres, sports clubs, neighbourhood centres, community health centres or senior citizens clubs. Your local council may also have its own physical activity directory.

Fitness Australia

fitness.org.au, 1300 211 311

The national health and fitness industry association. Go to the 'Start Exercise' section for tips on physical activity and information on community events.

Lift for Life

liftforlife.com.au, 1300 733 143

A structured, evidence-based strength-training program for people with type 2 diabetes or at risk of developing diabetes, developed by experts from Baker IDI Heart and Diabetes Institute and available in fitness centres across Australia. If there is a Lift for Life provider in your local area, ask your doctor for a referral, then call the provider for an initial assessment.

Council on the Ageing (COTA)

cota.org.au, (08) 8232 0422

Australia's leading senior's organisation, COTA promotes the wellbeing of seniors through a range of activities, including Living Longer Living Stronger (lllswa.asn.au), an affordable strength-training program for older people offered in community venues. The website has links to each state and territory branch.

Kinect Australia

kinectaustralia.org.au, (03) 8320 0100

Promotes health and wellbeing through a range of health-promotion activities. The website has information on local community programs and health coaching services.

10 000 Steps

10000steps.org.au

10 000 Steps is a free program for recording pedometer information. By increasing your daily steps, you increase your physical activity levels. The website has information on physical activity, including goal-setting, overcoming barriers, and tips and tricks.

Australian Bicycle Council

austroads.com.au/abc, (02) 9283 3389

Information on where to ride in your major capital city, with links to the cycling resource centre for further information.

Exercise and Sports Science Australia

essa.org.au

Visit the ESSA website to find a sports physiologist near you.

Nutrition and recipes

Dietitians Association of Australia (DAA)

daa.asn.au, (02) 6163 5200

Australia's leading nutrition organisation. Click on 'Smart Eating for You' for nutritional advice, healthy eating self-assessment activities, recipes and a virtual supermarket tour. A dietitian can assess your food intake and provide advice on food choices. Dietitians work in hospitals, community health services and private clinics. Use the website to find a dietitian in your local area.

Glycaemic Index and GI Database

glycemicindex.com

Information on the glycaemic index, including low-GI diets and a GI database.

Go for 2&5

gofor2and5.com.au

Information on increasing fruit and vegetable intake, with a variety of nutritious recipes.

SaltMatters

saltmatters.org/site

Information on salt and blood pressure can be found from the Menzies Research Institute and the University of Tasmania.

Books

These books contain suitable recipes for people with diabetes and are available at most leading bookshops.

The CSIRO Healthy Heart Program, Dr Manny Noakes & Dr Peter Clifton, Penguin, Melbourne, 2008.

The CSIRO Total Wellbeing Diet, Dr Manny Noakes with Dr Peter Clifton, Penguin, Melbourne, 2005.

The CSIRO Total Wellbeing Diet Book 2, Dr Manny Noakes with Dr Peter Clifton, Penguin, Melbourne, 2006.

The CSIRO Total Wellbeing Diet Recipe Book, Penguin, Melbourne, 2010.

Delicious Living, Peter Howard, New Holland, Sydney, 2006.

Deliciously Healthy Cookbook, Jody Vassallo, National Heart Foundation, Sydney, 2001.

Diabetes: Eat & Enjoy, 4th edition, Christine Roberts, Margaret Cox & Jennifer McDonald, New Holland, Sydney, 2009.

Eat to Beat Cholesterol, Nicole Senior & Veronica Cuskelly, New Holland, Sydney, 2007.

Eat Well Live Well with Diabetes, Karen Kingham, Murdoch Books, Sydney, 2007.

Fast Living, Slow Ageing, Kate Marie, Mileage Media, Sydney, 2009.

The Low GI Family Cookbook, Kaye Foster-Powell, Anneka Manning, Jennie Brand-Miller & Philippa Sandall, Hachette, Sydney, 2008.

The Low-GI Shopper's Guide to GI Values, Jennie Brand-Miller & Kaye Foster-Powell with Kate Marsh & Philippa Sandall, Hachette, Sydney, yearly.

The Low GI Vegetarian Cookbook, Jennie Brand-Miller & Kaye Foster-Powell with Kate Marsh & Philippa Sandall, Hachette, Sydney, 2006.

Depression and anxiety

BeyondBlue
beyondblue.org.au, 1300 224 636

Provides a range of information on depression, mental illness, and finding a doctor or mental health practitioner in your local area.

Black Dog Institute
blackdoginstitute.org.au, (02) 9382 4523

Attached to the Prince of Wales Hospital in Sydney. Advice and information on depression and bipolar disorder, where to go for help and community programs.

Diabetes education

Australian Diabetes Educators Association (ADEA)
adea.com.au, (02) 6287 4822

Australia's leading organisation for health professionals who provide diabetes education and care. Provides basic information on living with diabetes and how to access a qualified diabetes educator in your local area.

Smoking

Quit Now
quitnow.info.au, 131 848

The National Tobacco Campaign website has information for helping you quit, including online Quit coaches. Click on 'Links' for the Quit organisation in your state or territory, which provides facts sheets, information packs and other support and guidance.

Foot care

Australasian Podiatry Council
apodc.com.au, (03) 9416 3111

Click on 'Member Associations' for your state-based podiatry association, information on diabetes and foot care, and finding a podiatrist in your local area.

Glossary

A1C – see HbA1C.

ACE inhibitor – a blood-pressure-lowering medication that can also protect the kidneys.

angiotensin-receptor blocker (ARB) – a blood-pressure-lowering medication that can also protect the kidneys.

aspirin – A medicine used to prevent blood clots. Also used for headaches and as an anti-inflammatory.

beta-blocker – A medicine that slows down your heart rate and lowers blood pressure by blocking the action of the hormones noradrenaline and adrenaline, which usually make your heart beat faster.

capillaries – Very small blood vessels.

cholesterol – A fatty material made in the body and absorbed from the diet.

diabetes care team – Generally this includes your doctor, other medical specialists, diabetes educator, dietitian and podiatrist, but many people only use a doctor for most of their diabetes care with occasional use of other health professionals as needed.

diabetologist – A doctor specialising in diabetes (see also **endocrinologist**).

diuretic – A medicine that increases the amount of urine you pass and lowers blood pressure.

endocrinologist – A doctor specialising in endocrine disorders, including diabetes.

haemoglobin – A protein that carries oxygen in the blood.

HbA1c – A blood test that measures your average blood glucose levels over the past few months.

HDL cholesterol – 'Good' cholesterol; high levels reduce the risk of heart disease.

hyperglycaemia – A condition where blood glucose levels are too high.

hypertension – High blood pressure; the smaller blood vessels become contracted and cause a build-up of pressure in the bloodstream.

hypoglycaemia – A condition where blood glucose levels are too low.

insulin – A hormone that decreases glucose levels in the blood.

LDL cholesterol – 'Bad' cholesterol; high levels increase the risk of heart disease.

microalbuminuria – Small amounts of protein found in the urine, indicating that the kidneys are not functioning properly.

neuropathic pain – Pain caused by a problem with the nerves.

ophthalmologist – A health-care professional who specialises in eye diseases.

orthopaedic surgeon – A surgeon who specialises in conditions of the bones.

orthotist – A specialist in designing shoes for people with foot problems.

pancreas – The gland behind the stomach that produces insulin.

peripheral arterial disease – A disease of the arteries that supply blood to the limbs that causes pain in the buttocks or legs.

podiatrist – A health-care professional who specialises in assessing, diagnosing and treating legs, ankles and feet.

proteinuria – A condition where protein leaks from your bloodstream into your urine.

retinopathy – An eye disease that affects the blood vessels supplying the eye.

self-monitoring – Checking your own blood glucose levels at regular intervals.

statins – Medications used to reduce blood cholesterol levels.

triglycerides – Fats circulating in the blood and used for energy; high levels are a risk factor for heart disease.

vascular surgeon – A surgeon who specialises in problems of the veins or arteries, clearing blockages with surgery, stents or other devices.

Modified from *Managing Diabetes: A Booklet for Patients and Carers*, Scottish Intercollegiate Guidelines Network, Edinburgh, 2010.

About the authors

Dr Grant Brinkworth – A senior exercise and nutritional research scientist at CSIRO Food and Nutritional Sciences, he is responsible for developing and leading several large-scale clinical studies into the role of diet and exercise on weight loss and the prevention and treatment of lifestyle diseases, including obesity, diabetes and cardiovascular disease. He has published more than 40 scientific papers and is an adjunct research fellow at the University of South Australia. He received a CSIRO Medal for Research Excellence in 2005 and the CSIRO Julius Career Development Award for outstanding scientific achievement in 2008.

Jing Hui (Jillian) Chin – An Accredited Practising Dietitian working as a research dietitian in the Clinical Research Unit of CSIRO Food and Nutritional Sciences. Jillian's work involves the development, delivery and analysis of diets for clinical trials. She has a strong interest in the use of sustainable diets in diabetes management.

Professor Peter Clifton – A high-profile clinical and nutrition researcher for more than 20 years, he joined Baker IDI in July 2009. While he was at CSIRO, he co-authored *The CSIRO Total Wellbeing Diet* books. His primary research interest is the use of diet in the prevention and treatment of cardiovascular disease and its risk factors: obesity and diabetes. Peter has a clinical practice specialising in lipid management at the Flinders Medical Centre and in diabetes and cardiovascular disease at the Royal Adelaide Hospital. He has written articles for newspapers and medical magazines, discussion papers for food companies and books for the public. He is on the editorial board of four journals, a reviewer for 20 others and a reviewer for grant bodies in Australia, New Zealand, South Africa, Israel and Austria.

Associate Professor David Dunstan – A VicHealth Public Health Research Fellow and Co-Director of the newly established Healthy Lifestyle Research Centre at the Baker IDI Heart and Diabetes Institute. His research focuses on the role of physical activity and sedentary behaviour in the prevention and management of chronic diseases. He leads the collaborative group that is analysing the lifestyle risk factor data collected from the Australian Diabetes Obesity and Lifestyle (AusDiab) study. He is also the creator of the physical activity program Lift for Life.

Associate Professor Jennifer Keogh – A dietitian with more than 35 years' experience, she was a research dietitian and research scientist at CSIRO's Food and Nutritional Sciences before moving to Baker IDI. Her current research interests are in weight-loss surgery in the treatment of obesity and the effects of salt on blood vessel function. She has published more than 50 scientific papers and is an associate editor of the Dietitians Association of Australia's journal, *Nutrition & Dietetics*. At the time of writing she is Associate Professor Dietetics and Nutrition at the University of South Australia.

Dr Lance Macaulay – The Theme Leader of Obesity and Health in CSIRO's Preventative Health Flagship, he has more than 32 years' research experience. His interests lie in understanding the mechanisms of insulin action, diabetes and obesity. He served on the editorial boards of the journals *Endocrinology* and *Frontiers in Biosciences*. His father had diabetes for 80 years and was one of Australia's longest-surviving people with diabetes. This continues to ignite Lance's passion to help other diabetics live long and healthy lives.

Sonia Middleton – An Accredited Practising Dietitian who specialises in diabetes management in the Education Services arm of Baker IDI. Her role includes clinical diabetes education, health-professional training, research and commercial projects. In 2009 she was the national trainer for the Reset Your Life Type 2 Diabetes Prevention Program.

Dr Phil Mohr – The senior behavioural scientist at CSIRO Food and Nutritional Sciences, where he leads the Diet, Exercise and Behaviour Research Team. He currently leads research projects for CSIRO's Preventative Health Flagship and CSIRO's Food Futures Flagship. His research into how people reason and make decisions about health, products and lifestyle choices applies his knowledge of psychology and methodology to produce practical outcomes. He is affiliated with the University of Adelaide and the University of South Australia, contributes to the South Australian Health Literacy Alliance and serves on the Social Science Expert Advisory Group for Food Standards Australia and New Zealand (FSANZ).

Associate Professor Manny Noakes – Manny is currently responsible for Capability Management in the CSIRO Food Nutrition and Health Science Program and is Stream Leader for Diet and Lifestyle Programs within the CSIRO Preventative Health Flagship. Manny has more than 30 years' experience in nutrition and has published more than 100 scientific papers. She has a strong interest in diets for weight management, including the role of protein and other dietary factors in appetite regulation. She co-authored the bestselling *CSIRO Total Wellbeing Diet* and has received several awards for research excellence, including two CSIRO medals and an Outstanding Achievement Alumni Award from Flinders University.

Pennie Taylor – An Accredited Practising Dietitian, she is the Senior Research Dietitian for the Clinical Research Unit at CSIRO Food and Nutritional Sciences. She also works part-time in diet clinics and private practice, specialising in weight management, weight-loss surgery and diabetes care. Her role at CSIRO is to liaise with senior scientists to develop and deliver designer diets for clinical trials, analyse dietary data and prepare scientific and commercial publications. Pennie has a strong interest in dietary patterns associated with weight-loss surgery and the impact of surgery on dietary tolerance and long-term weight loss.

Professor Merlin Thomas – A nephrologist (kidney specialist) at the Baker IDI Heart and Diabetes Institute. He has published close to 150 scientific papers and has received a number of awards, including the 2005 Victorian Premier's Award for Medical Research. His ongoing research focuses on the mechanisms of vascular and kidney damage in diabetes.

Professor Paul Zimmet AO – Director Emeritus and Director of International Research at the Baker IDI Heart and Diabetes Institute, he has an outstanding international record in diabetes and obesity research. In 2008 he was appointed to the Federal Government's Preventative Health Taskforce. His research in Australian, Pacific and Indian Ocean populations provided new insights into the causes of type 2 diabetes. In 2000 he led the first-ever national diabetes and obesity study in Australia (AusDiab). Paul has published more than 650 scientific papers, chapters and reviews. He is co-editor of the widely used *International Textbook of Diabetes Mellitus* and *The Epidemiology of Diabetes Mellitus: An International Perspective*.

Index